This series seeks to go beyond a traditional focus on the virtues of intra-regional and inter-regional trade agreements, liberal economic policies, and a narrow security agenda in Latin America. Instead, titles deal with a broad range of topics related to international cooperation, global and regional governance, sustainable development and environmental cooperation, internal displacement, and social inclusion in the context of the Post-2015 Development Agenda – as well as their repercussions for public policy across the region. Moreover, the series principally focuses on new international cooperation dynamics such as South-South and triangular cooperation, knowledge sharing as a current practice, and the role of the private sector in financing international cooperation and development in Latin America. The series also includes topics that fall outside the traditional scope of studying cooperation and development, in this case, (in)security and forced internal displacement, cultural cooperation, and *Buen Vivir* among indigenous peoples and farmers in Latin America. Finally, this series welcomes titles which explore the tensions and dialogue around how to manage the imbalance between state, markets, and society with a view to re-articulating cooperation and governance dynamics in the 21st century.

More information about this series at
http://www.palgrave.com/gp/series/15135

Alejandro Angel

Consolidating Economic Governance in Latin America

palgrave
macmillan

Alejandro Angel
Universidade Federal de Santa Catarina
Florianópolis, Santa Catarina, Brazil

Governance, Development, and Social Inclusion in Latin America
ISBN 978-3-030-64521-2 ISBN 978-3-030-64522-9 (eBook)
https://doi.org/10.1007/978-3-030-64522-9

This Palgrave Macmillan imprint is published by the registered company Springer Nature Switzerland AG
The registered company address is: Gewerbestrasse 11, 6330 Cham, Switzerland

A la memoria de mi mamá

Acknowledgments

This has been a long journey. From the early ideas for my doctoral dissertation to the completion of this book the debts I have accumulated are numerous. The loneliness of this process was easier to endure thanks to people who were kind enough to share their time with me. Their help was crucial for me to get to this point.

First and foremost, I would like to thank my advisor Philippe Faucher for all his dedication to this work. He had the patience to deal with me and was always available, well beyond the call of duty, to discuss and advise when I was his doctoral student. From the linguistic confusions to the sometimes-overcomplicated lines of reasoning I came up with, he invariably showed patience, kindness, and willingness to understand what I was thinking but was incapable of expressing. Many of his insights have shaped, and sharpened, my thoughts in ways that I am still discovering. Matthew M. Taylor gave me important insights that allowed me to improve my arguments substantially.

The first part of this odyssey took place at the *Département de science politique* of the *Université de Montréal*. The commitment to academic excellence of its members, as well as their openness, disposition to help, and their sense of community provided me with a stimulating and nurturing environment as a doctoral student. Among the members of the *Département*, special thanks go to Professors Françoise Montambeault and Denis Saint-Martin who believed in me as a researcher and scholar. Their support in many dimensions made that part of the journey possible, from the mundane financial concerns with many research contracts to the instances in which we have had the possibility to share and collaborate, I am very grateful for having the opportunity to learn from them throughout all these years. When I was in Montreal Professors Jane Jenson, Graciela Ducatenzeiler, Christine Rothmayr, Jean- Philippe Thérien, and Martial Foucault also provided generous advice in many occasions.

At the *Instituto de Estudos Sociais e Políticos* of the *Universidade do Estado do Rio de Janeiro* in Rio de Janeiro I had the opportunity to meet with Professor Fabiano Santos who offered advice and helped me to make important contacts to the advancement of my research. At the *Colegio de México* in Mexico City I am grateful for the help of Gerardo Esquivel, who provided invaluable information and contacts for my interviews. Despite the short sojourns in each institution, I always felt myself at home. Financial support for my stay in Mexico was provided by the *Chaire d'études du Mexique contemporain* of the Center for International Studies of the University of Montreal—CERIUM. For all the people who accepted to answer my questions about their work of many years ago I am very thankful. I know their agendas were always full and this work, and the dissertation on which it is based, could not have seen the day without their help. I can only hope it does not question too much their vision of their own work.

Brazilian taxpayers have been very generous. The transformation from a doctoral dissertation to a published book would have been impossible without their financial support provided through a postdoctoral fellowship from the *Programa Nacional de Pós-doutoramento*—PNPD of the *Coordenação de Aperfeiçoamento de Pessoal de Nível Superior*—CAPES. The opportunity that the *Programa de Pós-Graduação em Relações Internacionais*—PPGRI of the *Universidade Federal de Santa Catarina* offered me to return to Brazil was essential for the completion of this book. The intellectual, and physical, space that the PPGRI provided were fundamental in this process. Special thanks to the editorial team of Palgrave Macmillan who were very helpful in bringing this last step to fruition.

Júlia Riscado and her family made the time in Rio a once-in-a-lifetime experience. All my Brazilian family, as always, provided a rare blend of care and support for which I do not have enough words. The casual way in which we met with Laura Ballén in Mexico City is something that we will take to posterity; those months in *el DF* would have never been what they were without her presence. Also in Mexico, my cousins Bela and Yo, and their families, made an already great experience, even better. Finally, El Mono in Santiago who opened the doors of his house for me deserves more than what I can say. His joy of life and his bottomless good humour made of Santiago a wonderful time. I am grateful for his companionship throughout all these years.

Special thanks go to Daniel Marcelino with whom I shared the uneasiness of being far from home at first, and who made me laugh in countless moments, making the first part of this journey enjoyable; Nordin Lazreg with whom I share many interests, and laughs, helped me to see things in perspective. I was fortunate for the innumerous occasions in which I asked him to edit and correct my written and oral French as well as many of the series that I have watched all these years. I am happy that we have continued our friendship and professional partnership. I enjoyed all the moments that we had with Kaisa Vuoristo that made me feel myself at home in Montreal as well as her encouragement to return there.

Margarita was an important part in the first stages of this journey. She offered many ideas, insights, references, and above all, care and support. Her parents, Aura and Edgar, were also very generous. All my family and friends back in Colombia, especially Jaime and Doris, Bubé and his family, and Sumercé and Rafa who have been holding my back during all these years abroad; I cannot thank them enough for being there for me when I needed most.

Unë nuk flas shqip, Zemër flet. Zemër has been an essential part in this endeavour. Her support has been unshakable even when my forces faltered. Her delicious lunches, salads, and numerous flowers have made me smile innumerous times. Words are not enough to express how grateful I am for having her in my life.

The greatest example of scholarship and research I have ever received came from my father. His curiosity, even in a completely different field, put the seed of who I am now; his example of integrity in his work continues to guide my practice as a scholar. Finally, the memory of my mother gives me the strength I need to keep fighting.

Contents

Acronyms

AFP	Administradoras de Fondos de Pensiones (Chile)
ARENA	Aliança Renovadora Nacional (Brazil)
Banamex	Banco Nacional de México
Banxico	Banco de México
BNDE(S)	Banco Nacional de Desenvolvimento Econômico (e Social) (Brazil)
BNDESPAR	BNDES Participações (Brazil)
BRL	Brazilian Real
CANAEMPU	Caja Nacional de Empleados Públicos y Periodistas (Chile)
CENDA	Centro de Estudios Nacionales de Desarrollo Alternativo (Chile)
CEO	Chief Executive Officer
CIEPLAN	Corporación de Investigaciones Económicas para América Latina (Chile)
CLP	Chilean Peso
CNC	Confederación Nacional Campesina (Mexico)
CODELCO	Corporación del Cobre de Chile
CORFO	Corporación de Fomento de la Producción (Chile)
CPI	Comissão Parlamentar de Inquérito (Brazil)
CPIn	Consumer Price Index (Chile)
CPMI	Comissão Parlamentar Mista de Inquérito (Brazil)
CSN	Companhia Siderúrgica Nacional (Brazil)
CTM	Confederación de Trabajadores Mexicanos
CVRD	Companhia Vale do Rio Doce (Brazil)
DC	Democracia Cristiana (Chile)
Diprés	Dirección Nacional de Presupuesto (Chile)
ECLA(C)	Economic Commission for Latin America (and the Caribbean)

EMPART	Caja de Previsión de Empleados Particulares (Chile)
ENAP	Empresa Nacional de Petróleo (Chile)
FAT	Fundo de Amparo ao Trabalhador (Brazil)
FSE	Fundo Social de Emergência (Brazil)
GATT	General Agreement on Trade and Tariffs
GDP	Gross Domestic Product
GNP	Gross National Product
IBGE	Instituto Brasileiro de Geografia e Estatística (Brazil)
IBRD	International Bank for Reconstruction and Development (The World Bank)
IMF	International Monetary Fund
IPCA	Índice de Preços ao Consumidor Amplo (Brazil)
ISI	Import Substitution Industrialization
ITAM	Instituto Tecnológico Autónomo de México
IUPERJ	Instituto Universitário de Pesquisas do Rio de Janeiro (Brazil)
Mercosur	Mercado Común del Sur
Morena	Movimiento de Regeneración Nacional (Mexico)
n.d.	No data
NAFTA	North American Free Trade Agreement
ODEPLAN	Oficina de Planificación Nacional (Chile)
OECD	Organization for Economic Co-Operation and Development
ORTN	Obrigações Reajustáveis do Tesouro Nacional (Brazil)
PAN	Partido Acción Nacional (Mexico)
PAYG	Pay-As-You-Go
PDS	Partido Democrático Social (Brazil)
PEMEX	Petróleos Mexicanos S.A.
Petrobrás	Petróleo Brasileiro S.A.
PMDB	Partido Movimento Democrático Brasileiro (Brazil)
PND	Programa Nacional de Desestatização (Brazil)
PPD	Partido por la Democracia (Chile)
PRD	Partido de la Revolución Democrática (Mexico)
PRI	Partido Revolucionario Institucional (Mexico)
PROER	Programa de Estímulo à Reestruturação e ao Fortalecimento do Sistema Financeiro Nacional (Brazil)
PROES	Programa de Incentivo à Redução do Setor Público Estadual na Atividade Bancária (Brazil)
PRSD	Partido Radical Social-Demócrata (Chile)
PS	Partido Socialista (Chile)
PSDB	Partido da Social Democracia Brasileira (Brazil)
PT	Partido dos Trabalhadores (Brazil)
PUC/RJ	Pontifícia Universidade Católica do Rio de Janeiro (Brazil)
SAFP	Superintendencia de Administradoras de Fondos de Pensiones (Chile)

SBIF	Superintendencia de Bancos e Instituciones Financieras (Chile)
SIDERBRAS	Siderurgia Brasileira
SINAP	Sistema Nacional de Ahorro y Préstamo (Chile)
SNTE	Sindicato Nacional de Trabajadores de la Educación (Mexico)
SSS	Servicio de Seguridad Social (Chile)
STN	Secretaria do Tesouro Nacional (Brazil)
URV	Unidade Real de Valor (Brazil)
US	United States of America
USD	United States' Dollars
USIMINAS	Usinas Siderúrgicas de Minas Gerais (Brazil)

List of Figures

List of Tables

CHAPTER 1

Introduction

The political, economic, and social transformations of the last decades of the twentieth century were the culmination of a process of exhaustion of political and economic models in place, in various forms, since the middle of the century. The seismic changes were not limited to a single arena; indeed, they were multidimensional and often overlapped. These included transitions to democratic rule in Southern Europe, Latin America, and Eastern Europe (O'Donnell, Schmitter, and Whitehead 1986); a pivot from a strong state intervention in the economy toward a free-markets approach (Barr et al. 1996; World Bank 1981); and a less hierarchical exercise of authority (Rhodes 1997). In the realm of economic policy, broadly speaking, these transformations represented for Latin American states a shift from the role of player in the marketplace to that of its referee.

Institutions were said to play a fundamental role in that shift, both in the region and abroad. They would represent the main tool with which states could still retain some control of economic processes without the drawback of relying solely on their authority. This had as a corollary a reform of the state that would transform heavy bureaucratic structures into light enterprise-like organizations with similar managerial instinct and acumen (Saint-Martin 2000). If institutions, and the reforms that would put them in place, were well crafted and implemented, so the argument

A. Angel, *Consolidating Economic Governance in Latin America*, Governance, Development, and Social Inclusion in Latin America, https://doi.org/10.1007/978-3-030-64522-9_1

went, economies would grow and create prosperity, once again. The challenge for governments was to put in place the best possible institutions to generate growth. Given the different nature of the task at hand—from exercising authority that creates growth, to creating ideal conditions for individuals to generate growth—governments, and the technocrats at their helm, attempted to shift their tools from instruments of power to the technology of control (Levi-Faur 2012, 3).

Governing was no longer to exercise power but to steer societies; governance had replaced government (Pierre 2000). In parallel, international organizations were active in the promotion of "best practices" to enhance and facilitate the new array of tasks that governments faced at the time (Bernstein and van der Ven 2017). In principle, relying on those practices would build good governance because they represented the best available technologies. In the case of economic policy, there was not much debate about what the best practices were, particularly during the 1990s, due in part to the triumph of liberalism at the end of the Cold War. Then, good economic governance consisted in the implementation of policies allowing market forces to allocate resources, thus replacing the state, which had usually played that role. Moreover, liberalizing reforms would bring the results that previous policies did not, mainly, because they would help national economies to grow, creating significant spillovers. Economic governance was, in that vision, a technocratic affair concerned exclusively with selecting the best technology available to do the task at hand. Following that reasoning, good economic governance leads to good economic performance. However, problems with that relation are evident.

The process of liberalization represented considerable political challenges since economic policy was only one among many arenas being reformed (Teichman 2001). Despite the fact that Latin American governments, more often than not, implemented a set of "best practices"—which in that context meant liberalization—as a response to the exhaustion of the previous model, they did not experience the expected outcome in terms of growth. The alleged relation between reforms and economic performance became less obvious. On the other hand, other economies—e.g., those in Continental Europe—resisted, to a significant extent, the kind of liberalizing reforms, considered as examples of "best practices," without experiencing bad economic performance. That outcome also questioned the relation between economic performance and liberalizing reforms, i.e., "best practices." In consequence, the relation between the notion of economic governance, focused on the implementation of "best practices," and economic performance is problematic.

Economic governance should not be the expected outcome of implementing "sound" economic policies. After all, economic performance is beyond the control of governments. Instead, economic governance should be the result of political processes concerning the economy rather than the technocratic view that has traditionally been associated with that notion. Authority arguments are no longer feasible, nor desirable, in the context of a liberalized economy. Thus, economic governance should refer to the order that exist in a political economy. I argue that economic governance refers to the predictability and stability within a political economy to the extent that economic policies are both accepted by political and economic actors and effective—i.e., they deliver the expected results within reason.

In turn, the question that this book, therefore, seeks to answer is how Latin American economies consolidate economic governance. As mentioned above, economic performance figures prominently as a criterion in the assessment of economic governance insofar as growth is presumed to be the consequence of having good governance (Knack and Keefer 1995). However, as crises are becoming more frequent, performance cannot be said to depend entirely on a government's actions. Thus, a more productive view of economic governance should produce an account of the organization and predictability of political economies, both of which are political outcomes. I seek to examine the question of economic governance through the concept of institutional complementarity because of how it describes the existence of stability and order in the economy. The link between economic governance and institutional complementarity offers a more robust theoretical underpinning to economic governance, independent from performance. I argue that the consolidation of economic governance indicates that no actor can simultaneously avoid complying with institutions and not have to pay the cost.

Institutional complementarity describes a situation where a given institutional arrangement imposes unavoidable rigidities (Aoki 1996). Therefore, when institutions are complementary, the cost of non-compliance increases. Thus, limiting the possibility that vested interests may disregard economic policies and their regulations, at their discretion, is key to the consolidation of economic governance. Debates surrounding institutional complementarity focused on its connection to economic performance

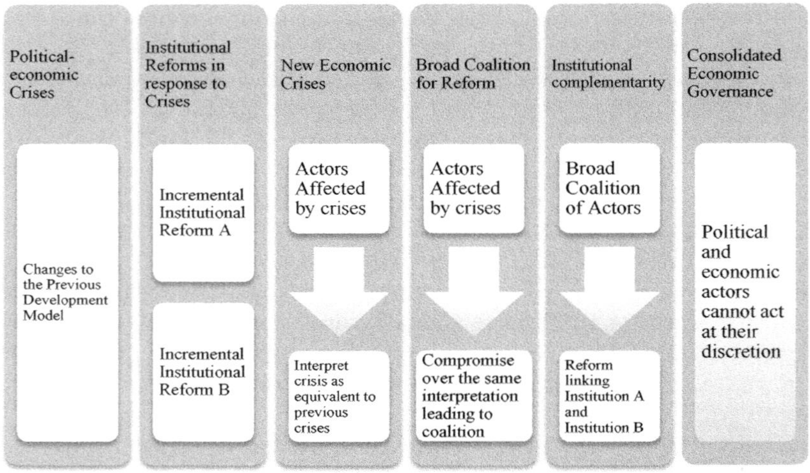

Fig. 1.1 Mechanism of Consolidation of Economic Governance (*Source* Own elaboration)

(Crouch et al. 2005). Instead, this study will analyze how institutions continue to evolve over time and continue to provide stability to the political economy in a way that does not depend on past or present performance. Furthermore, it advances the notion that economic governance is a function of the creation of a set of limits to the discretion of political and economic actors relative to different economic policies, rather than a measure of economic performance. Such limits are represented, essentially, by complementary institutions.

In order to explain how Latin American economies consolidated economic governance I focus on those instances that recast the mores of economic policymaking. Frequently, those were moments of profound economic crisis. Critical situations forced actors to launch reform processes that would eventually lead to the consolidation of new patterns of economic governance (Fig. 1.1). These crises not only had an immediate trigger effect, instigating an initial transformation, but remained in the background of economic policymaking for years to come. Thus, economic crises constitute a key part of the scope conditions for the process of consolidation of economic governance. First, they create the circumstances under which the reforms that will eventually lead to the consolidation of economic governance take place (Ragin 2000, 61). Then, they play several other roles later in the consolidation process. Most notably, economic crises had distributional consequences, both economic and political, affecting many actors across the board and exposing those who could, at their discretion, take advantage of past arrangements. Actors tend to respond to previous traumatic experiences because they do not want to repeat them; such is the legacy of crises past.

While crises are a normal feature of modern capitalist economies (Frieden 2006), some are more consequential than others. In response to the events of the early 1980s, Latin American countries embarked on a series of reforms that attempted to reestablish a sense of order while coping with the worst effects of those crises. After successive incremental reforms that significantly limited the abilities of powerful actors to act at their discretion, new crises arose, with the potential to send into disarray the milestones of stability that were buttressed by those very reforms. The extent to which new crises would destabilize the newly established policymaking routines depended on how actors evaluated their severity and how they responded to them (Widmaier, Blyth, and Seabrooke 2007). In addition, since incoming crises are often analyzed in light of previous traumas, measures in line with those analyses were usually taken, in an effort to prevent their worst effects.

The key role of subjective appraisal in the model presented here highlights the relevance of the points of view of the people involved in processes of institutional change. As a result, interviews with actual and former policymakers are of prime importance for the analysis presented in the empirical chapters. With that in mind, I have conducted several interviews with people involved in those institutional reforms analyzed in the present study. In most cases, they were directly involved in pushing for the reforms, but there are also some who opposed them, or at least were critical of them. These attempts to avoid bias have not ruled them out, however; interviewed supporters and critics do not always match up in terms of rank. This is partially a consequence of the difficulty in gaining access to high-ranking officials.[1] Taken as a whole, the interviews allowed me to assess the subjective appraisal that policymakers had over the threats, or the way in which they understood each reform's role in the transformation of the institutional architecture of their country.

[1] Even if many of them no longer hold responsibilities, some were reluctant to share information. This withholding of information promotes an even greater degree of asymmetry within the study. This is one among many difficulties of interviewing elites (Harvey 2011).

Whether past and present crises are truly similar or not, actors tend to make connections between them, and respond in turn with new reforms intended to avoid the most catastrophic outcomes. This can be in the interest of key actors insofar as the general uneasiness around past crises can help encourage the construction of coalitions supporting reforms that might be especially beneficial to them. In other words, actors interpret new crises by associating them with previous crises. Certain interpretations would legitimize different uses of existing institutions. Moreover, this new interpretation could facilitate the joint use of other institutions in the political economy in an effort to broaden the necessary coalitions. These actions might turn out to be crucial to the constitution of an institutional complementarity since their effective enforcement requires the use of other institution in the political economy. The openness of such institutional interpretation aligns with recent institutional theories that emphasize the political character of agency in processes of change (Mahoney and Thelen 2010).

Because the severity of crises and the extent to which they relate to previous events are open to interpretation but nonetheless have a real impact, institutions can be used by actors at their convenience and according to their own best interests. This instance constitutes the second part of the mechanism for the consolidation of economic governance. In effect, actors are motivated to prevent outcomes that in their eyes could cause significant disruptions to policymaking routines. Consequently, the interpretation of any new crisis in Latin America involves an association between previous crises and the subsequent discretionary actions of key vested interests. In the case of this study, the relevant crises are those of the early 1980s. Subsequent crises, such as those of the global financial crisis or the shock caused by the pandemic, however, can also be associated with further reforms, depending on how each set of crises and reforms will affect interested political and economic actors.

It is important to highlight the role of agents' interpretation in the consolidation of economic governance through the formation of an institutional complementarity. Associations between past and present crises do not always result in such complementarities. There are a number of reasons for this. First, there might not be institutions available to help sustain the proper functioning of other institutions that are crippled by the crisis; second, even when institutions are available, the implemented reforms themselves might fall short of what is needed to prevent another crisis, which would mean, again, that the institutions concerned would no longer be able to operate; and third, sometimes actors do not interpret the new crisis as important enough to act upon, and consequently, they do not mobilize any resources in response. This wide variety of possible challenges shows that neither the theoretical model nor the hypotheses proposed within this framework lead directly to functionalist explanations, as had been argued about studies drawing on the theory of institutional complementarities (Callaghan 2010; Howell 2003).

Even once actors associate current economic crises with previous ones, there is still one final component before an institutional complementarity is created. When new crises are reminiscent of critical moments lived in the past, reformers are in a position to gather political coalitions that would consolidate reforms in a way that makes them complementary to one another. Such a coalition would require a reform that links at least two institutions that are dependent on one another in order to function properly. It is because these actors have a common understanding of the situation that they are willing and able to coalesce and reform institutions in a way that is satisfactory for the members of the coalition. This final reform effectively reduces opportunities for vested interests to exercise their power as they had done in the past, because this would imply substantial political costs given the new link between institutions. Because of the complementarity between institutions, reforms are brought about not by their independent attempts, but only by their combined effort, taken as a whole.

What holds these coalitions together is the need to respond to what is perceived as the repetition of a previous crisis. Even if this forces them to adopt changes that have negative effects in the short term—for instance, because they impose previously unforeseen costs—they accept the reforms with the hope that previous crises do not recur. The broader and stronger the coalition behind the necessary changes, the higher the likelihood of constituting an institutional complementarity and consolidating economic governance. The scope of the coalition is crucial, since changes to the rules might not restrain the actions of other key actors—or, even if the changes do take place, they can be contested later if actors do not perceive them as satisfactory, legitimate, or in correspondence with the previous crisis.

This kind of reform, then, is characterized by compromise among a broad range of actors. The support of these actors, materialized in a heterogeneous coalition, guarantees that they will act within the limits imposed by the reform. Moreover, since this type of reform will prevent another economic crisis, actors have a powerful interest in keeping the institutional complementarity in place. A broad coalition buttresses the consolidation of economic governance because it includes many actors under the reformed institutions that comprise the institutional complementarity. That is, the foundation of economic governance is the existence of a strong political support for a given order to be predictable and stable. This wide inclusiveness helps to prevent cases where, for instance, a particular vested interest might cheat in order to gain advantages in other institutional arenas. In other words, institutional complementarities limit the ability to counter institutions that some actors have enjoyed in the past, and this allows for the consolidation of economic governance. Indeed, actors will abide by the rules when they perceive that in so doing, they will preserve their interests in the long run.

When institutions function properly, they establish guidelines that actors cannot work around. If this is the case with an institution that requires the presence of other institutions to be effective or vice versa, we are in the presence of an institutional complementarity. The creation of an institutional complementarity ensures the simultaneous operation of several institutions within the political economy, which limits opportunities for vested interests to externalize their costs by working around them. Since economic governance relies on the presence of institutional complementarities, the association of current crises with previous ones is a fundamental step of the consolidation of economic governance.

Although the coalitions mentioned above are forged in narrow policy circles or in a parliamentarian context, the actors involved in such reforms must enjoy significant political support from the population at large. Whether that is manifested through direct electoral support in the form of electoral victories or, to the very least, in the absence of open popular contestation of the order the reforms in question uphold, that point is unavoidable. In democratic contexts, even if somehow limited, the explicit or tacit support of a plurality of citizens must be continuously granted. Even in authoritarian contexts, the continuous support of the regime's partners is essential for an order to uphold. For instance, if a given issue is recurrent both as a reason for popular mobilizations, in electoral campaigns, or through changes in the authoritarian support, that is a sign that there is enough discontent with the status quo. Sooner or later, if left unaddressed, such concerns will eventually emerge to the political agenda forcing a change in the institutional underpinnings of that economic order. Even though the in-depth analysis of those dynamics is very important as macro-indicators of the completion of the political process leading to the consolidation of economic governance, the focus of this study is on the political dynamics that put the stage for those debates.

Such caveat does not mean that macro-dynamics are not considered here; in fact, they are discussed through the use of primary sources—i.e., press articles or government documents—to further assess if economic governance has indeed consolidated. A thorough discussion of those processes would involve an entire study on the political support that institutional reforms enjoy in the mid- to long-run.[2] It's important to emphasize the different nature of the political processes in question because they represent different political struggles: the first set—that is, the focus of this study—refers to how certain political actors clash over the contours of institutional reforms so they can indeed be enacted; the second set—the macro-indicators mentioned above—refers to how the population at large perceive those reforms and accept, or contest, them. Both dynamics tend to be different, even if they can overlap.

1.1 Plan of the Book

The next chapter will focus on the debate around institutional complementarity and economic governance. It first presents the theoretical debate about institutional complementarities that took place in response to the liberalizing policies during the 1990s. Within those debates the hypothesis of institutional complementarity explained the persistence of good economic performance in advanced capitalist economies in spite of having institutional structures different to those present in the biggest advanced liberal economies. The chapter argues that instead of focusing exclusively on economic performance, institutional complementarities were also related to stability and predictability of political economies. This role entailed a constant adaptation of the constitutive institutions of the complementary relation because they experienced incremental change through time. The point about how institutional complementarities are the foundation of predictable political economies comes from the fact that for them to hold, actors cannot countervail them.

The third chapter discusses the evolution of economic governance in Latin America, starting with an analysis of how Latin American economic governance consisted, from the mid-twentieth century until the 1980s, on

[2] Armijo and Faucher (2002) discuss the support for liberalizing reforms in Latin America.

the basic model of the developmental state with heavy intervention in the economy. Furthermore, the chapter discusses how the crumbling of the developmental project forced political and economic actors to implement reforms in order to cope with the crises that brought down that model. It emphasizes how vested interests affected the processes of reform insofar as these continuously attempted to steer reforms in such a way that the benefits they derived from previous policies remained almost untouched. Therefore, this had an impact on how crises affected national political economies in the long run because powerful actors resisted reforms. After years of reform, new crises stroke, compelling a wide range of actors to deepen reforms in an attempt to consolidate economic governance.

Chapters 4–6 present the empirical cases. Chapter 4 presents the Brazilian struggle against inflation, which included not only a monetary reform, but a complete reorganization of the country's political economy. Chapter 5, in turn, presents the case of Chile, which implemented the first mandatory pension system based on capitalization, which has been reformed several times responding to recurrent market failures as well as legitimacy deficits of that particular reform. Chapter 6 focuses on Mexico which reformed its central bank, making it independent, and created a fiscal rule, in the middle of a contentious presidential campaign, in order to reduce the discretion of the President. Finally, Chapter 7 presents the conclusions and discusses the evolution of economic governance in Latin America until the late 2010s through the lens of institutional complementarities and the struggle of limiting the discretion of political and economic actors.

References

Aoki, Masahiko. 1996. "Towards a Comparative Institutional Analysis: Motivations and Some Tentative Theorizing." *The Japanese Economic Review* 47 (1): 1–19. https://doi.org/10.1111/j.1468-5876.1996.tb00031.x.

Armijo, Leslie Elliott, and Philippe Faucher. 2002. "'We Have a Consensus': Explaining Political Support for Market Reforms in Latin America." *Latin American Politics and Society* 44 (2): 1–40. https://doi.org/10.2307/3177093.

Barr, Nicholas, Stijn Claessens, Alan Harold Gelb, Cheryl Williamson Gray, Peter C. Harrold, Françoise M. Le-Gall, John R. Nellis, Zhen Kun Wang, and Ulrich Zachau. 1996. *World Development Report 1996: From Plan to Market*. Washington, DC: The World Bank.

Bernstein, Steven, and Hamish van der Ven. 2017. "Best Practices in Global Governance." *Review of International Studies* 43 (3): 534–556. https://doi.org/10.1017/S0260210516000425.

Callaghan, Helen. 2010. "Beyond Methodological Nationalism: How Multilevel Governance Affects the Clash of Capitalisms." *Journal of European Public Policy* 17 (4): 564–580. https://doi.org/10.1080/13501761003673351.

Crouch, Colin, Wolfgang Streeck, Robert Boyer, Bruno Amable, Peter A. Hall, and Gregory Jackson. 2005. "Dialogue on 'Institutional Complementarity and Political Economy'." *Socio-Economic Review* 3 (2): 359–382. https://doi.org/10.1093/SER/mwi015.

Frieden, Jeffry A. 2006. *Global Capitalism: Its Fall and Rise in the Twentieth Century*. New York: Norton.

Harvey, William S. 2011. "Strategies for Conducting Elite Interviews." *Qualitative Research* 11 (4): 431–441. https://doi.org/10.1177/1468794111404329.

Howell, Chris. 2003. "Varieties of Capitalism: And Then There Was One?" *Comparative Politics* 36 (1): 103–124. https://doi.org/10.2307/4150162.

Knack, Stephen, and Philip Keefer. 1995. "Institutions and Economic Performance: Cross-Country Tests Using Alternative Institutional Measures." *Economics & Politics* 7 (3): 207–227. https://doi.org/10.1111/j.1468-0343.1995.tb00111.x.

Levi-Faur, David. 2012. "From 'Big Government' to 'Big Governance'?" In *The Oxford Handbook of Governance*, edited by David Levi-Faur, 3–18. New York: Oxford University Press.

Mahoney, James, and Kathleen Thelen. 2010. "A Theory of Gradual Institutional Change." In *Explaining Institutional Change: Ambiguity, Agency, and Power*, edited by James Mahoney and Kathleen Thelen, 1–37. Cambridge: Cambridge University Press.

O'Donnell, Guillermo A., Philippe C. Schmitter, and Laurence Whitehead. 1986. *Transitions from Authoritarian Rule, Comparative Perspectives*. Baltimore: Johns Hopkins University Press.

Pierre, Jon, ed. 2000. *Debating Governance: Authority, Steering, and Democracy*. Oxford: Oxford University Press.

Ragin, Charles C. 2000. *Fuzzy-Set Social Science*. Chicago: University of Chicago Press.

Rhodes, R. A. W. 1997. *Understanding Governance: Policy Networks, Governance, Reflexivity, and Accountability*. Buckingham and Philadelphia: Open University Press.

Saint-Martin, Denis. 2000. *Building the New Managerialist State: Consultants and the Politics of Public Sector Reform in Comparative Perspective*. Oxford: Oxford University Press.

Teichman, Judith A. 2001. *The Politics of Freeing Markets in Latin America*. Chapel Hill: The University of North Carolina Press.
Widmaier, Wesley W., Mark Blyth, and Leonard Seabrooke. 2007. "Exogenous Shocks or Endogenous Constructions? The Meanings of Wars and Crises." *International Studies Quarterly* 51 (4): 747–759. https://doi.org/10.1111/j.1468-2478.2007.00474.x.
World Bank. 1981. *World Development Report*. Washington, DC: The World Bank.

CHAPTER 2

Complementarity and Economic Governance

After the capitalist crises of the 1970s and 1980s, there was an increase in preoccupations about the causes behind the difference between the industrial performance of the United States, on the one hand, and Japan and Germany, on the other (Amable 2005, 8). This concern evolved in the 1990s with the Asian crisis, as it became increasingly evident that institutions—those "sets of regularized practices with a rule-like quality, [that] structure the behavior of political and economic actors" Hall (2010, 204)—have an impact on economic practices and performance (Morgan et al. 2010a, 6). In parallel, there was the implicit acknowledgment that economic performance could be delivered through a wide array of institutional arrangements rather than a single one. The concept of comparative institutional advantage captures this acknowledgment well, as it describes the conditions under which different economies excel in a diversity of industries (Aoki 1994, 675). However, these realizations contrasted heavily with the dominant wave of liberalization of the 1990s, which seemed to signal a convergence toward a single economic model (La Porta, Lopez-De-Silanes, and Shleifer 1999).

These new realities of capitalism had differing impacts on different economies. In some cases, particularly in advanced capitalist societies, the question was whether technological progress and globalization were enough to inspire institutional convergence (Hall and Soskice 2001a,

A. Angel, *Consolidating Economic Governance in Latin America*, Governance, Development, and Social Inclusion in Latin America,
https://doi.org/10.1007/978-3-030-64522-9_2

1). In developing economies, exacerbated by significant debt loads, the crises of 1970s–1980s exhausted the development model that had been in place since at least the 1930s (Cardoso and Helwege 1992). These diverging realities were reproduced by the different research and policy agendas concerned with those changes and their consequences. The interest of research into advanced capitalist societies was precisely to explain the persistence of different institutional arrangements (Albert 1991), whereas the objective relating to developing economies was to explain the processes of institutional reform and transformation (Frieden 1991; Haggard and Kaufman 1992a). Behind this difference in research agendas was the divergent performance of advanced and developing capitalist economies. Moreover, economic performance also affected the political salience of such agendas in their respective regions.

Institutions and institutional dynamics were, however, at the core of both research agendas.[1] In relation to developed economies, research sought to explain the lack of change in institutional arrangements across a plurality of economies, i.e., the lack of institutional convergence. Simultaneously, these economies maintained economic performance to a significant extent, which implied that different institutional arrangements could produce similar economic performance. Part of the answer was that capitalism rested on specific social relationships in different parts of the world; those relationships were systematized in institutions regulating specific arenas. Therefore, the main goal of such an ambitious research agenda was precisely to compare how capitalisms differed. Many perspectives approached this question emphasizing a range of social relations within capitalism (Boyer 1990; Campbell and Pedersen 2001; Hall and

[1] Three different types of new institutionalism appeared in the 1980s, each one stemming from different scholarly traditions. The difference can be appreciated when the definition of an institution is analyzed according to each tradition. First, in the case of historical institutionalism: institutions are defined as "formal or informal procedures, routines, norms and conventions embedded in the organizational structure of the polity or political economy" (Hall and Taylor 1996, 938). Rational choice institutionalism, in turn, has a less complex definition. Institutions, here, are described as "humanly devised constraints that shape human interaction" (North 1990, 3), although they can also be conceived of as working rules organizing information about decisions as well as the payoff matrix derived from such decisions (Ostrom 1990, 51). Finally, the tradition of sociological institutionalism understands institutions as "not just formal rules, procedures or norms, but the symbol systems, cognitive scripts, and moral templates that provide the 'frames of meaning' guiding human action" (Hall and Taylor 1996, 947). In a later synthesis between these traditions, Hall (2010) offers the definition quoted above.

Soskice 2001b). Although these approaches were fairly different from one another, there were collaborations and cross-breeding between them (Boyer 2002–2003; Hollingsworth and Boyer 1997), defying the sense of "gated communities" (Amable 2005; Crouch et al. 2005).

Conversely, what drew the attention of research into developing economies was the process of reform and how different factors affected it. Moreover, in many of these countries there had been important political changes arising from recent transitions to democracy (O'Donnell 1993). The focus of this work was the processes of that change, both political and economic, in the way each dynamic affected the other (Domínguez 1998; Remmer 1990). Institutions were key to the processes of reform that Latin American economies had launched (Haggard and Kaufman 1992b). Elsewhere, the focus was on the role of institutions in the impressive economic change that Asian economies experienced during the second half of the twentieth century (Johnson 1987). This interest in economic performance resonates with research interests described above in relation to developed economies. The issue indeed remained the impact that institutions have on economic performance and, as such, the reforming of institutions was seen as a response to the economic crises affecting developing economies in Latin America, during the 1980s, and in Southeast Asia, through the 1990s (Kohli 2012).

In the case of advanced capitalist systems, the comparison between its different variants privileged more holistic views of the institutional settings and social relationships underlying productive activities (Jackson and Deeg 2008). These institutional settings created a pattern in each society, or each group of societies. These patterns were a consequence of the unique combination of complementary institutions in each national setting. Thus, the field of comparative capitalism sought to explain how private economic activity was organized nationally, referring to the complementarity between the institutions that regulate different arenas. A key aspect of this literature on comparative capitalism is that such complementary institutions provided a degree of economic stability to the extent that, given their social embeddedness and path dependency, they would only change incrementally (Jackson and Deeg 2008). Later on, such studies of institutions, which focused mainly on national-level cases, were subject to criticism (Lane and Wood 2012).

Thus, the comparative capitalisms approach to political economy argues that the distinct institutional arrangements that exist in every economy provide for corresponding routines and decision-making patterns. Such routines create predictable frameworks of behavior (Jackson and Deeg 2008, 703 fn. 1). While some variants of comparative capitalism focused on the mechanisms allowing for enforcement of such institutional arrangements (Crouch 2005), the main focus of this literature was elsewhere. The predictability and order implied in that body of literature has elicited criticisms about its implicit functionalism (Howell 2003), the absence of a perspective on institutional change (Deeg and Jackson 2007), and its perceived need to account for the role of politics within those dynamics (Jackson and Deeg 2008). Many of those criticisms have, to a significant extent, been subsequently addressed (Boyer 2015; Hall and Thelen 2009; Hall 2018).

The literature on comparative capitalism, with its emphasis on the role of institutions and the order they produce, has also turned to the study of developing or transitional economies (Feenstra and Hamilton 2006; King 2007; Schneider 2012). In the case of Latin American economies, these efforts have also broadened perspectives on the distinctiveness of capitalist relations in the region, focusing mainly on its biggest economies (Bizberg 2015b, 2019; Boschi 2011b; Schneider 2013). These works have identified and emphasized different institutional regularities, depending on their approach and theoretical framework. In some cases, these institutions are inserted into a longer-term perspective, whereby effects are seen to persist despite the successive changes in policy priorities over the years (Schneider 2013, 4). In others, the focus turns toward the new configurations that appeared and crystallized after several years of institutional change (Bizberg 2015a; Boschi 2011a).

The predictability that institutional arrangements can generate, through their complementarity, along with the stability of economic performance, has largely been absent in the more recent discussion of Latin American cases. Naturally, since economic performance has not been stable in the region, this absence is justified; although, depending on the criteria with which performance is evaluated, some outcomes have remained through the successive changes these economies have endured (Schneider 2009b). Actually, the significant transformations of Latin American economies have attracted the attention of scholars interested in the changing role of the state. This has been the case with both the process of liberalization during the 1990s (Fanelli 2007) and state activism seen in the first decade of the present century (Levitsky and Roberts 2011).

However, these successive changes to the role of the state have led to a new organization of economic activity in the region, involving new routines, actors, and priorities. This means that reforms that sought to respond to the collapse of the previous development model substantially modified the organization of economic activity. As a result, as the organization of Latin American economies went through significant changes, we could reasonably expect that the underlying social relationships supporting them would also change. If we consider that such relationships are fundamentally political, the changes in the organization of economic activity have also had political consequences that go beyond the change embodied by transitions to democracy mentioned earlier. In this sense, because they are at once the product of political struggles and the buttress of economic activity, institutions must also have changed substantially, as well as in relation to one another. These changes mean that new institutional complementarities would have appeared, although unevenly across the region.

While in many ways these ideas seem uncontroversial (i.e., institutions changed in response to the social and political transformations of the region), a key question remains: What are the implications of the new institutional complementarities observed in Latin American countries? There are at least two controversies in question here. First, since institutional complementarities have served to identify models or types of capitalist organization and given them an air of permanence, moreover, their role in the radical transformation of Latin American economies has been contentious. Second, is not clear whether such new complementarities have actually established themselves or whether they are still in flux, not yet fully consolidated. Therefore, reconsidering institutional complementarities with their sense of economic organization and governance in Latin America is interesting because it addresses the transformations of Latin American economies without falling into the trap of evaluating their economic performance. Such a perspective, furthermore, brackets discussions of the political cycles that have been common in the study of Latin American political economies. A focus instead on how economic governance has changed in the region provides a more comprehensive view of these issues.

The present chapter will present the debates surrounding the concept of institutional complementarities and its relation to economic performance, stability, and the possibilities of institutional change. The subsequent section of the chapter deals with the importance of limiting the discretion of political and economic actors so that economic governance can consolidate. The final section offers some preliminary conclusions.

2.1 Institutional Complementarities

The concept of institutional complementarity first appeared in the work of Aoki (1994), who studied Japanese corporate governance arrangements. His model offers a theoretical foundation for a feasible solution to the free-rider problem appearing in team-oriented organizations where individual efforts are not discernable. The solution is an intermediary monitoring agent, who would take over for the team's manager if performance is not satisfactory. The main bank system, for instance, constitutes just such a solution to the free-rider problem among team members because the bank could take control of the underperforming firm. Because the team-oriented organization is prevalent in Japan, these analyses resonate with Japanese experiences. This kind of arrangement was prevalent during the transitional phase of the Japanese economy, in part because the banks and the imperfect labor market were complementary.

This seminal argument about the interaction between the labor market and corporate governance, in the particular case of Japan, contributed to the debate about the diversity of institutional arrangements prevalent in advanced forms of capitalism. The field of Comparative Institutional Analysis developed as a response to the narrowness of the institutional analysis that was common in economics at the time, and in an effort to better understand the policy implications of the resulting diversity (Aoki 1996, 12). Institutional complementarity describes a situation in which a particular institutional arrangement imposes rigidities to such an extent that an exit strategy is increasingly difficult to implement. This occurs because, once selected, the equilibrium strategies are mutually complementary and because institutions as such become complementary (Aoki 1996, 15). Complementary institutions can be identified when the presence of one increases the returns of the other.

This conception of institutional complementarities is explicitly embraced in a book about the Varieties of Capitalism (Hall and Soskice 2001a, 17). The volume studies firms' problems of coordination with workers or providers of capital, both of which are essential for their existence. Coordination in one sphere of the economy is complementary with coordination in other spheres, reinforcing the efficiency of each one and, by implication, of the entire economy. Examples of such spheres are corporate governance and industrial relations. The argument focuses on efficiency, whereby one institution, creating a specific set of incentives, will reproduce those incentives in other arenas of the economy, creating an equilibrium. If one of the coordinating institutions fails to provide the same kind of incentives to relevant actors within the economy, the efficiency and performance of the whole will be affected. Therefore, those economies with coordinating institutions giving different sets of incentives underperform relative to those that offer the same set of incentives across the board (Hall and Gingerich 2009). Thus, the institutional basis for economic activity in a given economy should offer one kind of incentives.

From the perspective of Regulation Theory (Amable 2000; Boyer 2004), the conversation starts with the premise that neither the neoclassical concept of spontaneous interaction between agents (Boyer 2004, 17), nor the Marxist premise that the capital-labor nexus is the same across time and space[2] (Boyer 1990, vii; 2004, 17) can fully account for capitalism. Essentially, what Regulation Theory provides is an account of how social relations determine capitalism's singularities. The regulation mode—the set of rules, procedures, and behavior of actors, both individual and collective—has the possibility of reproducing fundamental relations such as the capital-labor nexus and, therefore, constitutes a key element of analysis. These rules and procedures are historically determined and seek to support and reproduce a contingent accumulation regime by ensuring the dynamic compatibility of the whole set of individualized decisions (Boyer 2004, 20). Such rules and procedures are enshrined in different institutional forms, the most important of which are the monetary form, the capital-labor nexus, the form of competition, the form of adherence to the international regime, and the form of the state (Boyer 1990).

Regulation Theory follows a deductive strategy to arrive at the concept of institutional complementarity. Its starting point is the general premise that regulation modes must involve the close interaction of different institutional forms. In principle, the interaction of institutional forms affecting the whole economy would produce many different types of capitalism, including a significant number that do not actually exist. Conversely,

[2] The term in French is *rapport salarial*. Jackson and Deeg (2008, 683) use the expression wage/labor nexus; however, in subsequent paragraphs capital-labor nexus will be used.

convergence toward one single type of capitalism has not been verified. Therefore, there should be a limited number of capitalisms (Amable 2000, 657; Boyer 2002–2003, 137). The existence of a reduced number of capitalisms is precisely due to the existence of complementarity between institutional forms. The concept of institutional complementarity here is the same as that described by Aoki (1996).

Complementarity between institutional forms is what differentiates each observable type of capitalism. Here, Regulation Theory concurs with the argument in Varieties of Capitalism, both of which suggest that there can be no single benchmark or superior model of capitalism. Moreover, Varieties of Capitalism agrees with the perspective of Regulation Theory in its assertion that complementarity is what holds capitalisms together. In this sense, the similarity between the two perspectives is striking to the extent that an inductive procedure and a deductive procedure, respectively, produce the same conclusion: complementarity occurs when the efficiency (presence) of one institution (institutional form) enhances or allows for the efficiency (presence) of another. From the perspective of both Varieties of Capitalism and Regulation Theory, complementarity is seen to explain both the existence and persistence of different types of capitalism. Instead of merely the interaction of individuals, specific social relationships and arrangements are foundational to capitalism itself.

Another group of scholars, called the Governance Approach,[3] advance a more complex conception of complementarity. This group focuses on the governance of economic activity via generic coordination mechanisms, including the market, the state, and communities. The meaning of governance embraced here refers to "those mechanisms by which the behavioral regularities that constitute institutions are maintained and enforced" (Crouch 2005, 20). This definition suggests that such a perspective reprises the "logic of appropriateness" (March and Olsen 1989) since it seeks to identify regularities across different settings that follow similar working patterns. Within this approach, complementarity operates according to three logics (Crouch 2005, 50): the logic of

[3] Despite the multiple meanings that governance might imply (Levi-Faur 2012a; Rothstein 2014, 738–739), including the one adopted in the present work, and regardless that this polysemy may be inconvenient, in the literature concerning the study of capitalism these works are regrouped under such label (Jackson and Deeg 2008, 688–689).

compensation; the economists' sense[4]; and mutual effects. First, complementarity as compensation is a more straightforward concept. A rounded object (like a ball) is a classic illustration of two components complementing one another and forming a predetermined whole. Institutional analysis is arguably more complex but the illustration works in that it is easy to visualize and understand. Two (or more) institutions are considered complementary, in this sense, when the elements of one counter the limitations of the other (Crouch et al. 2005, 359).

Examples of compensatory characteristics are, for instance, the series of institutions that constrained the excessive risk-taking attitude demonstrated by the US banking industry in the years leading up to 2006–2008. These institutions were, however, consistently weakened over that period by decisions that, coupled with the incentives offered to homeowners to take out large loans, created an unbalanced situation that eventually led to the financial meltdown (Campbell 2011). Moreover, compensation can exist between two or more closely related institutions, as in the case of the Danish "flexicurity" model that seeks to increase workers' market exposure while keeping several of the welfare protections characteristic of corporatist arrangements (Campbell and Pedersen 2007). The criterion for each compensation is rather clear from the point of view of the entire political economy, if not also from the point of view of the actors involved.

The Governance Approach conceives of complementarity also in the economists' sense, referring to the description, within microeconomics, of a specific relationship between two goods within a utility or production function.[5] Two commodities are complementary when the demand for Commodity 1 decreases as the price of Commodity 2 increases, or if demand for Commodity 1 increases as the price of Commodity

[4] More precisely, this refers to the notion of complementary goods as used in microeconomics.

[5] This condition refers to the Hicksian demand function, which follows the expenditure minimization problem (Mas-Colell, Whinston, and Green 1995, 69–70). Although this seems to be a negligible detail, it is actually of the utmost importance. The expenditure minimization problem implies that the utility of agents remains constant and that agents possess information about what satisfies them. This information can also refer to the relative proportion of two different goods that is most likely to maintain the desired level of utility.

2 decreases.[6] Crouch (2010, 133) argues that this understanding of complementarity can provide the theoretical foundation for a thicker discussion if it is used in combination with the notion of mutual effects. In an earlier part of the text, Crouch's (2010, 124) use of the arguments advanced by Aoki (1994, 670; 2000, 13; 2001) to explain the economists' sense of complementarity reflects the trickiness of such an interpretation.[7]

Crouch (2010, 124) adds a further layer to the debate where he relies on other descriptions of other types of complementarity,[8] including the increasing-returns or efficiency enhancement sense defined in Varieties of Capitalism and Regulation Theory. The use of the same practical situation to explicate two different ideas shows how slippery the economists' conception of complementarity is when applied to institutional analyses. More generally, this slipperiness demonstrates that debates about complementarity have also focused on the interpretation of institutional arrangements and their consequences for the political economy.

The third, mutual effects sense of complementarity is a softer version of the increasing-returns definition, whereby the efficiency of institution 1 is enhanced by the presence of institution 2 and vice versa. According

[6] An example often used is that of the tomato and flour in the making of a pizza. When the price of one of the two commodities rises, the demand for the other decreases. Yet, it is rather difficult to apply this argument to a definite set of institutions. In the context of institutional theory, the operationalization of the microeconomic definition of complementarity would require that we could determine in advance the relationship between two institutions that keep social utility constant. However, Arrow (1950) shows that a social utility function is not feasible and, therefore, that is not possible to maximize such a function. Furthermore, we neither know in advance the desired outcome of institutions (the pizza), e.g., either growth or equality, or both, even something else, nor what institutions (the tomatoes and the flour) are needed in order to produce such an outcome, e.g., rigid labour markets, progressive taxation, or fluid capital markets.

[7] Aoki's (1994, 674–675) reasoning leads to confusion. In the concluding summary of the article, he states: "This paper investigated the second-best solution for the moral hazard problems of teams. It indicated that complementary institutional arrangements are necessary for controlling internal moral hazard problems," pointing toward the compensatory role of the contingent governance structure of main banks in relation to the team-work characteristic of Japanese firms. In the next paragraph, however, he seems to lean toward a definition based on increasing returns: "Specifically, it was pointed out that the emergence of the main bank system in Japan was related to the strongly 'team' nature of the internal organization, while the team oriented organization were incentive wise supported by the main bank system and the imperfect labor market. *There were mutually reinforcing effects*" (emphasis added).

[8] "Different institutions are brought together, (…) because when they occur together they produce a stable model that is mutually reinforcing" (Crouch 2010, 124).

to Crouch (2005, 54), the fact that many authors (Amable 2000, 657; Pierson 2000b, 492; Whitley 2005) use the term complementarity to describe this phenomenon is misleading because the sense of compensation is much stronger. The weak link between two institutions that "affect" one another might be identified as many things, creating a certain degree of confusion. Nevertheless, Crouch recognizes that the idea that two institutions can affect each other is a powerful one. Indeed, in 2005, he expressed concern about how the idea that institutions can mutually affect one another, were to be widely adopted as in fact it now has, would make it hard to distinguish similarity from complementarity, which for Crouch also includes the notion of compensation.

Furthermore, for Crouch (2005, 48–50), similarity refers to the presence of the same kind of incentives in different spheres of the economy. Crouch's characterization of the debate is precisely that economies presenting similar incentives and institutions perform better than those that do not; which is precisely what Hall and Gingerich (2009) find. Clearly, the concept of similarity described by Crouch is strikingly alike, if not actually identical to, the definition of complementarity found within both Varieties of Capitalism and Regulation Theory. In one passage about similarity, Crouch (2005, 49) cites the same pages quoted by Hall and Soskice (2001a, 17–21) in their explanation of complementarity and its significance. This instance of the debate is one of many in which the scope and meaning of complementarity have been discussed and analyzed.

The debate so far has revolved around a clashing of different concepts, interpretations, and examples. The empirical record is conceptualized in different ways; interpretations of the Japanese institutional arrangements emphasizing efficiency (Aoki 1994; Hall and Soskice 2001b) versus the economist's conception of complementary goods (Crouch 2010, 124).[9] What is conceptualized as complementarity in the seminal works of Aoki (1994, 1996), in Varieties of Capitalism (Hall and Soskice 2001b), and in Regulation Theory (Amable 2005; Boyer 2004) is reworked and rearticulated by Crouch (2005) into something called similarity (48–50) and in a softer version, called mutual effects (54).

[9] While the example provided here is that of the Japanese economy with its system of banks and long-term job tenure in industrial firms, accounts of other economies are characterized by the same kind of polysemy. Boyer lists the case of the German economy which also generated numerous different interpretations (in Crouch et al. 2005, 368–370).

This debate was part of a broader debate in the 1990s on the subject of capitalism, in which the relationship between complementarity, cohesion, and co-evolution was equally important (Amable 2000). As mentioned above, the starting point for all of these concepts was an acknowledgment of the existence of a variety of different arrangements across the landscape of contemporary capitalism. What was not clear was why these arrangements continued to hold in the wake of liberalization. Was it because they embodied such abstract properties as complementarity and cohesion, or simply because they had evolved together, historically? Furthermore, whether the simultaneous presence of a given pair of institutions evolved as a mere coincidence or rather because of more abstract causes, several other properties can serve to explain the same set of outcomes.[10]

Thus, until the mid-2000s, complementarity was discussed by several different traditions as one of a number of relevant concepts in the study of the sociopolitical relations of capitalism. It even arguably attracted more attention than those other concepts. Many works situated their analyses of complementarity in relation to other studies of the same kind (Amable 2000, 2005; Amable, Ernst, and Palombarini 2005; Aoki 1994, 1996, 2000; Boyer 2002–2003, 2004, 2005; Crouch 2005; Hall and Soskice 2001b; Höpner 2005b; Thelen 1999, 2004). Alongside these contributions, there has been an attempt to create common ground about what constitutes institutional complementarity and how it differs from other institutional phenomena (Crouch et al. 2005). Implicit here is the notion that complementarity leads to better performance. Höpner (2005a, 383) even attempts to settle the debate by offering that complementarity means that "the functional performance of an institution A is conditioned by the presence of another institution B and vice versa" (emphasis in the original).

[10] Boyer (2005) argues that the presence of a pair of institutions and their possible interaction should not be at first glance thought of as complementarity. Similar concepts also serve to explain the same phenomena of institutional interaction that would produce a presumed good outcome. However, there is also the problem of the criterion used to decide whether one pair of institutions has performed better than another. For instance, supermodularity implies that there is no better combination than the one that outperforms every other possibility. Moreover, compatibility is the single coexistence of two institutions that does not produce any particular outcome (Boyer 2005, 48–49). The difference between the two is the performance criteria. Whereas compatibility does not involve any other criterion than coexistence, both supermodularity and complementarity require a criterion to judge their relative performance.

This relation between complementarity and performance remained at the core of institutional debates about capitalism. Complementarity served to explain how multiple forms of capitalism persisted in the wake of liberalization and maintained their performance. Its definition was the subject of much debate, as shown above, but these were largely inconclusive given that various understandings of the concept were in circulation. Broadly considered, capitalist survival and performance were deemed a consequence of complementarity; however, the question of whether institutions lead actors to use the same kind of social skills across different economic dimensions because of similar incentives or, rather, by counterbalancing them was never settled. Thus, institutions in different spheres could lead actors to adopt two kinds of behavior: either a single pattern of economic interaction across different dimensions, including labor relations, corporate financing, and training, or multiple such dimension-specific patterns as close networks in corporate finance and loose labor relations.

Whether the mongrel or the pedigreed animal had led to greater performance outcomes continued to be the main debate through the late 2000s (Campbell 2011, 213 fn. 1), with evidence supporting both claims (Campbell and Pedersen 2007; Hall and Gingerich 2009). This debate uses complementarity as an explanation for economic performance with all the limitations that such a practice entails. These limitations have to do with the crucial fact that a measure of performance depends on the criteria used to evaluate it. Furthermore, the performance of capitalist economies is not stable; that is, capitalism is characterized by cycles. Definitions of complementarity based on performance, therefore, are not adequate given that it varies greatly over time, even when its cycles are accounted for.

In parallel, the main use of the concept of complementarity has been to articulate notions of increasing returns or similarity (Amable and Palombarini 2009; Deeg 2007; Deeg and Jackson 2007; Kang and Moon 2012; Schneider 2009a). Complementarity was increasingly used to describe situations in which two institutional spheres within an economy exhibited the same behavioral patterns. Büthe and Mattli (2011) explain the different private governance arrangements that operate in finance and in industrial standards according to the relative institutional strength of those involved. Because the financial sector in the United States was institutionally strong, its standards were adopted as the benchmark for financial reporting. Conversely, because the manufacturing sector in

Continental Europe was strong, its standards were adopted as a benchmark for that sector. While it is difficult to give a definite explanation for the generalized adoption of the definition of complementarity as efficiency, it is useful to consider the impact of Varieties of Capitalism (Hall and Soskice 2001b) on the works of political economy that followed (Ebenau 2012; Hancké, Rhodes, and Thatcher 2007; Lane and Wood 2009, 2012; Sánchez-Ancochea 2009; Schneider and Paunescu 2012; Schneider 2013; Schrank 2009).

The core debate on complementarity, then, moved one step forward with the typology of complementarity provided by Crouch (2010) in the *Oxford Handbook of Comparative Institutional Analysis*. Instead of separating the concepts of "similarity" and "complementarity" as in previous works (Crouch 2005, 50–52), he would now propose that "similarity" is, in fact, a type of complementarity. Compensation, too, which is to say the two parts that make a whole and complement one another, is identified as another type of complementarity. The third type of complementarity is the one used by economists. This new development concerning the definition of complementarity clears up the confusion, at least to some extent, giving it more analytic leverage. Instead of having numerous concepts with analogous definitions, we now had a single (albeit nuanced) concept. Crouch (2010, 117) recognizes that the notion of complementarity is of significant value for institutional analysis and for the field of political economy in general; although, for him, it remains difficult to grasp.

Part of the difficulty in assessing complementarity derives from the fact that its definitions have been tied to outcomes. While a definition should provide sufficient information as to how the set of institutions considered to be complementary can create outcomes such as better performance, efficiency, or stability, the definition should not depend on these outcomes. This is clear insofar as complementarity between institutions can also reinforce undesired outcomes such as poor performance or instability at the macro-level. Hence, the notion of institutional complementarity should account for institutional interactions regardless of the outcome these produce; once the interaction between actors and institutions stands on its own, it is possible to produce an explanation of the outcome. In other words, accounting for the interaction between agents and institutions should prevent functionalist arguments from appearing, as has frequently been pointed out of theories that have institutional complementarities as a core argument, including Varieties of Capitalism (Howell 2003).

Therefore, complementarity between two institutions happens when one institution needs the presence of another to function in a certain way in the political economy. This definition adheres to Hall's definition of institutions as sets of regularized practices with a rule-like quality (2010, 204). At the core of this definition is the way in which institutions regulate agents' behaviors within the political economy. In addition, we should ask, what behaviors do we take into account when studying the relationship between institutions? According to a variety of traditions (Crouch 2005, 88–93; Mahoney and Thelen 2010, 10–14), institutions have different dimensions that actors could take advantage of, depending on their interests. This diversity underscores the fact that choosing any particular dimension essentially involves a political choice, which has an incidence on the complementarities that might appear between two given institutions.

Although such a complex debate makes definitive judgments difficult, we concur with Höpner (2005a, 383) that complementarity refers to how the functional performance of "Institution A" is conditioned by the presence of "Institution B," and vice versa. This would imply that each institution buttresses the other, for instance, by foreclosing the possibility that some actors might evade the negative effects of "Institution A" by escaping into the arena that "Institution B" regulates. If each institution represents a local equilibrium where actors maximize their utility (Aoki 1994), then in the case of institutional complementarity, the absence of the other institution would prevent the existence of such internal equilibrium, creating externalities and impeding an actor's utility maximization. Without the inputs provided by the second institution, the payoff matrix would not have a solution. The Pareto efficiency would never be attained since some actors could be better off by changing the system. In other words, the Pareto equilibrium can only be attained via the introduction of a new institution.

Furthermore, this sort of equilibrium would prevent actors from creating an effective exit strategy (Aoki 1996). Indeed, the existence of complementary institutions forces actors to comply, simultaneously, with both sets of rules, rather than abiding only by one and disregarding the other. If agents do not abide by one dimension of a given institution, such a dimension cannot be complementary with other institutions with regard, precisely, to compliance. In fact, non-compliance can render such an institution complementary with another dimension of the political economy. It is entirely possible that compliance with "Institution A" will make it complementary with "Institution B" while non-compliance will make it complementary with "Institution C." The key to understanding complementarity is to note the relative difficulty of exiting the equilibrium created by a given set of institutions. If there were a way to avoid one institution (i.e., if there were an exit strategy), then there would remain neither equilibrium nor complementarity.

Beyond the debate concerning what complementarity means, we still need to clarify how complementarity relates to outcomes of interest in political economy. In particular, we need to address how the stability that complementary institutional arrangements produce can also account for the cyclicality of economic performance. This is a tension that needs to be accounted for in order to consider the debate advanced. One way to address the tension between the sets of institutions that create stability and the dynamism of capitalist economies is to incorporate the study of institutional change, mainly those changes that do not imply institutional breaks. The next section will discuss how economic performance, institutional stability, and change are related to institutional complementarity.

2.2 Economic Performance, Stability, and Institutional Change

Attempts to simplify the discussion presented in the previous section were grounded in the notion that institutional complementarities positively affect economic performance, recalling the original debate around institutional differences in capitalism in the wake of liberalization policies (Albert 1991; Aoki 1994; Hollingsworth and Boyer 1997). Nevertheless, while some elements remain from past discussions about complementarity, there have since been other important contributions. Bringing in an argument developed by Aoki (1994, 2000, 2001), Crouch (2010, 124) asserts that the concept of a market for institutions might contribute to a better understanding of complementarity.[11] In such a market, actors would search for other institutions that would help to sustain the one.

[11] In a previous work, Crouch (2005, 53–54) had argued against a market for institutions: "There is no real market for institutions: there are too few producers and too few consumers of institutions. The observation that two institutions tend to be found together therefore tells us little in itself; the same producer might have made them all; there might be simple imitation among a small number of institutional producers and consumers."

Campbell (2011, 212–213) concurs with Crouch (2010) that the debate was reduced to the question of whether complementarities produce good results because they provide the same kind of incentives or because they compensate for the deficiencies of their counterparts. Nevertheless, he contends further, complementarities have also produced bad results. Campbell (2011) makes his point with reference to American financial markets and the way in which the financial crisis unfolded in 2006–2008. While this is not the first time institutional complementarity has been used to explain a negative outcome (Schneider 2009b), it is the first time that someone like Campbell makes the point, close as he is to the complementarities debate (Crouch et al. 2005), given his discussions of the Danish case (Campbell and Pedersen 2007) and his work in the field of Comparative Institutional Analysis (Morgan et al. 2010b).

However, if the results of institutional complementarities can be either positive or negative, depending on the empirical case, the concept tends to lose its appeal as an explanation of the level of economic performance. In this sense, complementarity could not really be classified among other institutional notions like supermodularity, as had been the case in the past (Boyer 2005). To identify and work with the concept of institutional complementarity, we would first have to measure such institutional outcomes as how institutions function in relation to one another, before asking about what macro-results appear as a result of those institutional outcomes. As to the matter of economic performance, such an assessment is harder still to make because performance can be good for a time, and at other times not, while the whole institutional arrangement underlying such opposing results remains unchanged.

That preoccupation about economic performance has taken over another dimension of the study of institutional complementarities. In the "similarity" or "increasing-returns" version of the concept, institutional complementarity serves to explain the organization of capitalist economies in their different incarnations. Thus, in Varieties of Capitalism, the complementarity between institutions in different spheres is linked to the notion of a distinct variety; whereas for Regulation Theory, the complementarity between the different institutional forms refers to an accumulation regime. In part because debates about comparative capitalism and Comparative Institutional Analysis sought to explain the resilience and good performance of different economies that did not strictly adhere to the American model during the 1990s,[12] the importance of the performance criterion has persisted. Even if it has only been in the background, this question of the organization and stability of an economy remains relevant.

Complementarity between institutions in different arenas, whether they are defined as spheres, as in Varieties of Capitalism, or as institutional forms, in Regulation Theory, is what gives an economy a sense of unity. In fact, as Amable (2005, 14) argues, *models* of capitalism are not random institutional arrangements. Instead, the close-knit status of complementary institutional forms gives a sense of *coherence* to the specific institutions of each model. This sense of coherence should be taken with caution, though. Crouch (2005) has reminded us about the flexibility that actors must possess in order to transform their institutional environment in unexpected ways, dampening in turn the degree of coherence of these institutional environments. Therefore, institutional complementarities can explain the links that organize economies without necessarily defining a model of capitalism. The next step should be to insert a dynamic element into the conversation that incorporates the transformative possibilities of changing institutions that may already be linked to others. Indeed, we need to be able to account for processes of institutional change that create institutional complementarities and transform already existing ones.[13]

Institutional analyses of capitalism that have focused on the existence of different models, which by their very nature tend to express a kind of stability, need also to account for the dynamic nature of capitalism (Crouch 2010, 134).[14] Thus, there is a tension between the stability of capitalist models and capitalism's continued evolution, which is operationalized by the actions of economic agents who seek to maximize their

[12] Economies outside the Anglo-Saxon world did not converge to liberal-type capitalisms because they had different institutional arrangements and complementarities that were equally efficient, however in different sectors and with a different balance between growth and equality (Hall and Soskice 2001b; Hollingsworth and Boyer 1997). Thus, convergence toward a liberal capitalism across the Atlantic, not to mention other regions, was unlikely.

[13] Deeg and Jackson (2007) also made this suggestion. However, that discussion was focused on Varieties of Capitalism and its counterparts, rather than on institutional complementarity itself as a concept.

[14] The way in which Crouch (2010, 134) expresses this idea is as follows: "The stability of institutions and their complementarities is the stability of the person riding a bicycle, not that of the person standing still."

own advantage. The stability to which Crouch refers seems more a rigid set of arrangements constraining actors than a relative freedom to work within a given pattern. This point should not, however, make us lose sight of the critical role that institutional complementarities play in such a difficult balancing act. First, they should account for agency and allow for change while, second, they should also account for the order that constrains actors to abide by existing rules (Deeg 2007).

The different orders that institutional complementarity supports have been interpreted as models of capitalism. Because actors in a given society are seen to follow a particular set of patterns, which clearly differ from the patterns of behavior in other societies, it is tempting to assume that there is a model here. However, as discussed above, the notion of model should be approached with caution. In a way, a number of the criticisms leveled against Varieties of Capitalism point to the fact that defining a model entails analytical consequences. Indeed, a model tends to be static, which leads us in the direction of institutional determinism (Jackson and Deeg 2008). At the same time, is difficult to assess what should be the limit of regional or sectoral diversity within a certain model for it to be still considered as such (Hudson 2012; Lane and Wood 2009). Furthermore, in many ways, such models have been associated with a particular country or a relatively small cluster of countries (e.g., Bizberg 2015a; Molina and Rhodes 2007), which tends to reproduce a problem that the field of Comparative Institutional Analysis has tried to address in the past. Indeed, such was the case when the sort of capitalist activity observed in the United States, and in other Anglo-Saxon economies, was taken as *the* model of capitalism.

Thus, analyzing the links that hold economies together is not exactly straightforward. There is some agreement that the very notion of complementarity between institutions implies that several institutions might have interdependent impacts over people's behavior, though it is difficult to assess what constitutes such an impact (Amable 2005, 13–14; Campbell 2011, 212). Moreover, the relationship between institutions and economic actors is not simply one-sided. Indeed, institutions that may constitute enduring arrangements are themselves subject to change. This of course is well understood since the explanation for the resilience of different economies in the face of liberalization has referred precisely to the existence of institutional complementarities. This implies that institutions may change, to some extent, while they continue providing a stable framework within which actors maintain the same kind of strategies that have been developed in the past.

A part of the answer to this conundrum will come from an analysis of the different hypotheses about the constitution of institutional complementarities. To avoid the functionalist position that considers institutional complementarities as the product of an heroic mastermind, we should consider the broader perspective of institutional evolution over time (Pierson 2004; Thelen 2004). Because institutional complementarities happen when the functioning of one institution depends on the presence of another (Höpner 2005a, 383), their constitution should imply an ability to adjust to another. Arguably, such change is likely to be incremental to the extent that institutions are already playing a role in the political economy when it happens. That is, they are not created from scratch.

Thus, another way to study institutional complementarities is to ask how the links between economic arenas or spheres (i.e., the instances where institution "A" depends on institution "B") shape actors' behavior. To do so would be to put this study of institutional complementarity, and to some extent that of institutions as well, on what Regulation Theory calls a meso-level of analysis.[15] In addition, and in an attempt to establish a connection between different levels of analysis, Hall (2010, 214–215) proposes a series of steps meant to integrate both the rational choice and historical variants of institutionalism.[16] This is another way of integrating the agency of rational actors at the micro-level with a macro-perspective on institutions. Some of those steps point to the environment within which institutional reform takes place, and particularly to the way institutional reforms affect other institutions. That is, institutional change can result in broader consequences where more than one institution is accounted for in the process. Considering, for example, the fact that actors may be more likely to invest in institutional changes that enhance their position in other institutional realms and, as a corollary, may feel disinclined to promote reforms that would negatively affect their position in such secondary arenas.

[15] Institutional forms constitute the meso-level of analysis in Regulation Theory, since these create a link between the individual decisions of economic agents in the regulation modes, which is the micro-level of analysis, and in accumulation regimes, the macro-level of analysis (Boyer 2004, 18–19).

[16] See footnote 1.

These general equilibrium effects of institutional change are one way in which institutional complementarities come into being (Hall 2010, 212–214). Schneider (2013, 192–193), on his part, suggests that the institutional complementarities underlying Hierarchical Market Economies, the Latin American Variety of Capitalism, were formed less by an equilibrium-driven process (Aoki 2001) than by the unintended consequences of other reform processes and the creation of institutions for other purposes (Thelen 2004). Indeed, the point these authors are making is precisely that institutional complementarities are not previously designed; actors use institutions in unexpected ways, bringing their attention (and ours) to aspects of institutions that were previously ignored or untapped. These unexpected uses and consequences, in turn, lead them to adapt both behaviors and institutions themselves. Thus, as Crouch (2010, 134) suggests, institutional complementarities and institutional change are two phenomena that go hand in hand. The first instance of this relation would be the institutional changes that bring about complementarities.

Schneider (2013, 196) suggests that the institutional complementarities underlying Hierarchical Market Economies have been changing recently, and in a piecemeal process driven rather by drift and displacement[17] than by a logic of punctuated equilibrium. Therefore, because both institutional change and the formation of institutional complementarities are closely related, they could, in principle, be explained using similar analytical tools. For instance, both could be explained by a process of punctuated equilibrium, where change is seen to happen over a short period of time, or in a piecemeal process with relatively unpredictable consequences for the actors involved. Nevertheless, the main purpose of such a discussion is to point to the way agents are able to build a complex set of institutions when institutional change takes place. The broader scope of this discussion though involves the way a set of institutions is affected by changes that happen to one or more of its components.

We have, thus far, advanced three explanations for the constitution of institutional complementarities. First, the existence of a market for institutions where actors search for available institutions that could guarantee political and economic stability (Crouch 2010, 124); second, a strategy of

[17] Although they will be explained in detail below, drift refers to "the change impact of existing rules due to shifts in the environment" (Mahoney and Thelen 2010, 16) while displacement refers to "the removal of existing rules and the introduction of new ones" (Mahoney and Thelen 2010, 15).

general equilibrium where actors chose the most efficient means of maximizing their interests in the political economy (Hall 2010, 212–214); and third, the incremental process of institutional change that has unintended consequences on actors who, in turn, take advantage of these new, unexpected situations (Schneider 2013, 196). These three explanations are not mutually exclusive. Indeed, the idea of a market for institutions entails the idea that incremental change produces unexpected consequences. Institutions may change incrementally, through different mechanisms, and transform themselves in ways that actors can use in their attempts to create stability in the political economy.

Nevertheless, given the range of possibilities for how institutional change might impact institutional complementarities, more detailed discussion is required. Doing so, moreover, will help untangle the possible contradictions between the notion of stability and the possibility of change and, as mentioned above, part of the answer to that question resides in a discussion about institutional evolution. There are, of course, different understandings of what constitutes an institution, each of which may lead toward different accounts of what constitutes change and what mechanisms bring it to fruition. Naturally, the mechanisms in question are not necessarily independent from one another. Indeed, accounting for both stability and change, and working toward a kind of synthesis, requires that we draw from different traditions and their different views of institutions, their production of stability, and their notions of change.

Underlining both the strengths and weaknesses of rational choice and sociological institutionalisms, these synthetic objectives will however tend to favor the strengths while downplaying the weaknesses. It is said that rational choice institutionalism offers powerful insights into how institutions work although its characterization of institutional change is not as effective. Conversely, sociological institutionalism conceives of a world full of institutions, downplaying the relevance of their inception, but underscoring how institutions are open to interpretation and accounting, in that sense, for the ambiguities that may open opportunities for enacting changes. Hall (2010, 205–206) proposes the strategy of expanding on the rationalist theme by including elements from historical institutionalism, taking the best of both traditions. This combination between institutionalist traditions implies that agents should act strategically when interacting with institutions. The result of such integration takes into account different aspects of the interaction between actors and institutions.

From the perspective of rational choice institutionalism, change has to come from outside because institutions are seen as formed in response to collective-action problems that set up a Pareto-optimum equilibrium. This condition recalls the argument for punctuated equilibrium in which short periods of intensive change are followed by long periods of institutional stability because change is seen to happen in the wake of such external perturbations (Howlett and Migone 2011). Furthermore, even where analyses of both rationalist choice and historical institutionalism face the same kind of problem, authors in the latter tradition produce a set of theoretical tools that deal only with slow institutional change. Despite the common ground between sociological and historical institutionalist analyses, as in their view that actors face a world full of institutions, their common ground does not mean a straightforward integration of both traditions. Take, for instance, the concept of institutions as resources or instruments (Hall and Thelen 2009; Hall 2010),[18] which complements the view of institutions as embodiments of a "logic of appropriateness" (March and Olsen 1989). Institutions are not only important because of actors' adherence to them, but mainly because actors can take advantage of them to advance their interests, which goes in line with the "logic of consequences" (March and Olsen 1989).

There is a multiplicity of ways in which institutions and actors influence one another. If institutions constrain the behavior of actors by structuring their actions, actors can also change institutions.[19] This transformation is operated also by changes in the use of institutions rather than exclusively through consciously intending to do so, as is suggested by rational choice theories. This use-driven mode of transformation represents a case of compliance as a political variable insofar as actors have the ability to effect changes rather through their uses than through explicit design (Mahoney and Thelen 2010, 10–14). While institutions structure the interaction of agents in the political economy, these interactions are subject to change

[18] "Although some institutions rely on sanctions for their operation, the varieties-of-capitalism approach moves away from a view of institutions purely as factors that constrain action toward one that sees them also as resources, providing opportunities for particular types of action, and especially for collective action" (Hall and Thelen 2009, 10).

[19] This argument is reminiscent of the theory of structuration (Giddens 1984).

if actors feel that they are on the losing end of the equation, or even that they could be gaining more.[20]

Nevertheless, the usefulness of a synthesis between historical and rational choice institutionalisms is that, while the latter provides powerful insights into how institutions work, limitations remain in their explanations of institutional change. Hall (2010, 206–216) proposed six steps within a broader rationalist model of institutions that could be fully integrated into a research agenda on institutional change, which could advance the above-mentioned synthesis. These elements offer insights into the integration of different schools of thought across institutional traditions (e.g., Peters 2005; Powell and DiMaggio 1991; Scott and Meyer 1994); they also allow for a broader view of how actors interact with institutions. Such interactions, moreover, are central to any understanding of the ways in which a set of institutions can evolve over time regardless of whether they share any such common objective as the constitution of an institutional complementarity.

Hall's six steps allow for the integration of both traditions. The first step is to acknowledge that a precondition for institutional change is the assembling of a coalition. Depending on the institution in question, the nature of such coalitions may vary. The main point is that institutional change is contingent upon political support. That is, the simple desire for change is not enough. Because institutions structure the behavior of actors within the political economy, they will (or not) come to favor change depending on how their interests are affected. If changes were guided only by efficiency, coalitions would not be necessary. Second, instrumental beliefs about the possible effects of these changes are a powerful driver for change, just as uncertainty about the possible results of reform is a driver for stability. This point underscores how, given that change brings with it an amount of instability, the more it can be controlled, through some reassurances based on experience, for instance, the more likely is it that change will be fostered.

Third, the relative power among actors interested in a given institution is fundamental to assessing its potential for change. For instance,

[20] Interactions refers to the way in which agents' actions are affected by institutions when the latter play their structuring role as well as the way in which actors can modify those same institutions. It is precisely this double influence that is being remarked upon here, as otherwise it would be just influence of institutions over actors or deliberate changes of institutions enacted by actors.

when opposing forces are balanced there is a collective-action problem instead of a clear majority. This means that even in the case of a level playing field, with agents similarly endowed, the solution to collective-action dilemmas rests on power dynamics, established and reinforced by organizations. Fourth, even when there is coordination among actors, there are distributive problems around institutions. This last point is in part a consequence of the former, and its recognition of the fact that the solution to a conflict between different actors may involve both winners and losers. Every actor involved in the process of change may try to avoid being the loser and such efforts should be accounted for in the study of institutional change.

The last two steps in Hall's six-step proposal focus on the existence of a plurality of institutions in a political economy. Plurality is the basic condition for the existence of institutional complementarities. This fact is of prime importance to our theoretical framework. The fifth step therefore concerns the fact that change in one institution is affected by those other institutional arenas in which the same actors participate. Thus, actors' preferences are understood to be multidimensional. Finally, the sixth step focuses on how proposals for reform are mediated through other institutions which are not themselves the object of reform (Hall 2010, 214–215). The non-reformed institution serves as leverage in the process of institutional change and becomes itself another condition for it.

In spite of the different attempts described above to create a synthesis between different institutionalisms, the most common explanation of institutional change has been the punctuated equilibrium model, with its descriptions of moments of substantial change followed by periods of stability (Katznelson 2003). Moments of institutional change are normally considered critical junctures in which structural political forces are, for a short period, relaxed (Capoccia and Kelemen 2007, 343), allowing agents to mobilize resources that would otherwise be unavailable. Capoccia and Kelemen (2007, 348) emphasize that critical junctures are those brief moments when choices have a higher probability of being consequential in determining the outcome of interest. The significance of such relatively brief moments in the long history of an institution depends to a large extent on their ability to trigger an enduring process of path dependency (Pierson 2000a). Critical junctures can occur within one institution but not in others (Capoccia and Kelemen 2007, 349–350). Whether they affect just one of the components of a set of linked institutions or the set itself is often difficult to determine. Equally difficult to prove is how a set could avoid being affected by a change in one of its components.

By contrast, gradual institutional change, with all its mechanisms, is meaningful in spite of the speed at which it takes place. These modes of gradual change have been characterized variously by Streeck and Thelen (2005), and by Mahoney and Thelen (2010) as "displacement," "layering," "drift," and "conversion." All these modes of change take into account the conflictual character of political economies by arguing that institutions are contested by actors, or that their existence and persistence is a political outcome (Mahoney and Thelen 2010, 7–10). Further, they highlight the various ways in which actors maximize their strategies for bringing about institutional change depending on how well the institutional status quo serves their interests. The advantage of this analysis of institutional change is its ability to account for the dynamic element within institutions, which contrasts with the static vision of punctuated equilibrium.

"Displacement" refers to the process through which actors take advantage of an institution's lack of coherence by making strategic use of those features that benefit them most (Streeck and Thelen 2005, 19–20). Once such actors have taken advantage of this incoherence, the institutional features that have been left aside become less important. Then, they are effectively but not formally replaced with new ones, which implies a break in the institutional path. In other words, the salience of one institutional feature increases while the other simultaneously decreases until the political environment allows for a formal change in the whole set of rules. Once the rules are changed, displacement is said to have taken place (Mahoney and Thelen 2010, 15). Displacement, in this sense, is often associated with a political context or state of affairs that does not offer actors much discretion in the interpretation of the rules that they would seek to subvert.

"Layering," in turn, refers to the process of adding a new rule *on top* of another. Instead of the blunt replacing of one institution with another, layering adds a new institution alongside an existing one that, over time, can alter the evolution of the former. The classic example in the literature on the welfare state is the introduction of voluntary pension systems on top of a public universal one (Streeck and Thelen 2005, 23). These new systems can be framed as adjustments of the old rules but, because they are based on different logics, they eventually end up undermining the pre-existing institution. Therefore, layering is used when there are strong veto powers attached to an existing institution that cannot for that matter prevent the enactment of new rules either because the possibility of such change was not evident enough to be noticed in time or because it became politically impossible to prevent it. It is a form of political compromise.

"Drift," in turn, happens when an already existing institution does not adapt to new realities that are affecting its performance. Although the existence of the institution as such is not compromised, its responsiveness to the new environment can imply a loss of relevance for the actors involved who in turn will be forced to ignore it. While the lack of adaptation seems to imply a lack of political will, it is precisely this lack that leads to institutional change (Hacker 2005; Streeck and Thelen 2005, 24–25). The political context in which drift is most likely to appear is one in which strong veto powers are present, which is to say, when the institution has a constituency strong enough to block more direct attempts to make changes.

"Conversion" is the process through which an institution is redirected toward a goal that was not originally intended. First, this can happen when unintended institutional consequences (Pierson 2004, 115–119) become apparent, but also when actors not originally involved with the creation of the institution take over and redirect it to their own ends (Streeck and Thelen 2005, 26). Thus, there are two possible origins for conversion, one strategic in which actors actively seek to redeploy an institution created with a different goal in mind (Mahoney and Thelen 2010, 17–18), and another that results when an institution has outlived its creators or somehow no longer reflect its origins (Streeck and Thelen 2005, 27–28). Thus, if institutional preservation, albeit with a different interpretation of its objectives, works better, they would more likely seek conversion than institutional replacement (Mahoney and Thelen 2010, 26–27).

From the perspective of Regulation Theory, on the other hand, institutional change includes mechanisms like "recombination" and "hybridization." "Recombination" refers to the process by which a set of supposedly independent institutions change the links and relations between them. These changes can completely redefine the set as a whole, in part because what delineates the set are precisely the links and relations established between its constituent parts (Boyer 2004, 193). Examples of this type of institutional change are those occurring in transitional economies where a broad change in the whole institutional apparatus is triggered in part by substantial changes in one part of the apparatus. What happened in Russia with the demise of the Soviet Union, for example, when property rights were supposed to bring in capitalism along with them but did not, shows how this change was not quite significant enough to trigger full regime change. Instead, what remained at the end of the 1990s were elements of the former system combined with that of the new one (Boyer 2004, 190–192).

"Hybridization" refers to the unintended consequence of an attempt at imitation, where an institution conceived for one context is implemented in another but it proves less useful (Boyer 2004, 197). Hybridization implies the existence of a given set of institutions with a common logic that is modified by the introduction of an exogenous institution. Following the *régulationiste* agenda, both recombination and hybridization try to capture institutional change on a macro-level, in contrast to the micro-level analysis that has thus far been the focus in this section. In fact, rather than being mutually exclusive, these two levels of analysis complement one another.

Incremental institutional change allows for a more dynamic characterization of the ensemble of institutions that buttress the sense of order in a given political economy. Depending on the set of institutions at play, and the political struggles surrounding them, available types of institutional change may vary. Institutional complementarities would transform but continue to uphold the order and routines they represent. This means that actors interacting with institutions would seek to change them to better serve their interests. Nevertheless, these changes must continue to uphold the order in place, otherwise the institutions involved would be facing a bigger breakup. The continuity of the order in place means that actors continue to abide, at least to a significant extent, by the institutions with which they are interacting.

When actors continue to abide by institutions the consequence is the continuity of the order they stand for. As Jackson and Deeg (2008) argue in their discussion of the literature on comparative capitalism, institutional configurations impose a certain logic of economic action when characterizing national economies. However, a logic for economic action does not necessarily imply the existence of a model, given the arbitrariness of that definition (Amable 2005). And as signaled by the *régulationistes* when discussing the gap between the action of economic agents (the regulation modes) and the inner working of the whole economy (the accumulation regime), it is not clear how the continuous interaction of agents and institutions could build a national economic model. I argue instead that a more productive task would be to examine how those processes of institutional change consolidate around a particular logic of economic action, meaning that actors comply with the institutions that govern economic activity.

Therefore, we should consider institutional complementarities as a key feature of economic governance. If institutional complementarities mean that the functioning of "Institution A" depends on the functioning of "Institution B" and vice versa (Höpner 2005a, 383), then actors are effectively abiding simultaneously by two institutions, probably because they cannot avoid one without also avoiding the other. In this sense, neither complementarities nor economic governance can hold if economic actors can at their discretion decide not to comply with a given institution. Conversely, when we examine the same problem from a macro-perspective we cannot escape the simple fact that economic governance exists if only because important economic actors comply with the institutions that govern economic activity. Therefore, institutional complementarity and economic governance are related to the extent that the existence of an order of economic activity passes through the consolidation and upholding of rules that effectively regulate economic activity.

The next section discusses the theme of economic governance and institutional complementarity in more detail, therefore, emphasizing how the functional connection between institutions prevents actors from acting in such a way that others end up paying for the costs of their actions.

2.3 Economic Governance: Limits on Discretion

The concept of governance alone points to different social phenomena and its use has increased over the last quarter of the twentieth century, eliciting much interest from scholars in several disciplines (Bevir 2011; Levi-Faur 2012b). In general, it refers to a pattern of rules and social coordination within a given realm or subject. Concerning the economy, there are four main conceptions deriving from the use of the term in other contexts. The first focuses on the effective implementation of rules and the second on the way in which rules governing economic activity are made and by whom. The third refers to a set of preferred practices that have traditionally been promoted by international organizations because of their efficiency and effectiveness and the fourth refers to both the rules themselves and their enforcement, which in a way returns us to the first of these four conceptions. In the next paragraphs, I will briefly outline these definitions and, subsequently, will present the connection between economic governance and the possibility of limiting the discretionary powers of economic actors.

First, economic governance is considered the effective implementation of rules, referring to the degree to which the ruling of authorities is enforced and implemented in a predictable and routine-like fashion (Faucher 1999, 129). This conception relates to the degree to which authorities are able to act reasonably and in a previously defined way, and to avoid having to change course due to serious questions being raised about their authority. This notion by no means implies the perfect rationality of decision-makers as a result of which all problems could be anticipated; instead, it states that policy decisions are put in place without being directly voided by other actors' strategies. This notion of effectiveness means that it can be measured, although not necessarily with a definite metric. The emphasis for this conception is on the predictability with which economic policy is put into practice, which in turn is supported by the implementation of a given set of rules.

Second, governance is also said to be the means by which rules are produced through the interaction of a set of actors, who could be either public or private (Bartolini 2011, 8; Héritier and Rhodes 2011, 164). When applied to the economic arena, governance refers both to those who produce the rules that govern economic activities and to the way such rules are made. This conception of governance more broadly is found in other arenas where the authority of the state has to be shared with new actors, normally organized in networks around specific issues (Rhodes 1997). It is in opposition to the traditional notion of government where decisions depend on hierarchies instead of on more horizontal ways of exercising power. When applied to the economy, governance characterizes the interaction of economic actors who produce rules and the institutions that regulate a set of economic arenas.

The third sense of governance refers to a series of practices that are worth reproducing elsewhere because of their effectiveness in one particular arena. Since the mid-1970s, international organizations have used this notion of governance as a way to assess government performance (Norris 2011). Indeed, it evolved into a whole body of literature on economic development in which the presence of certain institutions played a significant role in increasing income levels (Acemoglu, Johnson, and Robinson 2001; Rodrik, Subramanian, and Trebbi 2004). It was in this particular tradition that the link between institutions, governance, and economic performance was strongest. In a way, it seemed that the silver bullet for economic development and well-being had been found. The notion of "best practices" (Bernstein and van der Ven 2017; Overman and Boyd 1994) was prevalent in policy circles that applied such prescriptions with more or less enthusiasm. Within this notion, economic governance was a consequence of getting the "right" institutions and reforms (Islam et al. 2002). This approach to economic governance has however shown its limitations (Rodrik 2006).

The fourth and final conception of economic governance to be itemized here is very broad, indeed. In this case, economic governance refers both to the rules governing economic activities and the way in which the state uses its power to enforce them, thus shaping economic life (Centeno and Cohen 2010, 120). This definition puts the rules themselves at the center of the conversation, instead of the elements required for their creation. Moreover, it shares with the first definition a consideration for the role that the state plays in the shaping of economic activities and the regulation of economic life. While there is a difference between the effectiveness of a given policy and the manner of authorities' shaping of economic life, there remain common elements between these first and fourth definitions of governance. Indeed, both refer to the effect of economic policies, with a distinct emphasis on the role of authorities, instead of the simple implantation of "good institutions." This outcome-oriented emphasis allows us to consider the link between institutional complementarities and governance.

Thus, using the notion of institutional complementarities to explain how different societies organize economic activity is closely aligned with the definition of governance as the set of rules that organize economic activities. However, if we consider the definition of institutional complementarity that focuses on the functioning of institutions and their outcomes (Höpner 2005a, 383), it aligns with the definition of economic governance as the effective implementation of rules. Moreover, the effectiveness of a given rule depends on the actors concerned complying with it. As a result, institutional complementarities strengthen economic governance because actors comply with existing rules and authorities, as well as other economic actors, can reasonably expect a degree of predictability in how the economy is working.

While an actor's compliance refers to the way they behave as required by the rules in place, Mahoney and Thelen (2010, 10–14) remind us that compliance is also a political variable, such that actors have some discretion as to whether and how they will comply with the rules governing a given institution. The more actors consider themselves free to comply only at their own discretion, the more ineffective institutions tend to become as intended outcomes do not materialize. If this happens in a series of institutions across different economic arenas, we can reasonably argue that economic governance is weak and the rules in place are unable to govern the actions of economic agents. Therefore, reducing the extent to which economic agents are free to use their own discretion is key to forging effective economic governance. If institutional complementarities consolidate, economic governance would be strengthened as agents would be called upon to comply with a wider or more imposing set of rules. Alternately, we can say that the consolidation of economic governance can be assessed by how little economic agents can do at their discretion.

The link, therefore, between institutional complementarity and economic governance provides a robust theoretical framework for studying governance that does not depend on measures of economic performance, as some of the more traditional uses of the term do (e.g., Rodrik, Subramanian, and Trebbi 2004; Rodrik 2006). Although institutional complementarities refer to functional outcomes, they limit the scope of such outcomes to the institutional realm rather than to a more macroeconomic perspective. Once such institutional outcomes take place, economic policies can be seen as more effective and stable. Therefore, as institutional complementarities consolidate, their constituent institutions perform increasingly as expected and actors increasingly comply with two institutions, or more, simultaneously even if in some cases they would prefer to comply with only one. Such compliance means that the rules in question are effective, which is the key component of economic governance. In effect, institutional complementarities reduce an agent's discretionary power to choose.

In order to answer the question of how economic governance is consolidated, we need also to understand how institutional complementarities are consolidated, which involves the process of imposing limits on an agent's ability to use their own discretion. Doing so requires retracing long processes of institutional change that, in a moment of crisis, can gather a coalition around compromises that might not have occurred otherwise. Such changes are likely to have been incremental since they tend to create less resistance than tends to be generated by more abrupt breaks with convention. Following the lead of Hall (2010, 214–215), I suggest that coalition-building is therefore key insofar as such relatively slow processes of change create collective-action problems in those instances in which vested interests would try to resist change. These institutional reforms provide many actors with both opportunities and constraints; however, they may be organized differently.

Key to the process of consolidating complementarity is the moment in which actors interpret a looming crisis as a new version of previous ones that had generated considerable losses. Admittedly, such an exogenous event implies that the reason for institutional change is unexpected and in conflict with how changes usually take place. However, the fact that the change is exogenous does not necessarily mean that it represents a break from the incremental pace of institutional change, although such a possibility cannot be entirely dismissed. It only means that the process of formation of the institutional complementarities that help to consolidate economic governance can have either exogenous or endogenous causes. Thus, what seals the consolidation of economic governance is precisely the apparent need to change and the interpretation of that appearance because, otherwise, actors would not feel the incentive to coalesce around a reform that promises to defend against some looming crisis. The fear of a repetition of past crises, in this sense, will lead actors to commit to reforms that will constitute the consolidation of institutional complementarities and new patterns of economic policymaking and governance.

It is because such actors have such a common understanding of a given situation that they are able to coalesce around the need to reform an institution in such a way that will increase its dependence on other institution. Because there is a common interpretation of the threat faced by the political economy, the solution is a form of compromise in which the success of the reformed institution will further depend on the presence of another, that is, on institutional complementarity. This last moment leads economic actors to comply with two (or more) institutions, further relinquishing their ability to act at their own discretion. That renunciation is motivated, moreover, by the evident possibility of winding up in a worse position in the wake of the impending crisis, as had happened in the past. There is a combination of an incremental reduction of an agent's discretionary power that, while limiting it, still provided substantial opportunities for its exercise until the new crises force these actors to comply with the reformed institutions, limiting such discretionary power further. Therefore, the process of consolidating economic governance is also the process of limiting the ability of an economic agent to correspondingly reduce the effectiveness of economic policies.

In essence, the consolidation of economic governance depends on an institution's ability to harness enough political support for the order that the most significant economic-power holders abide by. This requires a combination of acquiescence and coercion; the former is produced by a coalition of willing participants in the consolidation of reforms, and the latter results from the possibilities of losses resulting from the refusal to comply with the re-organization of institutions that buttress economic governance. The success of a consolidation process is not bound by a definite amount of time, meaning that it might as easily take months as years. Similarly, as much as an economy without a consolidated pattern of economic governance can deliver good economic performance, an economy with a perfectly consolidated pattern of economic governance can lead to equally terrible economic performance (Amable 2016, 93–94). This underscores that the question of economic governance is a political one.

Institutional complementarities buttress economic governance because they reduce the possibility that economic agents will use their own discretion to resist it. Non-compliance with one of a set of complementary institutions leads to the non-functioning of the other related institutions, which in turn may lead to outcomes that conflict with that agent's own interests. Although these arrangements entail a high degree of path dependency, they are also subject to change over time. So is the formation of the coalitions that support the constitution of institutional complementarities. Just as some national models, buttressed by institutional complementarities, may not be able to adjust swiftly to change in the environment, the patterns of governance buttressed by institutional complementarities might also take time to adjust. One reason for this is that an economic agent's preferences are multidimensional, which implies that their adjustment strategies may take advantage of institutional arenas beyond those currently buttressing economic governance.

Moreover, since economies change, an order that holds at one point in time might cease to hold in the future. Other institutional arenas might, at that point, empower actors to such an extent that they become able to act to break with current patterns of governance. Economic governance, in this sense, can be either consolidated or weakened. Even such actors as are active participants in the consolidation of a pattern of economic governance, confronted by a moment of crisis, could try to undermine such order if they felt that their interests would no longer be served after the crisis had passed. The use of one's discretion is only limited by the extent to which one feels compelled to participate in the institutions mandated with preventing an impending crisis.

2.4 Conclusions

Institutional complementarities have been characterized in a variety of ways. They are at the core of the literature on comparative capitalism insofar as they explain the continuity characterizing the institutional organization of capitalist economies around the world. A key feature of this explanatory power is the relative centrality of economic performance in the debates about institutional complementarity. However, this association between the two concepts is seen to have been misleading where the former is intrinsically unstable and the latter refers to the relatively stable aspects of political economies. I argue, therefore, that a more productive way of taking advantage of the concept of institutional complementarity in a political economy is through the concept of economic governance. This particular association accounts for the dynamic role of institutions, which can continuously evolve and change according to the interests and needs of its economic actors.

This way of understanding the role that institutional complementarities play in capitalist economies does not pretend to replace the traditional use of the term. It does though assert that its association with economic governance represents a less complex operationalizing of the concept insofar as the outcome of economic governance has a more straightforward relation with the institutional realm than the notion of economic performance does. Indeed, if economic governance represents the effectiveness of institutional rules, then, institutional complementarity buttresses economic governance forcing actors to comply with a multiplicity of institutions. Moreover, the functional performance of institutions refers mainly to the fact that economic agents largely comply with those institutions as, otherwise, their rule-like quality would be void. Since agents abide repeatedly by the institutions, such situation brings stability and predictability to the political economy.

The next chapter deals with the structure of economic governance in Latin America from a historical perspective, emphasizing in the first part on how the political and economic project around development in the middle of the twentieth century constituted the organizing principle of economic governance in the region. In subsequent sections, is discussed the manner in which the crisis that finally brought down such a model affected the interests that had built around the policies implemented in those years as well as the reforms seeking to respond to the crisis itself. In each country, the crisis manifested differently depending on its particularities and left equally diverse legacies with which actors had to deal later in time. Depending on the construction of broad coalitions of reformers, new crises could be avoided and economic governance could be consolidated through the constitution of institutional complementarities. A key feature is that such coalitions prevent vested interests to act at their discretion, having as the main consequence the consolidation of an institutional complementarity and the upholding of a new economic order.

References

Acemoglu, Daron, Simon Johnson, and James A. Robinson. 2001. "The Colonial Origins of Comparative Development: An Empirical Investigation." *American Economic Review* 91 (5): 1369–1401. https://doi.org/10.1257/aer.91.5.1369.

Albert, Michel. 1991. *Capitalisme Contre Capitalisme*. Paris: Éditions du Seuil.

Amable, Bruno. 2000. "Institutional Complementarity and Diversity of Social Systems of Innovation and Production." *Review of International Political Economy* 7 (4): 645–687. https://doi.org/10.1080/096922900750034572.

Amable, Bruno. 2005. *Les Cinq Capitalismes. Diversité des Systèmes Économiques et Sociaux dans la Mondialisation*. Paris: Éditions du Seuil.

Amable, Bruno. 2016. "Institutional Complementarities in the Dynamic Comparative Analysis of Capitalism." *Journal of Institutional Economics* 12 (1): 79–103. https://doi.org/10.1017/s1744137415000211.

Amable, Bruno, Ekkehard Ernst, and Stefano Palombarini. 2005. "How Do Financial Markets Affect Industrial Relations: An Institutional Complementarity Approach." *Socio-Economic Review* 3 (2): 311–330. https://doi.org/10.1093/ser/mwi013.

Amable, Bruno, and Stefano Palombarini. 2009. "A Neorealist Approach to Institutional Change and the Diversity of Capitalism." *Socio-Economic Review* 7 (1): 123–143. https://doi.org/10.1093/ser/mwn018.

Aoki, Masahiko. 1994. "The Contingent Governance of Teams: Analysis of Institutional Complementarity." *International Economic Review* 35 (3): 657–676. https://doi.org/10.2307/2527079.

Aoki, Masahiko. 1996. "Towards a Comparative Institutional Analysis: Motivations and Some Tentative Theorizing." *The Japanese Economic Review* 47 (1): 1–19. https://doi.org/10.1111/j.1468-5876.1996.tb00031.x.

Aoki, Masahiko. 2000. *Information, Corporate Governance, and Institutional Diversity. Competitiveness in Japan, the USA, and the Transitional Economies*. Oxford: Oxford University Press. Original edition, 1995.

Aoki, Masahiko. 2001. *Toward a Comparative Institutional Analysis*. Cambridge, MA: MIT Press.

Arrow, Kenneth J. 1950. "A Difficulty in the Concept of Social Welfare." *Journal of Political Economy* 58 (4): 328–346. https://doi.org/10.1086/256963.

Bartolini, Stefano. 2011. "New Modes of European Governance." In *New Modes of Governance in Europe: Governing in the Shadow of Hierarchy*, edited by Adrienne Héritier and Martin Rhodes, 1–18. Basingstoke: Palgrave Macmillan.

Bernstein, Steven, and Hamish van der Ven. 2017. "Best Practices in Global Governance." *Review of International Studies* 43 (3): 534–556. https://doi.org/10.1017/s0260210516000425.

Bevir, Mark. 2011. "Governance as Theory, Practice, and Dilemma." In *The SAGE Handbook of Governance*, edited by Mark Bevir, 1–16. London and Thousand Oaks: Sage.

Bizberg, Ilán. 2015a. "Tipos de Capitalismo en América Latina." In *Variedades del Capitalismo en América Latina: los Casos de México, Brasil, Argentina y Chile*, edited by Ilán Bizberg, 41–94. México: El Colegio de México.

Bizberg, Ilán, ed. 2015b. *Variedades del Capitalismo en América Latina: los Casos de México, Brasil, Argentina y Chile*. México: El Colegio de México.

Bizberg, Ilán. 2019. *Diversity of Capitalisms in Latin America*. Cham: Palgrave Macmillan.

Boschi, Renato R. 2011a. "Introdução. Instituições, Trajetórias e Desenvolvimento. Uma Discussão a partir da América Latina." In *Variedades de Capitalismo, Política e Desenvolvimento na América Latina*, edited by Renato R. Boschi, 7–30. Belo Horizonte: Editora UFMG.

Boschi, Renato R., ed. 2011b. *Variedades de Capitalismo, Política e Desenvolvimento na América Latina*. Belo Horizonte: Editora UFMG.

Boyer, Robert. 1990. *The Regulation School: A Critical Introduction*. New York: Columbia University Press.

Boyer, Robert. 2002–2003. "Variété du Capitalisme et Théorie de la Régulation." *L'Année de la Régulation* 6 (Économie, Institutions, Pouvoirs): 125–194.

Boyer, Robert. 2004. *Une Théorie du Capitalisme Est-elle Possible?* Paris: Odile Jacob.

Boyer, Robert. 2005. "Coherence, Diversity, and the Evolution of Capitalisms—The Institutional Complementarity Hypothesis." *Evolutionary Institutional Economics Review* 2 (1): 43–80. https://doi.org/10.14441/eier.2.43.

Boyer, Robert. 2015. *Économie politique des capitalismes. Théorie de la régulation et des crises*. Paris: La Découverte.

Büthe, Tim, and Walter Mattli. 2011. *The New Global Rulers: The Privatization of Regulation in the World Economy*. Princeton: Princeton University Press.

Campbell, John L. 2011. "The US Financial Crisis: Lessons for Theories of Institutional Complementarity." *Socio-Economic Review* 9 (2): 211–234. https://doi.org/10.1093/ser/mwq034.

Campbell, John L., and Ove K. Pedersen. 2001. *The Rise of Neoliberalism and Institutional Analysis*. Princeton: Princeton University Press.

Campbell, John L., and Ove K. Pedersen. 2007. "The Varieties of Capitalism and Hybrid Success: Denmark in the Global Economy." *Comparative Political Studies* 40 (3): 307–332. https://doi.org/10.1177/0010414006286542.

Capoccia, Giovanni, and R. Daniel Kelemen. 2007. "The Study of Critical Junctures. Theory, Narrative, and Counterfactuals in Historical Institutionalism." *World Politics* 59 (2): 341–369. https://doi.org/10.1017/s0043887100020852.

Cardoso, Eliana, and Ann Helwege. 1992. *Latin America's Economy: Diversity, Trends, and Conflicts*. Cambridge, MA: MIT Press.

Centeno, Miguel A., and Joseph N. Cohen. 2010. *Global Capitalism: A Sociological Perspective*. Cambridge: Polity Press.

Crouch, Colin. 2005. *Capitalist Diversity and Change*. New York: Oxford University Press.

Crouch, Colin. 2010. "Complementarity." In *The Oxford Handbook of Comparative Institutional Analysis*, edited by Glenn Morgan, John L. Campbell, Colin Crouch, Ove K. Pedersen and Richard Whitley. Oxford: Oxford University Press.

Crouch, Colin, Wolfgang Streeck, Robert Boyer, Bruno Amable, Peter A. Hall, and Gregory Jackson. 2005. "Dialogue on 'Institutional Complementarity and Political Economy'." *Socio-Economic Review* 3 (2): 359–382. https://doi.org/10.1093/ser/mwi015.

Deeg, Richard. 2007. "Complementarity and Institutional Change in Capitalist Systems." *Journal of European Public Policy* 14 (4): 611–630. https://doi.org/10.1080/13501760701314433.

Deeg, Richard, and Gregory Jackson. 2007. "Towards a More Dynamic Theory of Capitalist Variety." *Socio-Economic Review* 5 (1): 149–179. https://doi.org/10.1093/ser/mwl021.

Domínguez, Jorge I. 1998. "Free Politics and Free Markets in Latin America." *Journal of Democracy* 9 (4): 70–84. https://doi.org/10.1353/jod.1998.0059.

Ebenau, Matthias. 2012. "Varieties of Capitalism or Dependency? A Critique of the VoC Approach for Latin America." *Competition and Change* 16 (3): 206–223. https://doi.org/10.1179/1024529412z.00000000014.

Fanelli, José María, ed. 2007. *Understanding Market Reforms in Latin America: Similar Reforms, Diverse Constituencies, Varied Results*. Houndmills, Basingstoke: Palgrave Macmillan.

Faucher, Philippe. 1999. "Restoring Governance: Has Brazil Got It Right (at Last)?" In *Markets and Democracy in Latin America: Conflict or Convergence?*, edited by Philip Oxhorn and Pamela K. Starr, 103–130. Boulder: Lynne Rienner Publishers.

Feenstra, Robert C., and Gary G. Hamilton. 2006. *Emergent Economies, Divergent Paths: Economic Organization and International Trade in South Korea and Taiwan*. Cambridge: Cambridge University Press.

Frieden, Jeffry A. 1991. *Debt, Development, and Democracy: Modern Political Economy and Latin America, 1965–1985*. Princeton: Princeton University Press.

Giddens, Anthony. 1984. *The Constitution of Society: Outline of the Theory of Structuration*. Berkeley: University of California Press.

Hacker, Jacob S. 2005. "Policy Drift: The Hidden Politics of US Welfare State Retrenchment." In *Beyond Continuity: Institutional Change in Advanced Political Economies*, edited by Wolfgang Streeck and Kathleen Thelen, 40–82. Oxford: Oxford University Press.

Haggard, Stephan, and Robert Kaufman, eds. 1992a. *The Politics of Economic Adjustment*. Princeton: Princeton University Press.

Haggard, Stephan, and Robert R. Kaufman. 1992b. "Institutions and Economic Adjustment." In *The Politics of Economic Adjustment*, edited by Stephan Haggard and Robert R. Kaufman, 3–37. Princeton: Princeton University Press.

Hall, Peter A. 2010. "Historical Institutionalism in Rationalist and Sociological Perspective." In *Explaining Institutional Change: Ambiguity, Agency, and Power*, edited by James Mahoney and Kathleen Thelen, 204–223. Cambridge: Cambridge University Press.

Hall, Peter A. 2018. "Varieties of Capitalism in Light of the Euro Crisis." *Journal of European Public Policy* 25 (1): 7–30. https://doi.org/10.1080/13501763.2017.1310278.

Hall, Peter A., and Daniel W. Gingerich. 2009. "Varieties of Capitalism and Institutional Complementarities in the Political Economy: An Empirical Analysis." *British Journal of Political Science* 39 (3): 449–482. https://doi.org/10.1017/s0007123409000672.

Hall, Peter A., and David Soskice. 2001a. "An Introduction to Varieties of Capitalism." In *Varieties of Capitalism: The Institutional Foundations of*

Comparative Advantage, edited by Peter A. Hall and David Soskice, 1–68. Oxford: Oxford University Press.

Hall, Peter A., and David Soskice, eds. 2001b. *Varieties of Capitalism: The Institutional Foundations of Comparative Advantage*. Oxford: Oxford University Press.

Hall, Peter A., and Rosemary C. R. Taylor. 1996. "Political Science and the Three New Institutionalisms." *Political Studies* 44: 936–957. https://doi.org/10.1111/j.1467-9248.1996.tb00343.x.

Hall, Peter A., and Kathleen Thelen. 2009. "Institutional Change in Varieties of Capitalism." *Socio-Economic Review* 7 (1): 7–34. https://doi.org/10.1093/ser/mwn020.

Hancké, Bob, Martin Rhodes, and Mark Thatcher, eds. 2007. *Beyond Varieties of Capitalism: Conflict, Contradictions, and Complementarities in the European Economy*. New York: Oxford University Press.

Héritier, Adrienne, and Martin Rhodes. 2011. "Conclusion: New Modes of Governance: Emergence, Execution, Evolution and Evaluation." In *New Modes of Governance in Europe: Governing in the Shadow of Hierarchy*, edited by Adrienne Héritier and Martin Rhodes, 163–174. Basingstoke: Palgrave Macmillan.

Hollingsworth, J. Rogers, and Robert Boyer, eds. 1997. *Contemporary Capitalism: The Embeddedness of Institutions*. Cambridge: Cambridge University Press.

Höpner, Martin. 2005a. "Epilogue to 'Explaining Institutional Complementarity'." *Socio-Economic Review* 3 (2): 383–387. https://doi.org/10.1093/ser/mwi016.

Höpner, Martin. 2005b. "What Connects Industrial Relations and Corporate Governance? Explaining Institutional Complementarity." *Socio-Economic Review* 3 (2): 331–358. https://doi.org/10.1093/ser/mwi014.

Howell, Chris. 2003. "Varieties of Capitalism: And Then There Was One?" *Comparative Politics* 36 (1): 103–124. https://doi.org/10.2307/4150162.

Howlett, Michael, and Andrea Migone. 2011. "Charles Lindblom Is Alive and Well and Living in Punctuated Equilibrium Land." *Policy and Society* 30 (1): 53–62. https://doi.org/10.1016/j.polsoc.2010.12.006.

Hudson, Ray. 2012. "Regions, Varieties of Capitalism and the Legacies of Neoliberalism." In *Capitalist Diversity and Diversity Within Capitalism*, edited by Christel Lane and Geoffrey Wood, 189–208. Abingdon and New York: Routledge.

Islam, Roumeen, Arup Banerji, Robert Cull, Asli Demirgüc-Kunt, Simeon Djankov, Alexander Dyck, Aart Kraay, Caralee McLiezh, and Russell Pittman. 2002. *World Development Report 2002: Building Institutions for Markets*. Washington, DC: World Bank.

Jackson, Gregory, and Richard Deeg. 2008. "From Comparing Capitalisms to the Politics of Institutional Change." *Review of International Political Economy* 14 (4): 680–709. https://doi.org/10.1080/09692290802260704.

Johnson, Chalmers. 1987. "Political Institutions and Economic Performance: The Government-Business Relationship in Japan, South Korea, and Taiwan." In *The Political Economy of the New Asian Industrialism*, edited by Frederic C. Deyo, 136–164. Ithaca: Cornell University Press.

Kang, Nahee, and Jeremy Moon. 2012. "Institutional Complementarity Between Corporate Governance and Corporate Social Responsibility: A Comparative Institutional Analysis of Three Capitalisms." *Socio-Economic Review* 10 (1): 85–108. https://doi.org/10.1093/ser/mwr025.

Katznelson, Ira. 2003. "Periodization and Preferences. Reflections on Purposive Action in Comparative Historical Social Science." In *Comparative Historical Analysis in the Social Sciences*, edited by James Mahoney and Dietrich Rueschemeyer, 270–301. Cambridge: Cambridge University Press.

King, Lawrence P. 2007. "Central European Capitalism in Comparative Perspective." In *Beyond Varieties of Capitalism: Conflict, Contradictions, and Complementarities in the European Economy*, edited by Bob Hancké, Martin Rhodes and Mark Thatcher, 307–327. New York: Oxford University Press.

Kohli, Atul. 2012. "Coping with Globalization: Asian Versus Latin American Strategies of Development, 1980–2010." *Revista de Economia Política* 32 (4): 531–556. https://doi.org/10.1590/s0101-31572012000400001.

La Porta, Rafael, Florencio Lopez-De-Silanes, and Andrei Shleifer. 1999. "Corporate Ownership Around the World." *The Journal of Finance* 54 (2): 471–517. https://doi.org/10.1111/0022-1082.00115.

Lane, Christel, and Geoffrey Wood. 2009. "Capitalist Diversity and Diversity within Capitalism" *Economy and Society* 38 (4): 531–551. https://doi.org/10.1080/03085140903190300.

Lane, Christel, and Geoffrey Wood, eds. 2012. *Capitalist Diversity and Diversity Within Capitalism*. Abingdon and New York: Routledge.

Levi-Faur, David. 2012a. "From 'Big Government' to 'Big Governance'?" In *The Oxford Handbook of Governance*, edited by David Levi-Faur, 3–18. New York: Oxford University Press.

Levi-Faur, David, ed. 2012b. *The Oxford Handbook of Governance*. New York: Oxford University Press.

Levitsky, Steven, and Kenneth M. Roberts, eds. 2011. *The Resurgence of the Latin American Left*. Baltimore: Johns Hopkins University Press.

Mahoney, James, and Kathleen Thelen. 2010. "A Theory of Gradual Institutional Change." In *Explaining Institutional Change: Ambiguity, Agency, and Power*, edited by James Mahoney and Kathleen Thelen, 1–37. Cambridge: Cambridge University Press.

March, James G., and Johan P. Olsen. 1989. *Rediscovering Institutions: The Organizational Basis of Politics*. New York: Free Press.

Mas-Colell, Andreu, Michael D. Whinston, and Jerry R. Green. 1995. *Microeconomic Theory*. New York and Oxford: Oxford University Press.

Molina, Oscar, and Martin Rhodes. 2007. "The Political Economy of Adjustment in Mixed Market Economies: A Study of Spain and Italy." In *Beyond Varieties of Capitalism: Conflict, Contradictions, and Complementarities in the European Economy*, edited by Bob Hancké, Martin Rhodes and Mark Thatcher, 223–252. New York: Oxford University Press.

Morgan, Glenn, John L. Campbell, Collin Crouch, Ove Kaj Pedersen, and Richard Whitley. 2010a. "Introduction." In *The Oxford Handbook of Comparative Institutional Analysis*, edited by Glenn Morgan, John L. Campbell, Collin Crouch, Ove Kaj Pedersen and Richard Whitley, 1–11. New York: Oxford University Press.

Morgan, Glenn, John L. Campbell, Collin Crouch, Ove Kaj Pedersen, and Richard Whitley, eds. 2010b. *The Oxford Handbook of Comparative Institutional Analysis*. Oxford: Oxford University Press.

Norris, Pippa. 2011. "Measuring Governance." In *The SAGE Handbook of Governance*, edited by Mark Bevir, 179–216. London and Thousand Oaks: Sage.

North, Douglass C. 1990. *Institutions, Institutional Change, and Economic Performance*. Cambridge: Cambridge University Press.

O'Donnell, Guillermo A. 1993. "On the State, Democratization and Some Conceptual Problems: A Latin American View with Glances at Some Post-communist Countries." *World Development* 21 (8): 1355–1369. https://doi.org/10.1016/0305-750x(93)90048-e.

Ostrom, Elinor. 1990. *Governing the Commons: The Evolution of Institutions for Collective Action*. Cambridge: Cambridge University Press.

Overman, E. Sam, and Kathy J. Boyd. 1994. "Best Practice Research and Post-bureaucratic Reform." *Journal of Public Administration Research and Theory: J-PART* 4 (1): 67–83. https://doi.org/10.1093/oxfordjournals.jpart.a037195.

Peters, Guy. 2005. *Institutional Theory in Political Science: The New Institutionalism*. London: Continuum.

Pierson, Paul. 2000a. "Increasing Returns, Path Dependence, and the Study of Politics." *American Political Science Review* 94 (2): 251–267. https://doi.org/10.2307/2586011.

Pierson, Paul. 2000b. "The Limits of Design: Explaining Institutional Origins and Change." *Governance* 13 (4): 475–499. https://doi.org/10.1111/0952-1895.00142.

Pierson, Paul. 2004. *Politics in Time: History, Institutions, and Social Analysis*. Princeton: Princeton University Press.

Powell, Walter W., and Paul J. DiMaggio. 1991. *The New Institutionalism in Organizational Analysis*. Chicago: University of Chicago Press.

Remmer, Karen L. 1990. "Democracy and Economic Crisis: The Latin American Experience." *World Politics* 42 (3): 315–335. https://doi.org/10.2307/2010414.

Rhodes, R. A. W. 1997. *Understanding Governance: Policy Networks, Governance, Reflexivity, and Accountability*. Buckingham and Philadelphia: Open University Press.

Rodrik, Dani. 2006. "Goodbye Washington Consensus, Hello Washington Confusion? A Review of the World Bank's 'Economic Growth in the 1990s: Learning from a Decade of Reform'." *Journal of Economic Literature* 44 (4): 973–987. https://doi.org/10.1257/jel.44.4.973.

Rodrik, Dani, Arvind Subramanian, and Francesco Trebbi. 2004. "Institutions Rule: The Primacy of Institutions Over Geography and Integration in Economic Development." *Journal of Economic Growth* 9 (2): 131–165. https://doi.org/10.1023/b:joeg.0000031425.72248.85.

Rothstein, Bo. 2014. "What Is the Opposite of Corruption?" *Third World Quarterly* 35 (5): 737–752. https://doi.org/10.1080/01436597.2014.921424.

Sánchez-Ancochea, Diego. 2009. "State, Firms and the Process of Industrial Upgrading: Latin America's Variety of Capitalism and the Costa Rican Experience." *Economy and Society* 38 (1): 62–86. https://doi.org/10.1080/03085140802560520.

Schneider, Ben Ross. 2009a. "A Comparative Political Economy of Diversified Business Groups, or How States Organize Big Business." *Review of International Political Economy* 16 (2): 178–201. https://doi.org/10.1080/09692290802453713.

Schneider, Ben Ross. 2009b. "Hierarchical Market Economies and Varieties of Capitalism in Latin America." *Journal of Latin American Studies* 41 (3): 553–575. https://doi.org/10.1017/s0022216x09990186.

Schneider, Ben Ross. 2012. "Contrasting Capitalisms: Latin America in Comparative Perspective." In *The Oxford Handbook of Latin American Political Economy*, edited by Javier Santiso and Jeff Dayton-Johnson, 381–402. New York: Oxford University Press.

Schneider, Ben Ross. 2013. *Hierarchical Capitalism in Latin America: Business, Labor, and the Challenges of Equitable Development*. New York: Cambridge University Press.

Schneider, Martin R., and Mihai Paunescu. 2012. "Changing Varieties of Capitalism and Revealed Comparative Advantages from 1990 to 2005: A Test of the Hall and Soskice Claims." *Socio-Economic Review* 10 (4): 731–753. https://doi.org/10.1093/ser/mwr038.

Schrank, Andrew. 2009. "Understanding Latin American Political Economy: Varieties of Capitalism or Fiscal Sociology?" *Economy and Society* 38 (1): 53–61. https://doi.org/10.1080/03085140802560512.

Scott, W. Richard, and John W. Meyer. 1994. *Institutional Environments and Organizations Structural Complexity and Individualism*. Thousand Oaks: Sage.

Streeck, Wolfgang, and Kathleen Thelen. 2005. "Introduction: Institutional Change in Advanced Political Economies." In *Beyond Continuity: Institutional Change in Advanced Political Economies*, edited by Wolfgang Streeck and Kathleen Thelen, 1–39. Oxford: Oxford University Press.

Thelen, Kathleen. 1999. "Historical Institutionalism in Comparative Politics." *Annual Review of Political Science* 2: 369–404. https://doi.org/10.1146/annurev.polisci.2.1.369.

Thelen, Kathleen. 2004. *How Institutions Evolve: The Political Economy of Skills in Germany, Britain, the United States, and Japan*. Cambridge: Cambridge University Press.

Whitley, Richard. 2005. "How National Are Business Systems? The Role of States and Complementary Institutions in Standardizing Systems of Economic Coordination and Control at the National Level." In *Changing Capitalisms? Internationalization, Institutional Change, and Systems of Economic Organization*, edited by Glenn Morgan, Richard Whitley and Eli. Moen, 190–231. Oxford: Oxford University Press.

CHAPTER 3

Economic Governance in Latin America

The study of Latin American capitalism has extended over almost a century. What exactly distinguishes capitalism in the region, if anything at all? By this point, it should be clear that, as Schneider (2012, 382) argues, Latin American capitalism is a moving target. To understand Latin American capitalism, scholars have often referred to capitalism in other regions as a kind of benchmark.[1] While there have been attempts to characterize Latin American capitalism without relying on pre-existing models, the region's position within an international context does make such benchmarks helpful.[2] However, by analyzing how institutional complementarities consolidate new governance arrangements in a number of

[1] Perspectives that consider Latin American capitalism as lagging behind in any of a number of dimensions (stages, institutions, completeness, and so on), normally measure capitalism in the region according to a set benchmark, therefore do not consider it as a different entity. Examples of such perspectives are modernization theory (Rostow 1971) and the Washington Consensus (Williamson 1990).

[2] This is epitomized in the concept of emerging markets that attempts to roughly characterize those economies not belonging to the Organization for Economic Cooperation and Development—OECD. Some exceptions apply even to this characterization, such as Turkey. However, most interesting for the present work are Chile and Mexico, which are already members, and also Brazil, which, after the election of Jair Bolsonaro as president in 2018, courted the US Administration of Donald Trump to receive approval for its bid to enter the OECD (Boadle 2020). China is another exception since its status

A. Angel, *Consolidating Economic Governance in Latin America*, Governance, Development, and Social Inclusion in Latin America, https://doi.org/10.1007/978-3-030-64522-9_3

Latin American countries, this work looks at Latin American capitalism from within.

This particular approach is challenging, since the region's capitalist development cannot be fully detached from that of the wider world, for at least two reasons. First, the regional economy has been integrated within the global economy for centuries; and second, previous scholarly attempts to explore regional particularities have used capitalism elsewhere as a reference. Any analysis of capitalist activity in Latin America must account for its integration with the world's economy, which after all is one of its defining characteristics; nevertheless, while having a reference point for comparison might explain some features, relying too heavily on comparative analysis actually obscures understanding of the Latin American economy itself. As Schneider (2012, 382–383) contends, the continent's capitalist history is a long one and it should be understood as independent.

In Latin America, the concept most closely associated with capitalism since at least the Great Depression is that of development, which encompasses a series of interventions normally carried out by the state.[3] Development and developmentalism both have an extensive intellectual tradition, and any attempt to explain it in a few pages will inevitably fall short of doing it full justice, nonetheless, a short discussion will be offered below. During the 2000s, after certain countries elected left-wing coalitions, discussions of the consequences of the previous decade's wave of market reforms concluded that their one-size-fits-all approach had had profound negative consequences.[4] As a result, several governments re-assumed the role of central actors within their respective economies while maintaining some of the market reforms enacted earlier.

Studying the region's experience of development is crucial to understanding the ways in which economic governance in Latin America

as emerging economy is debatable despite not being in the OECD (Barth, Caprio, and Phumiwasana 2009).

[3] The vastness of the continent, with hundreds of millions of inhabitants and a dozen and a half countries, reveals the challenges of classification and abstraction. Generalizing categories might help to grasp big trends, but one should not overlook the fact that such exercises are incomplete, inasmuch as they cannot account for the differences and nuances that exist within the Latin American capitalist context.

[4] About the left turn in Latin America and its consequences in different spheres, see Levitsky and Roberts (2011) and Cameron and Hershberg (2010).

consolidates. Development represented a promise of transformation of both economies and societies, justifying the mobilization of substantial political and economic resources. In the context of rapidly changing societies, and considering that the state itself was central to these processes, the idea of development was behind many of the states' policies and rules. Moreover, the developmental project, explained in more detail below, allowed for the effective implementation of such rules and policies: this constitutes the core of economic governance. Of course, this fact should not suggest that every policy or rule created in the context of the developmental project in Latin America was implemented effectively. The argument is simply that economic governance was related to development in Latin America for several decades. Thus, any analysis of economic governance in Latin America must begin with an analysis of development.

3.1 Development as Economic Governance

The Depression and the Second World War created a situation that legitimized the intervention of the state in the economy. In many countries around the world, this intervention resulted in what is known as the Developmental State (Woo-Cumings 1999).[5] The international context in which Import Substitution Industrialization—ISI—was implemented was relatively stable from the 1930s or 1940s to the 1970s. In Latin America, ISI and state capitalism appeared as a response to the economic crisis caused by the Depression and subsequently consolidated in the aftermath of the Second World War. The biggest Latin American economies implemented policies associated with ISI to varying degrees, responding to their own priorities, needs, and challenges without following a defined blueprint (Thorp 1992).

However, a key point in the region's developmental trajectory was the publication of the *Manifesto* by Raúl Prebisch, which describes the problems of Latin America in the context of a world economy (Prebisch and Martínez 1949). While these problems had already existed both in policy and in academic circles for many years, the text offers a helpful synthesis that applies in both arenas. For instance, one important argument mobilized by Prebisch, which came to be known as the declining terms of

[5] Even if it is tempting to assert that the Developmental State was a phenomenon of the Global South, its main example is Japan (Johnson 1982), which does not belong to that group of countries.

trade, proposes that raw materials producers would need to sell them in greater quantities to receive the same amount of manufactured goods in return. A strategy to break such a vicious circle would be to promote industrialization within individual countries and to encourage them in turn to rely on internal markets.[6]

Declining terms of trade were connected with balance of payments crises because they made it more difficult to gather hard currency to pay for imports. The lack of capital thus jeopardized efforts to invest in machinery that would improve productivity. In turn, low productivity prevented wage increases, causing the fragmentation of the consumer products markets, because there were not enough customers. While sectors such as agriculture were also among the many problems that development could have addressed, the point is that it was conceived of as a series of linkages among economic and policy arenas. Indeed, these points of connection were so important that the success of each policy was considered essential to the success of other policies.[7]

While it would be a stretch to argue that development problems or interventions were intended from the outset to create institutional complementarities, the importance of such relationships can nevertheless not be denied. Development as a project implies a comprehensive review of capitalism in Latin America, with emphasis on particular connections and dynamics. Several interventions were implemented in order to overcome the obstacles created by the region's position within the world

[6] Fajardo (2015), on whom the next paragraph relies, offers an in-depth discussion of how such intellectual and policy endeavors were linked. The wider literature on development is vast, covering several disciplines and years. Unfortunately, to do it full justice is well beyond the scope of the present work.

[7] Development is often associated with industrialization even if the existence of capitalist activities transforming inputs goes back to at least the late nineteenth century in Latin America. Rents also existed in countries that were rich in mineral resources and enclaves were pervasive in many countries, e.g., the Caribbean. These are also capitalist activities but differ qualitatively from the process of industrialization. One difference is their respective impact in the possibility of democratization (Rueschemeyer, Stephens, and Stephens 1992) as well as the type of incorporation of the labor force into the political systems (Collier and Collier 1991). Capitalist development in Latin America is said to depend on the economic structures put in place during colonial times, which is the traditional structuralist view epitomized in the classic works of Cardoso and Faletto (1976) and Furtado (1970). Moreover, in the mid-twentieth century, industrialization represented a substantial increase in the rate of economic growth, which would later become more important in the understanding of development.

economy, highlighting connections among policy arenas (Fajardo 2015). Moreover, to a large extent, these settings often resembled institutional complementarities, which were discussed in the previous chapter. Höpner (2005, 383) asserts that institutional complementarity refers to instances where the functional performance of one institution depends on the presence of another institution and vice versa; and, indeed, development involved some complementarity among its key policies.

Without falling into conceptual stretching (Sartori 1970, 1034–1035), is clear that the developmentalist project sought to address several challenges of Latin American economies simultaneously, and that some of the reforms it instituted were dependent on other reforms in order to succeed. This condition is similar to the concept of complementarity discussed in the previous chapter. However, practices such as offering subsidized credit to economic sectors, or creating new industries or companies—especially those that require substantial capital investments—cannot be considered as institutions in the sense of rules or rule-like regularized practices. Other policies, in turn, such as restrictive trade policies or a state monopoly over previously defined industries signaled the existence of rule-like provisions.[8] In addition, a position shared by the literatures on development and on the sociopolitical relations of capitalism is that social and political specificities determine economic outcomes.

Beyond the conceptual realm, however, crucial differences appear, and these suggest the limits of applying a concept such as complementarity to a literature on a different topic. Theories about sociopolitical relations within capitalism demonstrate that there are different ways of attaining good economic performance. For its part, the literature on development seeks to explain the lag in performance, among other dimensions, between non-advanced economies and advanced capitalist economies, and also to elucidate the strategies that would reduce such lag. Furthermore, this scholarly preoccupation around development was transformed into a series of policy prescriptions that later came to be known as developmentalism. This is yet another difference between the theories that discuss the social relationships within capitalism, such as Varieties of Capitalism

[8] A closed economy or the existence of a state monopoly on a given industry represent practices that structure agents' actions since the conditions to operate businesses with an open economy or competing in a market with a prevalent state presence modify the behavior of economic and political agents. These policies fit within the definition of institutions advanced by Hall (2010, 204).

and Regulation Theory, and the theories that focus on the relationship between development and capitalism in Latin America: scholarship in the first category does not conceive of capitalism (and its institutional bases) as a political project to transform society, whereas scholarship in the second category often justifies policy prescriptions to change a given state of affairs. Development as a theoretical endeavor evolved alongside policy practice, both before and after its recognition as a concept both in the academic and policy worlds.

The links among economic arenas most commonly addressed by the literature on development in its many stages are those involving foreign financing and jeopardized industrialization efforts (Fajnzylber 1980; Prebisch 1963). Since industrialization required significant resources, which Latin American countries did not possess, these had to come from abroad. However, foreign investment was scarce and exports were insufficient to fully finance domestic industrialization. When the state stepped in, it was able to mobilize resources—whether through taxation, multilateral credit, or, in many cases, outright monetary emission. Thus, the institutions governing relations between Latin American economies and the rest of the world were dependent on those institutions governing monetary and fiscal affairs: the presence and usage of the former led to specific results in the latter. Indeed, the relationships among different areas within Latin American economies clearly recall the concept of institutional complementarities, since the functional features of one institution depended on the presence of another institution, and vice versa.

As mentioned above, there was a crucial political dimension to the links among different arenas of Latin American economies, because the aim of the intellectual and political endeavors around development was also to devise a set of policies seeking to transform their current situation. This meant that there was an overlap between the conceptual and policy endeavors in which many policymakers participated. In consequence, because the defining characteristics of Latin American economies—exporters of raw materials and importers of capital and manufactured goods—were deemed counterproductive, they were the object of a thorough intervention by the authorities. This brings us back to developmentalism, which became the political project intended to transform that situation.[9] In principle, it was the role of the state to break

[9] Sampaio Jr. (2012, 674) asserts, from a critical perspective, that developmentalism was "an ideological weapon of social and economic forces that, at the moment of crystallization

the bottlenecks preventing Latin American economies from reaching their potential. Governments of the region would tackle these problems by implementing a series of economic policies which would allow them, or so the argument went, to improve the economic conditions in their countries.

Some policies had a dramatic impact while others remained inconsequential; however, all of them sought to encourage development.[10] Thus, development and its incarnation as a policy, developmentalism, not only involved the combination of ideas and institutions (Sikkink 1991), but could also be considered as an ideology (Limoeiro 1975). The intellectual and policy endeavors associated with developmentalism are closely related to the policies advocated by the Economic Commission for Latin America—ECLA, together forming a broad tradition known as structuralism.[11] While this policy tradition was commonly considered to be unified, both ideologically and in terms of the actual policies they mobilized, the tradition was in fact quite diverse, and involved significant debates both about the pace and order of policy implementation in different countries (Thorp 1992) and about the theoretical underpinnings of these policies[12] (e.g., Rodríguez 1980).

of the structures of the bourgeois economy and society, struggled for the utopia of a domesticated capitalism, subordinated to the interests of the national society" (Author's translation).

[10] Critical studies on development consider these interventions as attempts to "Westernize" Latin American societies while disregarding their particularities (e.g., Escobar 1995).

[11] Currently, structuralism is the label attached to the intellectual and policy efforts of Latin American policymakers to elucidate a model that would explain the conditions of Latin American economies and strategies for change. However, the term first appeared in the debates around the causes of Latin American inflation and its connection with industrialization and agrarian transformation. It was opposed to monetarism, which claimed that inflationary problems were more often linked to monetary issues than to the broader process of development (Boianovsky 2012, 284–286).

[12] ECLA has retained significant influence in several countries over the years. The organization successfully shifted its emphasis from the early years of industrialization in order to show stronger concern about inequality and its impact on growth (Love 2019). Following Stone (2008), we could argue that ECLA has played a significant role as a depository of ideas and information for economic policymaking in Latin America, even in more recent times, despite its diminished influence.

The goal of development was a broader transformation of Latin American societies, mainly through industrialization.[13] This view was also reflected in the intellectual tradition of modernization (Rostow 1971), in which the transformation of traditional societies into modern ones would follow from a series of stages fuelled by economic growth. Even if the idea of stages waned, economic growth remained as an enduring feature of economic policymaking and, in some ways, represented what development stood for.[14] As mentioned above, the relationship between the region's economy and the global economy was fundamental for two reasons: first, because on many occasions the constraints imposed by the latter negatively affected the former—for instance in the relation between balance of payments and industrialization initiatives; and, second, because the solutions offered were not enough to overcome the obstacles. In fact, sometimes the solutions even became part of the problem—as, for example, in the case of policies that tried to create trade surpluses that could also cause domestic inflation.

At the heart of this conundrum is the role of multinational corporations. In the early postwar period, they represented a most desirable source of foreign currency with their green-field investments, which also meant access to technology. For these corporations in turn, investments were a bet on promising rents that would derive from closed markets. Later on, the dual nature of multinational corporations' activities, both within and outside of the region, meant that their priorities no

[13] The most salient issue around industrialization was that it resonated with political and economic concerns in the middle of the twentieth century. Industrialization fitted within nationalist policies seeking more political autonomy as well as with the disruption to international trade caused by world conflicts, which forced many countries to create industrial sectors. In later years, the political weight of developmental policies waned with what were perceived as the flaws of inward-looking policies that governments across the political spectrum implemented indistinctly.

[14] The option for economic growth was not politically neutral. Instead, the argument in many countries was that policies had to focus on growth instead of redistribution, equality being another desirable outcome of development, since no distribution could take place without an available surplus. Besides the traditional view of modernization, other contemporary scholarship that explains the relation between growth and inequality includes the work of Kuznets (1955), with his idea of the inversed "U," meaning that inequality would increase in the first phases of economic growth, only to decrease later. An example of a statement on the secondary character of the inequality by a senior policymaker is that of Ortiz (1970). More recent research in the field of development (Sen 2000) has questioned that assumption, with mild success in influencing public policies.

longer corresponded to the needs of Latin American economies (Evans 1979). However, the relative importance of such companies *vis-à-vis* the host economies gave them a prominent place in the region's capitalism nonetheless. Indeed, some authors consider them to be definitive of Latin American economies to this day (Schneider 2013).[15]

Development gained significant legitimacy in part because it promised the kind of change Latin American societies hoped for, including better economic conditions as well as more political autonomy. Though the concept of development has many meanings, its most enduring definition probably refers to economic growth; this is also the case within the field of Development Economics (Collier 2007).[16] For this reason, market reforms were approved in part as a path to development, whether within an authoritarian regime, as in Chile, or as a response to authoritarianism, as in Brazil. This complex scenario underlines the differences among Latin American countries: in spite of their shared role as producers of raw materials, the implications of development or liberalization are different in each country. Nevertheless, it should be clear that while the policy implications are different throughout the region, the paradigmatic character of development remains similar.

Notably, the acceptance of developmentalism varied from country to country. For instance, while development as a goal still motivates significant political mobilization in Brazil even after several decades of economic transformations, this is not the case at all in Chile. The relationship of the region with the rest of the world, the relationships among different economic arenas, and the policies prescribed to change a given situation were all dimensions of the kind of development that characterized capitalism in Latin America in the second half of the twentieth century. However, what matters for the present discussion is that the concept of development, as well as developmentalism, provided a framework for organizing the capitalist sociopolitical relations created in Latin America to such an extent that it became the core of the region's economic governance for decades.

[15] The evidence as to whether foreign direct investment and multinational corporations produce a positive or negative net effect is context-dependent. A middle ground has emerged on the role of these companies, since a catch-all category does not do full justice to the broad range of experiences (Lipsey and Sjöholm 2005).

[16] Some debates remain in that field since economic growth does not account for all possible dimensions of development—e.g., fighting inequality (cf. Duflo 2010).

In more recent times, particularly in Brazil, where developmentalism has had the biggest influence, there has been an intellectual debate concerning the interventionist policies implemented in the first decade of the current century (Bresser-Pereira 2010). The main objective of these discussions is to determine the benefits of state intervention in the economy, in complete opposition to the market. This oppositional framework, "states vs. markets," has largely defined the political debates around economic policy in the country. In these debates, development is closely associated with the state's role in the allocation of resources, with the implication that an exclusive reliance on the market mechanism would lead to undesirable outcomes, or even to a reversal in development.[17] The states vs. markets dichotomy has been prevalent at least since the beginning of the transition to democracy in Brazil in the late 1970s, when a public campaign favored the "retreat of the state," implying both economic liberalization and the return of the military to the barracks (Payne 1994).

The relationship between the literature on developmentalism and that on comparative capitalisms, with institutional complementarities as a core concept, might be clearest in Boschi's (2011b) book, *Variedades de Capitalismo, Politica e Desenvolvimento* [Varieties of Capitalism, Politics, and Development]. Boschi tries to examine Latin American capitalism from the perspective of a renewed developmentalism by engaging in a debate with the broad literature of comparative capitalisms.[18] Unsurprisingly, the most salient issue in the examination of Latin American capitalism is the role of the state in it. Even if there are explicit attempts to downplay any apparent dichotomy between states and markets (Diniz 2011, 50–51), the discussion continues in that direction, partly because certain actors also framed it that way throughout the process of liberalization,

[17] Relying on the market while sidelining the state would imply a reversal of the process of development; this means that these authors' concept of development encompasses much more than economic growth or industrialization.

[18] *Variedades de Capitalismo, Política e Desenvolvimento* [Varieties of Capitalism, Politics, and Development] tries explicitly to engage in a debate with the work of Schneider and Soskice (2009) and Schneider (2009), who had as their goal to incorporate Latin American economies into the framework of Varieties of Capitalism (Hall and Soskice 2001; Hancké, Rhodes, and Thatcher 2007). Although the references to complementarities are scarce in this volume (Almeida 2011, 172; Santana 2011, 122), their efforts speak to the common ground between both literatures and the attempts to reinforce their dialogue.

including in the international arena.[19] Any argument that casts the state as a key, coordinating actor in the development process thus vindicates the state's historical role in instituting capitalism throughout Latin America, and particularly in Brazil.[20]

Indeed, the dominant theme of Boschi's volume is the centrality of the state as the main actor in such endeavors. The authors in this volume argue that the state should reprise the role that it had before international and domestic actors intervened to promote the supremacy of the market. Those who advocate for the supremacy of market mechanisms are represented by what is known as the "Washington Consensus" and its backers, mainly international financial organizations that encouraged liberalizing reforms during the 1990s, with less than convincing results, in their effort *to generate* development (Diniz 2011, 36).[21] In the domestic arena, a technocratic elite that embraced the vision of such organizations carried these actions out in different sectors. Subsequently, in the first decade of the twenty-first century, the backers of such policies suffered electoral defeats. The most significant change in that respect was the ascent to power of Luiz Inácio Lula da Silva (2003–2010), who won the Brazilian presidential election in 2002. It was after this political shift that the state was once again mobilized (Diniz 2011, 31).[22] This example underscores the political dimension of developmentalism—of its more recent incarnation, neo-developmentalism.[23]

[19] Diniz (2011, 36, 41) cites Krueger (1974) on her work concerning rent-seeking. However, the latter published during the 1990s on economic reform in developing economies (Krueger 1993).

[20] For an assessment of the traditional ISI model from the point of view of intellectual history in the light of the current model, see Kuntz Ficker (2005) and Love (2005).

[21] Emphasis added.

[22] This portrayal of such a change is oblivious to the fact that both Venezuela, with Hugo Chávez (1998–2013), and Chile, with Ricardo Lagos (2000–2006), elected presidents who tried to rebalance the relation between the state and the markets, although to different degrees depending on the circumstances of their respective countries, before Lula was elected in late 2002. This narrative reflects the way in which this account of the supposed debate between comparative capitalisms and development is centered in Brazil. For detailed analyses of the implications of Chávez's election, see Corrales (2010) and López-Maya (2011). In addition, for detailed analyses concerning Lagos's election, see Huber, Pribble, and Stephens (2010) and Roberts (2011).

[23] Nowhere is this clearer than in the doctoral dissertation of Mercadante (2010, 9–10), a politician from the *Partido dos Trabalhadores*—PT (Workers' Party) and candidate for the vice-presidency in 1994, who asserts that the notion of new development synthetizes

Therefore, three elements came together to allow for a resurgence of developmentalism within the policy agenda: a shift in the intellectual clout of liberalizing ideas in the international arena, which appears in Stiglitz's (2002) and Rodrik's (2007) criticisms; an electoral change that brought to power progressive governments; and a reconsideration of the role of the state. Nevertheless, the idea of a zero-sum game between the state and the market was rejected. This implied the acceptance of democratic rules and prevented authoritarian actions. Thus, in this context, the question was not whether the state should participate in the economy, but how it should do so (Diniz 2011, 41). A reinvigorated role for the state and a broad agenda in terms of its relationship with society therefore suggests that different types of capitalism are not only conceivable, but actually attainable (Diniz 2011, 39).[24]

In the early 2010s, Boschi (2011a, 13) argued that neo-developmentalism was still a model in the making. Broadly, this model postulates the possibility of coordination between public and private actors, with the aim of increasing economic growth alongside special attention to social well-being. However, given the changes in the world economy that followed the financial crisis of the late 2000s, any efforts in that direction toward actual policy reform had a significant negative impact for President Dilma Rousseff (2011–2016), who presided over Brazil when the world economy was weak (Singer 2015). On the other hand, there were lively intellectual debates surrounding neo-developmentalism, attempting to delineate its conceptual borders and

the economic policies of the Party during Lula's tenure as president. Others would disagree with such position arguing that neo-developmentalism is a theoretical framework rather than a set of policies or political program (Bresser-Pereira 2016). Moreover, an all-encompassing evaluation of Lula's government as neo-developmentalist tends to downplay the different policy priorities and instruments used during those years. In the first term (2003–2006), there was continuity with the previous government (Ban 2013), and only after a series of political and economic changes was neo-developmentalism given a new opportunity (Barbosa and Souza 2010). An account of neo-developmentalism and its connection with populism is provided by Bresser-Pereira and Theuer (2012).

[24]This idea of the multiplicity of ways in which capitalism is organized as a response to a presumably unique approach is reminiscent of the seminal arguments in Comparative Institutional Analysis concerning the comparison between European or Asian economies with that of the US, discussed in the previous chapter.

the possible consequences of its implementation as policy measures.[25] These discussions continued even after the premature end of Rousseff's second term. The main divide was between neo-developmentalism and social-developmentalism (Bastos 2012).

Neo-developmentalism re-centers the role of the state in leading a National Development Strategy capable of mobilizing significant resources, both human and material, to create a growth path that fits the needs of the country. In contrast to traditional developmentalism, the state under neo-developmentalism would be more strategic in selecting its interventions (Bresser-Pereira 2010, 98–99), focusing mainly on particular niches in a way that will guarantee a reasonable economic and social return.[26] Social-developmentalism, for its part, emphasizes the domestic market and the role of the state in redistribution (Bastos 2012, 794). In many respects, it tries to reposition classic developmentalism as a valid economic policy program, especially the conscious political act of placing the state above the market to advance the development process (Carneiro 2012, 776). The adjective *social* makes reference to the increased spending on social programs, such as *Bolsa Família*, that took place when Lula's government was in power; but its main emphasis is nevertheless undoubtedly on the role of the state as a privileged resource allocator.

The economic policies implemented in order to further the goal of development, through the political projects of classic developmentalism or neo-developmentalism, have attempted to address the connections among different arenas within the economy. Acknowledging these connections reveals that the normal functioning of a given policy or rule depends crucially on the presence of other policy to succeed. The policies I have discussed here arose from the rules and expectations that guided policy-makers in the middle of the twentieth century and the beginning of the twenty-first. However, given the dynamism and cyclicality of capitalism, profound crises throughout the last decades of the twentieth century forced countries to reroute, often starting a long process of reform. These

[25] An example of such attempts is the special issue of the *Revista de Economia Política* [Brazilian Journal of Political Economy] (Vol. 40(2)) on New Developmentalism published in 2020.

[26] In principle, the rationale of state intervention is to create the appropriate conditions (like innovation and investment) for the strengthening and correct functioning of the market, not to replace it (Bresser-Pereira 2010, 80).

crises interrupted previous arrangements insofar as the institutions and the complementarities supporting economic governance no longer functioned as expected. The next section will discuss the contours of such crises and the importance of their legacy for the future consolidation of economic governance in Latin America.

3.2 The Crises, Vested Interests, and Reforms

Latin American economies were transformed through liberalization policies during the 1980s and 1990s. These changes represented a shift in the development model that most countries in the region had adopted after the Depression. There was not, however, a conscious and deliberate attempt to change existing models of economic governance following a preconceived blueprint. In fact, observations show that the process did not follow such an *ex-post* sequence at all (Fanelli 2007). Throughout the operationalization process, the very concept of development was constantly redefined depending on domestic politics, as was the notion of reform. This is clear in the immediate goals of development strategies and policies previously implemented in each country, as emphasized in the previous section, as well as in the policies that would seek to reform them some years later. In some countries, there were significant accomplishments in terms of industrialization, notably in the cases of Brazil and Mexico (Schneider 1999), while others suffered a continuous decline, notably Argentina and Chile.

Brazil and Mexico were both large enough to accumulate scale economies within their domestic market. While big public investment projects took place in Brazil during Juscelino Kubitschek's presidency (1956–1961), the slogan of which was "50 years in 5,"[27] and Mexico's "Stabilizing Development" (1956–1970) represented a period of significant growth (Ortiz 1970), Chile lagged behind in that regard. Kubitschek's coalition represented an exercise in equilibrium, that involved promoting the projects of urban industrialists while continuing to protect rural interests (Skidmore 1967, 166–174).[28] "Stabilizing

[27] An excellent online dossier on the years of Kubitschek's presidency is offered by Ferreira (2002).

[28] The construction of the new capital was symbolically important in gaining support for the government's program. Kubitschek was clever in crafting coalitions in both the political arena and in society at large; however, a favorable economic environment helped.

Development" likewise represented a compromise between orthodox economic bureaucracy and those pursuing new industries and investments (Moreno-Brid and Ros 2010, 149–169).

Chile's "Commitment State" (1938–1970) represented an attempt to create an internal market in parallel with democratization (Gárate 2012, 128–130); however, these transformations required deep changes, such as agrarian reform and the state's acceptance of economic responsibilities. Such reforms were attempted during the government of Eduardo Frei Montalva (1964–1970), but they could only go so far.[29] In Argentina, meanwhile, the Peronist movement implemented a populist strategy for the incorporation of labor (Collier and Collier 1991), which radically changed the trajectory of the Argentinean economy. Among other things, the push for industrialization, and the policies required to successfully implement it, prevented sectors in which Argentina had a relative advantage, such as agricultural goods, from developing their full potential (Waisman 1987). In any case, the implementation of developmentalist policies in Argentina was informed by the traumatic experience of the Depression, following which policymakers had to find new ways of responding to economic challenges (Sikkink 1991).

In the 1970s, the international context changed adversely. Unsurprisingly, the responses in terms of economic policy varied depending on the political priorities of the authoritarian governments that were in place at the time. There are, however, some similarities to be found among them. Despite the changing conditions of the international economy during that decade, the existing patterns of economic policymaking remained in place throughout Latin America,[30] signaling that those global changes were

[29] Indeed, these attempts to avoid confrontation were limited. In fact, rather than continuing with the politics of compromise, new leaders sought to foster the tensions between political groups, which gave authoritarian groups within each society the opportunity to take power, successfully most of the time, in the name of stability and social order. In Brazil and Chile, coups d'état were made against João Goulart (Skidmore 1967), in office from 1961 to 1964, and Salvador Allende (Angell 1993), in office from 1970 to 1973, respectively, who embraced a more confrontational way of dealing with the contradictions created by the development process and its consequences. The case of Mexico also reveals similar confrontations, ever since the government of Luis Echeverría (1970–1976) took a populist turn in part as a response to the events of Tlatelolco in 1968, where police clashed violently with protesting students.

[30] Path dependency is part of the explanation, but there were also mitigating factors such as a favorable international credit market that, at first, eased the restrictive conditions of the oil shocks.

not initially considered to be as fundamental as they would turn out. The continuation of those existing economic policies, with, in fact, a significant deepening of their characteristics, created further vulnerabilities in big Latin American economies. Both Brazil and Mexico deepened their models of heavy intervention, with the *Plano Nacional de Desenvolvimento* (National Development Plan) in Brazil (Carneiro 1989) and the discovery of oil and the subsequent expenditures in Mexico (Lustig 2002, 41ff). In the case of Chile, the extreme liberal policies implemented by the military government were not adapted in light of the new international environment either (Ffrench-Davis 2014). In Argentina, while there were attempts to change the path of economic policymaking with a timid liberalization in the midst of the strong intervention represented by military expenditures, it was the military expenditures that prevailed (Canitrot 1994, 79). Throughout the 1980s, all of these countries suffered significant crises and the complete disruption of their patterns of economic governance.

This commitment to development and to the policies that would implement it had profound implications later on. While the debt crisis that affected the region in the early 1980s was a generalized problem, Brazil, Mexico, Chile, and Argentina were among the most affected. Since both investment and consumption depended on external financing, when the supply of international resources retracted, these policies had to contract as well, further deepening the crisis.[31] Despite the different ways in which liberalization policies were carried out, the economies of Brazil, Chile, and Mexico have experienced considerable success in maintaining a pace

[31] This trend will be analyzed at length in each empirical chapter. Briefly, in Brazil, the favorable conditions to borrow in international markets allowed companies, public and private alike, to make big investments that would mature in the middle of the crisis. In Chile, by contrast, a boom in consumption, fueled by the flow of international capital, caused a serious exchange rate crisis and forced a change in economic policy within the bureaucratic-authoritarian regime. Mexico's overreliance on oil exports with the subsequent fall in oil prices in 1981 also forced desperate measures such as the nationalization of banks, among others. In Argentina, meanwhile (though this case is not analyzed at length in the present study), when the military took power in 1976, they justified a change in the economic policy matrix by claiming that it was a way to discipline business through market forces (Canitrot 1981); these attempts to reshuffle the principles orienting economic policymaking were among the causes of the debt crisis of the early 1980s (Kaufman 1988).

of change—that is, without major discontinuities—whereas Argentina has not managed to observe a similarly steady pattern (Berbecel 2018).[32]

The fact that these countries continued along their previously established policy paths despite the economic turmoil reveals the interests that had arisen around these regulations. In other words, in spite of the changing environment, vested interests were capable of guiding progress along the established course of action. As well, to a significant extent, such continuity was possible because of policy feedback (Pierson 1993). Two mechanisms in particular are important in the present study: first, the creation of interest groups around the policies, and second, the importance of past experiences in defining the response to a situation that, despite initial appearances, differed substantially from previous cases. For instance, industrialists in several countries were adamant about the importance of subsidized credit, among other advantages, to the continuity of the development project regardless of the scarcity of resources to keep such subsidies in place. Furthermore, economic bureaucracies of all political stripes failed to grasp the severity of the crisis and the ways in which it would affect the economies of their respective countries, and they therefore interpreted it as a small and inconsequential deviation.

The crisis, which manifested differently in each country, disrupted previous policymaking routines in significant ways.[33] This in turn threatened vested interests, which tended to resist change. As a result, reforms took place by way of incremental changes, giving reformers more leverage in the struggle to change the institutions buttressing the long-standing interests. It is striking that despite the severity of the crises these countries were facing, such interests were powerful enough to maintain remarkable influence and, in some instances, even led to actions that deepened

[32]The obvious counterfactual would be the case of Brazil, which even suffered a process of impeachment in 1992. Despite such a traumatic political experience, however, the process of liberalization was not derailed and continued throughout the government of a president who was largely considered to be against such policies. Even in the 2000s when both countries elected a left-leaning government, Brazil's new government continued to follow the economic policies of its predecessor while Argentina changed them substantially. Thus, the evidence supports the claim that Brazil shows a stable pattern of economic governance whereas Argentina does not. About Argentinean economic policies and their frequent reforms, see Canitrot (1994) and Acuña, Galiani, and Tommasi (2007).

[33]The changes in the international environment affected countries across the board, but given the particularities of each country and the way in which each one was affected, is preferable to talk about a plurality of crises.

the crises and exacerbated their effects. And yet while it is tempting to blame particular groups for those negative outcomes, for the most part, they merely sought to maximize their gains in their own unique political and economic contexts, however authoritarian they might be. Emerging from these critical situations involved the consolidation of coalitions that supported minor changes spread out over several years.

Indeed, these changes both to policymaking routines and to the ways in which different interests participated in them constitute a critical juncture in the process of consolidation of economic governance in Latin America.[34] The disruptions brought about by the crises had lasting consequences, shaping both future decisions as well as the different reforms that were launched in more immediate response. While it is difficult to verify whether political or economic impacts were more influential in determining future assessments of similar events, the fact is that they were frequently referred to later on as reminders of conditions that should be avoided. In practice, evaluating whether the political or economic impacts were more important depends on the weight each actor, or group of actors, gave to their own relevance. Beyond that, the key to consolidating economic governance is an aversion to the kind of disruption these crises created. Each crisis had a high cost, and left a scar as a reminder that significant disruptions to policymaking routines should be avoided. In future crises, these costs would carry weight once more, as actors would again launch efforts to avoid incurring similar loses. Thus, the effects of the crises in the early 1980s are central in explaining the consolidation of economic governance in the following decades.

Following Pierson (1993), I will initially discuss the argument about vested interests as responsible for feedback effects that prevented a faster response to the crises; later on, I will discuss the role of bureaucracies as factors in feedback effects. When countries and societies face the challenge of economic crises, they must devise a response which not only attends to the mitigation of its effects but also maps out possible strategies for recovery. Economic policies take many different shapes, and their responses to crisis are informed by many different schools of thought

[34] I concur with Taylor (2009, 500 fn. 47) concerning the difficulty in pointing to a critical juncture, because it can only be labeled as such with reference to some other phenomenon of interest. However, these crises triggered a long process of institutional reform that transformed Latin American economies and, in some cases, led to the consolidation of economic governance.

(Gourevitch 1986). And while it would be very interesting to assess the extent to which these responses and the theories that support them actually fit with the crises they were intended to address, the present study focuses instead on how the reforms instituted in response to a seismic crisis consolidated a new pattern of economic governance. As mentioned above, crises were often political as much as economic, in that many actors had invested substantially in the institutions and policies that the crises brought down.

In normal times, vested interests try to maintain the benefits and advantages they enjoy from policies or established rules as much as possible, a tendency that constitutes the definition of such groups (Moe 2015).[35] But as a result of the crises of the early 1980s, these efforts to keep institutions in place in order to continue receiving certain benefits, were finally overwhelmed: existing policies crumbled as the previous model came to an end. In the cases studied here, then, vested interests had to cope with the effects of crises. In other words, whereas traditional vested interests try to prevent change, in these cases they had to adapt to changes that were exogenously imposed upon them.

There were two main types of vested interest, and each contended differently with the crises and their aftermath. First, there were those that benefited squarely from the status quo, and used their resources to steer reforms following the period of crisis so as to return to the conditions that had existed previously. Their interest in maintaining the status quo—that is, in encouraging the persistence of a policy that allowed them to benefit—likely arose from their own heavy dependence on that particular policy.[36] Second, there were vested interests created by policy responses that struggled to use reforms in order to maximize their benefits. These were newly created groups which coalesced around a recent policy response which helped to inspire collective action and provided them with key resources to mobilize. A common denominator for these types of vested interests is their access to privileged spaces of policy

[35] However, as Moe (2015, 289) contends, a more precise definition is a collective effort and should include different dimensions, however elementary, in order to advance theory.

[36] A classic example in the literature on policy feedback is that of the American Civil War Veterans (Skocpol 1992). More recent work has focused on businesses and their influence on policy, which derives from the ways in which they profit from the implementation of a given policy (e.g., Ledbetter 2011).

decision-making, which in theory would greatly enhance their potential for success (Pierson 1993, 600ff). However, they sometimes had different levels of access before and after the crises, which of course affected their ability to influence reforms. In some cases, crises provided more access, while in others, it was restrained.

Bureaucracies are also key actors in reform processes. They can be a source of policy feedback insofar as their existence is conditional upon the implementation of certain policies, or simply because they view the policies they implement in a way that does not necessarily align with the positions of their political masters, which adds an additional layer to the reform process. As stakeholders, they can be both for and against reform.[37] When they are in favor of reform, bureaucrats actively seek to advance changes and use their institutional position to increase opportunities for transformation to take place (Taylor 2009). When they consider that reform is not in their best interests, they can be a powerful source for institutional stability; this is the traditional view of bureaucracies as engines for policy feedback (DiSalvo 2015).

More broadly, it is possible to argue that those crises to which vested interests had to adapt were in large part caused precisely by the actions intended to protect them in the previous cycle. Although there are no great powers in Latin America, this argument resonates with that of Olson (1982) about technological decline. This kind of decline occurs when the interests that derive benefits from current technologies fail to adapt to a new technological revolution. In a similar fashion, many Latin American political and economic actors failed to grasp the depth of the crisis and continued to invest their resources as they had under the previous model. But such a model, in which the state played a significant role in the process of development, was no longer viable, and many did not adapt to the new environment. Therefore, in this case vested interests are no longer actors who wish to prevent change, but those who try to steer the reform process in order to minimize their losses.

Their success in limiting their losses depended sometimes on their relative strength and the coalitions they created throughout the processes of reform. Although certain critical events represented clear breaks with the

[37] This characteristic can even appear simultaneously and embody the main struggles in the process of reform. Nóbrega (2005, 298–302) shows how in the 1980s different groups of bureaucrats within the same institutions were both for and against the reform of the *Banco do Brasil*, the biggest state-owned retail bank in the country.

past and had significant consequences for these groups, their influence did not wane immediately. In many ways, they retained their power by trying to delay meaningful reforms as much as possible—or at least, they thwarted reform attempts, prolonging the crises for years. On the other hand, reformers had to unite in order to advance parts of the reform agenda that sought to address the challenges presented by the crises, even if there were some instances when reformers held substantial power and tried to use it to act without the support of a coalition. Nevertheless, coalitional dynamics were unavoidable: reformers had to convince other actors within the political economy that the reform they supported had the potential to benefit their partners.

As discussed in the previous chapter, incremental institutional change can take many forms but after some time, the accumulation of small incremental changes does eventually amount to significant and meaningful transformations. The institutional changes that take place in the context of political struggles concerning the response to crises are central to the consolidation of economic governance. These might result from the actions of vested interests trying to prevent meaningful reform at the outset of the crisis (Moe 2015, 284), or from instances in which those trying to keep the status quo are outmaneuvered and change takes place. In fact, there is little interest in defining what type of political struggle leads to, or at least facilitates, the consolidation of economic governance, since this process requires reforms in different institutional arenas, each with its own political dynamics and vested interests.[38] In those cases where vested interests are weak, change is easier; where they retain significant power, change is harder to effect.

As is traditionally the case in the creation of feedback effects, a series of interest groups sprang up around different developmental policies in Latin America. Many of the actors who took advantage of those policies did so at their own discretion, since once the privileges had been created there were no real limits to their use. As discussed above, these groups were prominent in the struggles around various reforms. However, the key to

[38] Given that several institutional arenas are in play when we consider the consolidation of economic governance, depending on the country in question or the sectors under consideration, the political struggles leading to its consolidation will likely be different in each context. Attempting to define a certain type might prevent us to grasp processes of consolidation of economic governance that do not necessarily fit within a theoretically expected pattern.

the consolidation of economic governance lies in effectively limiting the potential actions of those vested interests, or at least reducing their benefits. When reforms had advanced adequately in the same direction, vested interests no longer enjoyed the same benefits, and the possibility of taking discretionary action they previously enjoyed was reduced. This diminishment of benefits effectively leveled the playing field so that more actors had access to what was previously available only to a few. Institutional reforms constitute an institutional complementarity when there are limits on discretion, thus creating a level playing field.[39]

Interest groups are not the only explanation for feedback effects, however. Political and economic actors' reliance on previous experiences to assess current situations also explains policy feedback. This argument has a strong tradition in the field; indeed, much literature on public policy argues that policymakers use their past experiences to inform their responses to current problems. This idea dates from the 1950s, when the question of rationality in policymaking was at the core of disciplinary debates (Dahl and Lindblom 1953; Lindblom 1958). Lindblom (1959) established the terms of the discussion with his analysis of incrementalism. He begins by defining two different approaches of thinking about policy problems: by root or by branch. The former would require the relevant decision-maker to weigh all possible factors, both causes and effects, involved in the decision to move forward.[40] A central tenet of the root method is comprehensive rationality; the branch method, on the other hand, relaxes such conditions. More precisely, the branch method elaborates on the works of Simon (1955) concerning the bounded rationality of decision-makers. Lindblom (1959, 80–81) considers the branch method more realistic and also makes its formalization an explicit goal of his article. To reinforce this point, he asserts that the rational-comprehensive model "assumes intellectual capacities and sources of information that men simply do not possess" (Lindblom 1959, 80).

With the advancement in information processing technology and programming that took place in the middle of the twentieth century, it seemed that cognitive limits could be easily surmounted. In fact, economic models took the idea of comprehensive rationality to its limits

[39] On threshold effects, see Pierson (2004).

[40] Because the analysis by root is presumably well known, it is not analyzed in Lindblom's article. This analysis corresponds to the perfect rational agent as used in microeconomics and public choice.

with the adaptive expectations revolution (Lucas 1972). Unsurprisingly, economic policymaking embraced this path. The solution offered in the arena of macroeconomic policy was the establishment of rules that would moderate agents' expectations (Barro and Gordon 1983; Kydland and Prescott 1977). In theory, this would solve the instability generated by the maximizing behavior of policymakers. However, rules governing the economy are necessarily limited, since they are devised with the same cognitive limitations as those underscored by incrementalism. If rules are specific and try to account for every possible scenario, they will probably fail; more abstract or general rules leave more space for policy. The model of comprehensive rationality is nevertheless still a fiction that gives economic policymaking significant legitimacy.[41]

That said, there is ample evidence about how economic policymakers respond to contemporary challenges through their interpretation of previous experiences, in line with what Lindblom suggests. In Latin America, policymakers responded to successive crises in the second half of the twentieth century with the events surrounding the Great Depression and its aftermath as their template (Sikkink 1991, 246). They kept key parts of the ISI model even when its elements were no longer relevant or were counterproductive, given how economies had changed. In more recent times, there has been discussion about the response of central bankers all over the world to the 2007–2008 financial crisis, arguing that these responses were motivated by their understanding of the Great Depression—in particular that of former Federal Reserve Chairman, Ben Bernanke (Khademian 2010, 145). Chairman Bernanke's long-lasting interest in the effects of the Great Depression (Bernanke 2000) derived in part from the influence of the period on macroeconomists' beliefs, research agendas, and policy recommendations (Bernanke 1995, 1).

In sum, crises have lasting impacts on economic policymaking at least through two mechanisms. First, there are interests created around policies; this leads policymakers to consider the possible consequences of abrupt changes to existing policies and how these will affect such interests directly. Furthermore, those interests pressure governments to maintain the status quo as much as possible, in order to minimize their losses. Second, economic policymaking tends to respond to current challenges through explicit or implicit reference to previous ones. This approach

[41] This is also the case with the supreme audit institutions (Saint-Martin and Rothmayr-Allison 2011).

arises in part from the bounded rationality of policymakers; however, previous crises were also fundamental in creating the theoretical or practical frameworks that these professionals use to support their actions. Therefore, previous crises establish a precedent insofar as future actions depend on the ways in which they are interpreted by political and economic actors.

When changes actually occur, however, vested interests cannot profit as easily from institutions. More specifically, when reforms take place incrementally throughout different institutional realms, vested interests, at least in part, are no longer able to shift the cost of their actions to the rest of the society. These costs are often associated with upholding the previous model even when it is no longer viable. Notably, another key part of the dynamics of change is their complexity (Baumgartner and Jones 2009), which in turn prevents vested interests that are unable to see how all the reform in place might end up questioning privileges or strategic positions. Indeed, reformers would prefer to work under the radar without attracting the attention of vested interests that might try to prevent reform from taking place. The success of this strategy depends on the extent to which the changes proposed might affect the benefits derived by the vested interests.

In fact, sometimes policymakers attempt to effect change through grandiose policy initiatives that, if fully implemented, could radically transform entire economies. The chances of success of those initiatives depend on the power resources they are able to mobilize and the coalitions they are able to gather. While such schemes have succeeded in authoritarian regimes at first, eventually they have had to retract and negotiate with other social forces. In these cases, the construction of coalitions for reform was the best strategy to guarantee the long-term survival of institutional reforms. It is therefore no surprise that the consolidation of economic governance depends crucially on the politics of institutional change in the long term rather than the ability of one set of policymakers in devising the lines, however basic, of a new pattern of economic governance.

In successful cases of reform, there are numerous processes of institutional reform running simultaneously in diverse arenas. While coalitions vary and some actors participate in many alliances at once, these processes are not conducted as parts of a whole. While at first glance it might seem that even a large number of small reforms would not be enough to consolidate economic governance, these rather disparate struggles are in fact essential to achieving that goal. Since many reforms tackle institutions that create benefits for certain groups, the opposition against them would be stronger if these processes were connected. Moreover, as discussed in the previous chapter, institutional complementarities are not the product of a master design. Therefore, reforms follow the specific power dynamics of the institutional arena in which they are advanced. Successive reforms in each arena alone, however, are not enough to consolidate the institutional complementarities on which economic governance rests.

Evidently, something more is needed to consolidate economic governance. Since crises are recurrent in capitalist economies, they can often create new opportunities for realignment and accommodation as the process of institutional reform, initiated in response to the end of the previous model, is carried out. However, not all economic downturns have the potential to realign political and economic interests in a significant manner or to serve as catalysts for new reform processes. In the next section, I will discuss the role of crises in the consolidation of economic governance.

3.3 Legacies, New Crises, and Possibilities of Consolidation

As mentioned above, Brazil, Mexico, and Chile each faced a crisis in line with its own vulnerabilities. All of these crises had their roots in the increasing lack of correspondence between actors' expectations and the context surrounding them. The crises faced by Latin American countries were severe and had considerable repercussions beyond their national borders. Indeed, crises triggered by the international events of the late 1970s and early 1980s not only affected the markets—causing disruptions such as bankruptcies or bail-outs—but left lasting legacies in national political economies. Many economic actors would continue to resent these events for decades to come, partly because those critical moments created dismal conditions that lasted for years, but also because some actors exploited these conditions time and time again.

Although each national iteration of these large international crises had different characteristics depending on the conditions of the country in which it occurred, they do all share a key trait. In each case, previous policymaking routines and priorities were either disrupted or changed altogether. Given that numerous actors would have invested in the previous models and routines, such disruptions had significant effects on their continued ability to act meaningfully. The arenas in which those actors held sway were diverse, and the consequences were significant: companies went bust, privileges were revoked, and wealth changed hands. The effects were widespread, since economic crises affected the livelihoods of people from all walks of life. Beyond the economic effects, there were also political effects. The political dimension is equally important in explaining the fall-out of these crises, since power and resources shifted hands—even if at the top in many cases there was no movement.

For instance, hyperinflation in Brazil represented a recurring problem that policymakers and citizens alike wanted to solve permanently. And the changes implemented in Brazil to stop inflation were not simply a matter of monetary reform. On the contrary, controlling inflation required a profound transformation of the prevailing institutions in the Brazilian political economy. This was partly a result of the extent to which inflation was naturalized in the country. Indeed, many actors had learned to live with high levels of inflation, and some even derived significant rents from it. This state of affairs lasted for decades, until the situation grew out of control and inflation transformed into hyperinflation (Bresser-Pereira and Nakano 1984, 175ff). Even for a population used to high levels of inflation, hyperinflation represented a disruption to normal life in which there was no possibility to plan ahead. For businesses, hyperinflation represented both a blessing and a curse, since many companies depended on hyperinflation to survive, while others did not have enough sources of income to weather such a disruption.

The study of the Real Plan provides important insight into economic governance because it required numerous institutional reforms to achieve its objective, even if these reforms were not rationally planned nor conceived as a series of steps to follow. Privatization represented a transformation of the role of the state from owner to regulator; trade liberalization, in turn, represented a change in a fundamental characteristic of the economy: whether or not it was open to foreign competition. Different actors, though they followed their own paths, transformed these institutions until the interaction among them was considered fundamental to the stabilization effort. In other words, these transformations ran simultaneously but fairly independently from each other, though they were occasionally seen as a whole. And although the successes of the Real Plan often capitalized on those independent institutional transformations, there were still gaps to bridge.

In Chile, meanwhile, radical governments on both the left and the right implemented abrupt changes to economic policy, creating disruptions that exacerbated vulnerabilities that had been accumulating for decades. The Chilean pension reform, launched in the midst of twin crises (Diaz-Alejandro 1985), created a situation in which a group of actors tried to take advantage of the possible returns granted by new norms. Given the severity of the situation, the authoritarian government had to support both the financial and pension systems, both of which suffered greatly under the twin crises. In turn, the government nuanced many of its most radical economic measures. After the state provided support for those systems, they were incrementally reformed numerous times. The continuous state of flux left many actors in precarious positions. These changes came on top of the serious disruptions caused by a radical government a decade before. This complex set of political allegiances and responsibilities generated both costs and opportunities for actors to mobilize their political resources.

Later, once the peak of the crises had been left behind, the discourse around those reforms maintained that taking advantage of financial resources within the labor market, using it to finance productive activities, would improve economic growth through financial intermediation. Such cooperation did not exist by design, however; rather it was part of a political argument in favor of the pension system. While there have been some crossovers between the two systems, the main changes enacted in both spheres had to do with internal concerns rather than with the possibility of their influencing one another. After four decades of existence, the pension system is still a contentious issue in Chilean politics and has led to successive reforms in recent years. The complexity of the crises that Chile suffered, both political and economic, adds to the intricacy of their legacy in the process of consolidation of economic governance; tellingly, each crisis or subsequent policy measure to address it has been interpreted in a partisan way.

In Mexico, the response to the economic uncertainty brought on by the economic crises of the 1970s was to concentrate power in the hands of the president. However, this measure, which could potentially have allowed for a straightforward response in such critical moments, actually just caused even more instability. Although the discretionary actions of the Mexican president, as Head of State, appeared legitimate, these crises revealed that economic policy should not rest on the will of a single person. While the crises had a substantial international dimension, their handling by Mexican authorities worsened the effects of the disruptions to the country's economy. Moreover, economic actors, both within and outside of the state, came to realize that the existing arrangement represented a very high risk. After the crises had passed, in order to ensure stability following a period of serious financial turmoil, efforts were made to reduce presidential discretion over economic policy. After much debate, central bank independence was granted, so that monetary policy is no longer at the discretion of the Presidency.

Another major reform was the attempt to introduce a new fiscal rule that would restrict the federal government's ability to run deficits. The new rule required the explicit authorization of Congress. However, while central bank autonomy has been respected, Congress has continuously approved deficits, ultimately undermining the effectiveness of this fiscal rule. The central bank reform mobilized actors in the Mexican polity, not least the bureaucracy within the organization itself. In one sense, this reform was influenced by foreign precedents and it went through a long maturation process, lasting through more than one administration. On the other hand, the fiscal rule was the product of an ephemeral alliance against a political outsider in the context of a contentious presidential campaign. Above all, such reforms sought to change the fundamental rules governing the behavior of actors—specifically the president, in the case of Mexico—who, in the past, had worsened the already dire conditions of the Mexican economy. The legacy of these rules continues to pose important challenges despite several decades of continuous reform.

Yet, despite many reforms seeking to address the consequences of a disruption in the policymaking routines, crises came back. This had to do more with the global economy and its inherent instability than the simple mishandling of national economies (Frieden 2006; Reinhart and Rogoff 2009), although some mistakes did indeed happen. When confronted with new crises, governments had to devise responses in line with their interpretation of the causes and convince other actors that their interpretation would lead to a feasible solution. While this convincing might have involved some technocratic agreement on both the causes of the crises as well as the best possible way to address them (Blyth 2007), in the end the path to consolidation of economic governance depends on the citizens accepting the solutions offered, or at least not contesting their fundamentals.

Such acquiescence might come in the form of an electoral victory of a government within which solutions were devised and convinced other actors to support them as a response to the crises afflicting the country; or, simply by electing representatives that promise to support the solutions to the crisis that threatens to bring the problems supposedly left behind. However, if a solution might appear palatable to the elites, which are involved in intense political struggles when crafting it, it still depends on how the legacies of crises past affected large swathes of the population and how the elite-crafted institutional reforms effectively respond to the concerns of the majority. If the solutions do not work as intended, support will likely vanish and new solutions must be crafted. While the focus of this book rests on the politics behind institutional reforms that allow for the consolidation of economic governance, it also points out how such reforms are also accepted or contested through the participation mechanisms democracies provide, whether such mechanisms are institutionalized—e.g., elections, judicial reviews—or not—e.g., direct popular mobilization.

As will be briefly discussed in each empirical case, the concerns of economic governance do not necessarily run high in the priority list of electorates, in part because the terms of the political debates surrounding it are most of the time complex economic concepts. However, since the social outcomes of those institutional reforms' consequences are something with which citizens must deal, they will hold them accountable through the means mentioned above. Indeed, those political processes—i.e., elections or popular mobilizations—might not even have as a main feature if economic governance is consolidated or not. Instead, the topics around which those processes would revolve are how the state provides a reasonable rate of inflation that allows for economic planning, a reasonable expectation of retirement income, or reassurances that their livelihoods will not disappear because a single politician made a bad decision or was guilty of embezzlement, among other outcomes.

The mechanism proposed in this study for the consolidation of economic governance underscores how broad coalitions must be at play when reforming institutions that effectively reduced the uncertainty that a new crisis creates. While institutional reforms might gather enough political support to be enacted, it is the long-standing political support that would uphold those reforms in the mid- to long run. This characteristic of economic governance points to its political, rather than technocratic, character since no matter how economically elegant an institution might be, it will not last long if political and economic actors do not support it. The possibilities for the consolidation of economic governance lie precisely in gathering a coalition of actors that supports what they consider a feasible solution for a critical situation. Part of what hold such a coalition together is the fact that institutional complementarities imply that two institutions, regulating different economic arenas on which different actors have stakes, need the presence of the other to work properly. This requires a compromise insofar as every member of the coalition understands that their commitment to that arrangement involves no longer acting at their discretion in the same way they had done so in the past. Essentially, the compromise among those interests is behind the broad coalitions mentioned above. Economic governance is above all, a political outcome.

3.4 Conclusions

The consolidation of economic governance in Latin America has followed a distinct path. First, there was the need to respond to a crisis that questioned and broke previously existing policymaking routines. The response to such crises took the form of several institutional reforms. These incremental reforms spanned several years and tended to question vested interests that in the past had been able to significantly affect economic outcomes by shifting the cost of their actions to the society as a whole. Given both the nature of the reforms and the cyclicality of the economy, new crises arose, forcing actors to attempt to prevent or mitigate their consequences. In so doing, they created coalitions that made possible the reforms that would respond to this new crisis. The coalitions depended on the existence of a common interpretation of the relationship between the old and new crises. Because there is a common interpretation of the threat faced by each political economy, the solution is a compromise in which the reformed institutions reinforce each other—that is, they become complementary. Finally, through the constitution of institutional complementarities, which reduced the margins for discretionary action over economic policies, economic governance could be consolidated in Latin America.

Thus, the consolidation of economic governance is less a premeditated and organized attempt to rule over economic forces than it is a subjective appraisal of previous experiences. The model discussed above also presents a solution to the tension between path dependency arguments (Pierson 2000)—with their tendency toward social determinism, as signaled by Crouch and Farrell (2004)—and the potential for action that agents possess. Hall and Thelen (2009) respond to several criticisms concerning both the functionalism of the Varieties of Capitalism framework and the static conception of capitalism (Deeg and Jackson 2007; Deeg 2007; Jackson and Deeg 2008) by stating that institutions are resources that actors intentionally use to change the political economy. Within this model, political and economic agents use institutions to create rules that structure their behavior in the face of the threat of instability that new economic crises pose. In so doing, they consolidate a new pattern of economic governance through the constitution of institutional complementarities.

The next set of chapters present the empirical cases. The first case shows how economic governance consolidates when two institutions become complementary. This happened when the Brazilian institutional reforms that responded to the crumble of the previous development model required each other to continue playing their role. This was the case concerning the effective end of hyperinflation, which affected Brazilians after the country democratized in 1985. After several attempts and a succession of institutional reforms that transformed the role of the state in the economy, hyperinflation was finally controlled. The institutions regulating the international dimension of the Brazilian economy as well as the extent to which the state held direct responsibilities in the production of goods and services—i.e., privatization—required the presence of the other to keep going. Such arrangement prevented what at the time was a likely return of hyperinflation. Subsequent chapters will deal with the cases of Chile and Mexico.

References

Acuña, Carlos H., Sebastián Galiani, and Mariano Tommasi. 2007. "Understanding Reform: The Case of Argentina." In *Understanding Market Reforms in Latin America: Similar Reforms, Diverse Constituencies, Varied Results*, edited by José María Fanelli, 31–72. Houndmills, Basingstoke: Palgrave Macmillan.

Almeida, Rodrigo de. 2011. "Entrando no Clube. O BNDES e a Inserção Brasileira no Capitalismo Internacional." In *Variedades de Capitalismo, Política e Desenvolvimento na América Latina*, edited by Renato R. Boschi, 164–193. Belo Horizonte: Editora UFMG.

Angell, Alan. 1993. *Chile de Alessandri a Pinochet: En Busca de la Utopía.* Santiago: Editorial Andrés Bello.

Ban, Cornel. 2013. "Brazil's Liberal Neo-Developmentalism: New Paradigm or Edited Orthodoxy?" *Review of International Political Economy* 20 (2): 298–331. https://doi.org/10.1080/09692290.2012.660183.

Barbosa, Nelson, and José Antonio Pereira de Souza. 2010. "A Inflexão do Governo Lula: Política Econômica, Crescimento e Distribuição de Renda." In *Brasil: Entre o Passado e o Futuro*, edited by Emir Sader and Marco Aurélio Garcia, 57–110. São Paulo: Editora Fundação Perseu Abramo.

Barro, Robert J., and David B. Gordon. 1983. "Rules, Discretion and Reputation in a Model of Monetary Policy." *Journal of Monetary Economics* 12 (1): 101–121. https://doi.org/10.1016/0304-3932(83)90051-x.

Barth, James R., Gerard Caprio, and Triphon Phumiwasana. 2009. "The Transformation of China from an Emerging Economy to a Global Powerhouse." In *China's Emerging Financial Markets: Challenges and Opportunities*, edited by James R. Barth, John A. Tatom and Glenn Yago, 73–110. New York: Springer.

Bastos, Pedro Paulo Zahluth. 2012. "A Economia Política do Novo-Desenvolvimentismo e do Social Desenvolvimentismo." *Economia e Sociedade* 21 (Número Especial): 779–810. https://doi.org/10.1590/s0104-06182012000400004.

Baumgartner, Frank R., and Bryan D. Jones. 2009. *Agendas and Instability in American Politics*. 2nd ed. Chicago: University of Chicago Press. Original edition, 1993.

Berbecel, Dan. 2018. "The Politics of Policy Stability: Explaining the Levels of Volatility in Economic Policymaking in Argentina and Brazil Between 1990 and 2010." *Canadian Journal of Latin American and Caribbean Studies* 43 (1): 18–46. https://doi.org/10.1080/08263663.2018.1423795.

Bernanke, Ben S. 1995. "The Macroeconomics of the Great Depression: A Comparative Approach." *Journal of Money, Credit and Banking* 27 (1): 1–28. https://doi.org/10.2307/2077848.

Bernanke, Ben S. 2000. *Essays on the Great Depression*. Princeton: Princeton University Press.

Blyth, Mark. 2007. "Powering, Puzzling, or Persuading? The Mechanisms of Building Institutional Orders." *International Studies Quarterly* 51 (4): 761–777. https://doi.org/10.1111/j.1468-2478.2007.00475.x.

Boadle, Anthony. 2020. "U.S. Backs Brazil for OECD Membership Ahead of Argentina." *Reuters*. Last Modified January 14, 2020. Accessed April 16, 2020. https://www.reuters.com/article/us-brazil-oecd-usa/u-s-backs-brazil-for-oecd-membership-ahead-of-argentina-idUSKBN1ZE01Z.

Boianovsky, Mauro. 2012. "Celso Furtado and the Structuralist-Monetarist Debate on Economic Stabilization in Latin America." *History of Political Economy* 44 (2): 277–330. https://doi.org/10.1215/00182702-1571719.

Boschi, Renato R. 2011a. "Introdução. Instituições, Trajetórias e Desenvolvimento. Uma Discussão a partir da América Latina." In *Variedades de Capitalismo, Política e Desenvolvimento na América Latina*, edited by Renato R. Boschi, 7–30. Belo Horizonte: Editora UFMG.

Boschi, Renato R., ed. 2011b. *Variedades de Capitalismo, Política e Desenvolvimento na América Latina*. Belo Horizonte: Editora UFMG.

Bresser-Pereira, Luiz Carlos. 2010. *Globalization and Competition: Why Some Emergent Countries Succeed While Others Fall Behind*. Cambridge: Cambridge University Press.

Bresser-Pereira, Luiz Carlos. 2016. "Reflexões sobre o Novo Desenvolvimentismo e o Desenvolvimentismo Clássico." *Revista de Economia Política* 36 (2): 237–265. https://doi.org/10.1590/0101-31572015v36n02a01.

Bresser-Pereira, Luiz Carlos, and Yoshiaki Nakano. 1984. *Inflação e Recessão*. São Paulo: Editora Brasiliense.

Bresser-Pereira, Luiz Carlos, and Daniela Theuer. 2012. "Um Estado Novo-desenvolvimentista na América Latina?" *Economia e Sociedade* 21 (Número Especial): 811–829. https://doi.org/10.1590/s0104-06182012000400005.

Cameron, Maxwell A., and Eric Hershberg, eds. 2010. *Latin America's Left Turns: Politics, Policies, and Trajectories of Change*. Boulder: Lynne Rienner Publishers.

Canitrot, Adolfo. 1981. "Teoría y Práctica del Liberalismo. Política Antiinflacionaria y Apertura Económica en la Argentina, 1976–1981." *Desarrollo Económico* 21 (82): 131–189. https://doi.org/10.2307/3466539.

Canitrot, Adolfo. 1994. "Crisis and Transformation of the Argentine State (1978–1992)." In *Democracy, Markets, and Structural Reform in Latin America*, edited by William C. Smith, Carlos H. Acuña, and Eduardo A. Gamarra, 75–102. Miami: North-South Center Press.

Cardoso, Fernando Henrique, and Enzo Faletto. 1976. *Dependencia y Desarrollo en América Latina. Ensayo de Interpretación Sociológica*. Decimaprimera ed. México: Siglo Veintiuno Editores. Original edition, 1969.

Carneiro, Dionísio Dias. 1989. "Crise e Esperança: 1974–1980." In *A Ordem do Progresso. Cem Anos de Política Econômica Republicana 1889–1989*, edited by Marcelo de Paiva Abreu, 295–322. Rio de Janeiro: Editora Campus.

Carneiro, Ricardo de Medeiros. 2012. "Velhos e Novos Desenvolvimentismos." *Economia e Sociedade* 21 (Número Especial): 749–778. https://doi.org/10.1590/s0104-06182012000400003.

Collier, Paul. 2007. *The Bottom Billion: Why the Poorest Countries Are Failing and What Can Be Done About It*. New York: Oxford University Press.

Collier, Ruth Berins, and David Collier. 1991. *Shaping the Political Arena: Critical Junctures, the Labor Movement, and Regime Dynamics in Latin America*. Princeton: Princeton University Press.

Corrales, Javier. 2010. "The Repeating Revolution. Chávez's New Politics and Old Economics." In *Leftist Governments in Latin America: Successes and Shortcomings*, edited by Kurt Weyland, Raúl L. Madrid, and Wendy Hunter, 28–58. Cambridge: Cambridge University Press.

Crouch, Collin, and Henry Farrell. 2004. "Breaking the Path of Institutional Development? Alternatives to the New Determinism." *Rationality and Society* 16 (1): 5–43. https://doi.org/10.1177/1043463104039874.

Dahl, Robert A., and Charles E. Lindblom. 1953. *Politics, Economics, and Welfare: Planning and Politico-Economic Systems Resolved into Basic Social Processes*. New York: Harper & Brothers Publishers.

Deeg, Richard. 2007. "Complementarity and Institutional Change in Capitalist Systems." *Journal of European Public Policy* 14 (4): 611–630. https://doi.org/10.1080/13501760701314433.

Deeg, Richard, and Gregory Jackson. 2007. "Towards a More Dynamic Theory of Capitalist Variety." *Socio-Economic Review* 5 (1): 149–179. https://doi.org/10.1093/ser/mwl021.

Diaz-Alejandro, Carlos. 1985. "Good-Bye Financial Repression, Hello Financial Crash." *Journal of Development Economics* 19 (1): 1–24. https://doi.org/10.1016/0304-3878(85)90036-7.

Diniz, Eli. 2011. "Depois do Neoliberalismo. Rediscutindo a Articulação Estado e Desenvolvimento no Novo Milênio." In *Variedades de Capitalismo, Política e Desenvolvimento na América Latina*, edited by Renato R. Boschi, 31–55. Belo Horizonte: Editora UFMG.

DiSalvo, Daniel. 2015. *Government Against Itself: Public Union Power and Its Consequences*. New York: Oxford University Press.

Duflo, Esther. 2010. *Le développement humain: lutter contre la pauvreté I*. Paris: Seuil.

Escobar, Arturo. 1995. *Encountering Development: The Making and Unmaking of the Third World*. Princeton: Princeton University Press.

Evans, Peter. 1979. *Dependent Development: The Alliance of Multinational, State, and Local Capital in Brazil*. Princeton: Princeton University Press.

Fajardo, Margarita. 2015. "The Latin American Experience with Development: Social Sciences, Economic Policies, and the Making of a Global Order, 1944–1971." PhD, Department of History, Princeton University.

Fajnzylber, Fernando, ed. 1980. *Industrialización e Internacionalización en la América Latina*. 2 vols. México: Fondo de Cultura Económica.

Fanelli, José María, ed. 2007. *Understanding Market Reforms in Latin America: Similar Reforms, Diverse Constituencies, Varied Results*. Houndmills, Basingstoke: Palgrave Macmillan.

Ferreira, Marieta de Moraes. 2002. "O Governo de Juscelino Kubitschek" [Dossier]. Centro de Pesquisa e Documentação de História Contemporânea do Brasil-CPDOC. Accessed October 8, 2020. http://cpdoc.fgv.br/producao/dossies/JK/apresentacao.

Ffrench-Davis, Ricardo. 2014. *Chile entre el Neoliberalismo y el Crecimiento con Equidad. Cuarenta Años de Políticas Económicas y sus Lecciones para el Futuro.* 5th ed. Santiago: J.C. Sáez Editor. Original edition, 1999.

Frieden, Jeffry A. 2006. *Global Capitalism: Its Fall and Rise in the Twentieth Century*. New York: Norton.

Furtado, Celso. 1970. *Economic Development of Latin America*. Cambridge: Cambridge University Press.

Gárate, Manuel. 2012. *La Revolución Capitalista de Chile (1973–2003)*. Santiago: Ediciones Universidad Alberto Hurtado.

Gourevitch, Peter. 1986. *Politics in Hard Times: Comparative Responses to International Economic Crises*. Ithaca: Cornell University Press.

Hall, Peter A. 2010. "Historical Institutionalism in Rationalist and Sociological Perspective." In *Explaining Institutional Change: Ambiguity, Agency, and Power*, edited by James Mahoney and Kathleen Thelen, 204–223. Cambridge: Cambridge University Press.

Hall, Peter A., and David Soskice, eds. 2001. *Varieties of Capitalism: The Institutional Foundations of Comparative Advantage*. Oxford: Oxford University Press.

Hall, Peter A., and Kathleen Thelen. 2009. "Institutional Change in Varieties of Capitalism." *Socio-Economic Review* 7 (1): 7–34. https://doi.org/10.1093/ser/mwn020.

Hancké, Bob, Martin Rhodes, and Mark Thatcher, eds. 2007. *Beyond Varieties of Capitalism: Conflict, Contradictions, and Complementarities in the European Economy*. New York: Oxford University Press.

Höpner, Martin. 2005. "Epilogue to 'Explaining Institutional Complementarity'." *Socio-Economic Review* 3 (2): 383–387. https://doi.org/10.1093/ser/mwi016.

Huber, Evelyne, Jennifer Pribble, and John D. Stephens. 2010. "The Chilean Left in Power: Achievements, Failures, and Omissions." In *Leftist Governments in Latin America: Successes and Shortcomings*, edited by Kurt Weyland, Raúl L. Madrid, and Wendy Hunter, 77–97. Cambridge: Cambridge University Press.

Jackson, Gregory, and Richard Deeg. 2008. "From Comparing Capitalisms to the Politics of Institutional Change." *Review of International Political Economy* 14 (4): 680–709. https://doi.org/10.1080/09692290802260704.

Johnson, Chalmers. 1982. *MITI and the Japanese Miracle: The Growth of Industrial Policy, 1925–1975*. Stanford: Stanford University Press.

Kaufman, Robert R. 1988. *The Politics of Debt in Argentina, Brazil, and Mexico: Economic Stabilization in the 1980s, Research Series*. Berkeley: Institute of International Studies, University of California.

Khademian, Anne M. 2010. "The Pracademic and the Fed: The Leadership of Chairman Benjamin Bernanke." *Public Administration Review* 70 (1): 142–150. https://doi.org/10.1111/j.1540-6210.2009.02118.x.

Krueger, Anne O. 1974. "The Political Economy of the Rent-Seeking Society." *American Economic Review* 64 (3): 291–303.

Krueger, Anne O. 1993. *Political Economy of Policy Reform in Developing Countries*. Cambridge, MA: MIT Press.

Kuntz Ficker, Sandra. 2005. "From Structuralism to the New Institutional Economics: The Impact of Theory on the Study of Foreign Trade in Latin America." *Latin American Research Review* 40 (3): 145–162. https://doi.org/10.1353/lar.2005.0045.

Kuznets, Simon. 1955. "Economic Growth and Income Inequality." *American Economic Review* 45 (1): 1–28.

Kydland, Finn E., and Edward C. Prescott. 1977. "Rules Rather Than Discretion: The Inconsistency of Optimal Plans." *Journal of Political Economy* 85 (3): 473–492. https://doi.org/10.1086/260580.

Ledbetter, James. 2011. *Unwarranted Influence: Dwight D. Eisenhower and the Military-Industrial Complex*. New Heaven: Yale University Press.

Levitsky, Steven, and Kenneth M. Roberts, eds. 2011. *The Resurgence of the Latin American Left*. Baltimore: Johns Hopkins University Press.

Limoeiro, Miriam. 1975. *La Ideología Dominante. Brasil-América Latina*. México: Siglo Veintiuno Editores. Original edition, 1972.

Lindblom, Charles E. 1958. "Policy Analysis." *American Economic Review* 48 (3): 298–312.

Lindblom, Charles E. 1959. "The Science of 'Muddling Through'." *Public Administration Review* 19 (2): 79–88. https://doi.org/10.2307/973677.

Lipsey, Robert E., and Fredrik Sjöholm. 2005. "The Impact of Inward FDI on Host Countries: Why Such Different Answers?" In *Does Foreign Direct Investment Promote Development?*, edited by Theodore H. Moran, Edward M. Graham, and Magnus Blomström, 23–43. Washington, DC: Institute for International Economics. Center for Global Development.

López-Maya, Margarita. 2011. "Venezuela. Hugo Chávez and the Populist Left." In *The Resurgence of the Latin American Left*, edited by Steven Levitsky and Kenneth M. Roberts, 213–238. Baltimore: Johns Hopkins University Press.

Love, Joseph Leroy. 2005. "The Rise and Decline of Economic Structuralism in Latin America: New Dimensions." *Latin American Research Review* 40 (3): 100–125. https://doi.org/10.1353/lar.2005.0058.

Love, Joseph Leroy. 2019. "CEPAL as Idea Factory for Latin American Development: Intellectual and Political Influence, 1950–1990." In *State and Nation Making in Latin America and Spain: The Rise and Fall of the Developmental State*, edited by Agustín E. Ferraro and Miguel A. Centeno, 29–50. Cambridge: Cambridge University Press.

Lucas, Robert E. 1972. "Expectations and the Neutrality of Money." *Journal of Economic Theory* 4 (2): 103–124. https://doi.org/10.1016/0022-0531(72)90142-1.

Lustig, Nora. 2002. *México. Hacia la Reconstrucción de una Economía*. Translated by Eduardo L. Suárez and Peter Lustig. 2a ed. México: El Colegio de México/Fondo de Cultura Económica. Original edition, 1992.

Mercadante, Aloízio. 2010. "As Bases do Novo Desenvolvimentismo no Brasil: Análise do Governo Lula (2003–2010)." PhD, Instituto de Economia, Universidade Estadual de Campinas.

Moe, Terry M. 2015. "Vested Interests and Political Institutions." *Political Science Quarterly* 130 (2): 277–318. https://doi.org/10.1002/polq.12321.

Moreno-Brid, Juan Carlos, and Jaime Ros. 2010. *Desarrollo y Crecimiento en la Economía Mexicana*. México: Fondo de Cultura Económica. Original edition, 2009. Reprint, 2014.

Nóbrega, Maílson da. 2005. *O Futuro Chegou. Instituições e Desenvolvimento no Brasil*. São Paulo: Globo.

Olson, Mancur. 1982. *The Rise and Decline of Nations: Economic Growth, Stagflation, and Social Rigidities*. New Haven: Yale University Press.

Ortiz, Antonio. 1970. "Desarrollo Estabilizador: Una Década de Estrategia Económica en México." *El Trimestre Económico* 37 (146(2)): 417–449. https://doi.org/10.2307/20856136.

Payne, Leigh A. 1994. *Brazilian Industrialists and Democratic Change*. Baltimore: Johns Hopkins University Press.

Pierson, Paul. 1993. "When Effect Becomes Cause: Policy Feedback and Political Change." *World Politics* 45 (4): 595–628. https://doi.org/10.2307/2950710.

Pierson, Paul. 2000. "Increasing Returns, Path Dependence, and the Study of Politics." *American Political Science Review* 94 (2): 251–267. https://doi.org/10.2307/2586011.

Pierson, Paul. 2004. *Politics in Time: History, Institutions, and Social Analysis*. Princeton: Princeton University Press.

Prebisch, Raúl. 1963. *Hacia una Dinámica del Desarrollo Latinoamericano*. México: Fondo de Cultura Económica.

Prebisch, Raúl, and Gustavo Martínez. 1949. "El Desarrollo Económico de la América Latina y Algunos de sus Principales Problemas." *El Trimestre Económico* 16 (63(3)): 347–431. https://doi.org/10.2307/20855070.

Reinhart, Carmen M., and Kenneth S. Rogoff. 2009. *This Time Is Different: Eight Centuries of Financial Folly*. Princeton: Princeton University Press.

Roberts, Kenneth M. 2011. "Chile: The Left after Neoliberalism." In *The Resurgence of the Latin American Left*, edited by Steven Levitsky and Kenneth M. Roberts, 325–347. Baltimore: Johns Hopkins University Press.

Rodríguez, Octavio. 1980. *La Teoría del Subdesarrollo de la Cepal*. México: Siglo XXI Editores.

Rodrik, Dani. 2007. *One Economics, Many Recipes: Globalization, Institutions, and Economic Growth*. Princeton: Princeton University Press.

Rostow, W. W. 1971. *The Stages of Economic Growth: A Non-Communist Manifesto*. 2nd ed. Cambridge: Cambridge University Press. Original edition, 1960.

Rueschemeyer, Dietrich, Evelyne Huber Stephens, and John D. Stephens. 1992. *Capitalist Development and Democracy*. Chicago: University of Chicago Press.

Saint-Martin, Denis, and Christine Rothmayr-Allison. 2011. "Rationalism and Public Policy: Mode of Analysis or Symbolic Politics?" *Policy and Society* 30 (1): 19–27. https://doi.org/10.1016/j.polsoc.2010.12.003.

Sampaio, Plínio de Arruda, Jr. 2012. "Desenvolvimentismo e Neodesenvolvimentismo: Tragédia e Farsa." *Serviço Social & Sociedade* (112): 672–688. https://doi.org/10.1590/s0101-66282012000400004.

Santana, Carlos Henrique Vieira. 2011. "Conjuntura Crítica, Legados Institucionais e Comunidades Epistêmicas. Limites e Possibilidades de uma Agenda de Desenvolvimento no Brasil." In *Variedades de Capitalismo, Política e Desenvolvimento na América Latina*, edited by Renato R. Boschi, 121–163. Belo Horizonte: Editora UFMG.

Sartori, Giovanni. 1970. "Concept Misformation in Comparative Politics." *American Political Science Review* 64 (4): 1033–1053. https://doi.org/10.2307/1958356.

Schneider, Ben Ross. 1999. "The Desarrollista State in Brazil and Mexico." In *The Developmental State*, edited by Meredith Woo-Cumings, 276–305. Ithaca: Cornell University Press.

Schneider, Ben Ross. 2009. "Hierarchical Market Economies and Varieties of Capitalism in Latin America." *Journal of Latin American Studies* 41 (3): 553–575. https://doi.org/10.1017/s0022216x09990186.

Schneider, Ben Ross. 2012. "Contrasting Capitalisms: Latin America in Comparative Perspective." In *The Oxford Handbook of Latin American Political Economy*, edited by Javier Santiso and Jeff Dayton-Johnson, 381–402. New York: Oxford University Press.

Schneider, Ben Ross. 2013. *Hierarchical Capitalism in Latin America: Business, Labor, and the Challenges of Equitable Development*. New York: Cambridge University Press.

Schneider, Ben Ross, and David Soskice. 2009. "Inequality in Developed Countries and Latin America: Coordinated, Liberal and Hierarchical Systems." *Economy and Society* 38 (1): 17–52. https://doi.org/10.1080/03085140802560496.

Sen, Amartya Kumar. 2000. *Development as Freedom*. New York: Anchor Books. Original edition, 1999.

Sikkink, Kathryn. 1991. *Ideas and Institutions: Developmentalism in Brazil and Argentina*. Ithaca: Cornell University Press.

Simon, Herbert A. 1955. "A Behavioral Model of Rational Choice." *Quarterly Journal of Economics* 69 (1): 99–118. https://doi.org/10.2307/1884852.

Singer, André. 2015. "Cutucando Onças com Varas Curtas – O Ensaio Desenvolvimentista no Primeiro Mandato de Dilma Rousseff (2011–2014)." *Novos Estudos CEBRAP* 34 (2(102)): 43–71. https://doi.org/10.25091/s0101-3300201500020004.

Skidmore, Thomas E. 1967. *Politics in Brazil, 1930–1964: An Experiment in Democracy*. New York: Oxford University Press.

Skocpol, Theda. 1992. *Protecting Soldiers and Mothers: The Political Origins of Social Policy in the United States*. Cambridge, MA: Belknap Press of Harvard University Press.

Stiglitz, Joseph E. 2002. *Globalization and Its Discontents*. New York: W. W. Norton.

Stone, Diane. 2008. "Global Public Policy, Transnational Policy Communities, and Their Networks." *Policy Studies Journal* 36 (1): 19–38. https://doi.org/10.1111/j.1541-0072.2007.00251.x.

Taylor, Matthew M. 2009. "Institutional Development through Policy-Making: A Case Study of the Brazilian Central Bank." *World Politics* 61 (3): 487–515. https://doi.org/10.1017/s0043887109000161.

Thorp, Rosemary. 1992. "A Reappraisal of the Origins of Import-Substituting Industrialisation 1930–1950." *Journal of Latin American Studies* 24 (S1): 181–195. https://doi.org/10.1017/s0022216x0002383x.

Waisman, Carlos H. 1987. *Reversal of Development in Argentina: Postwar Counterrevolutionary Policies and Their Structural Consequences*. Princeton: Princeton University Press.

Williamson, John, ed. 1990. *Latin American Adjustment: How Much Has Happened?* Washington: Institute for International Economics.

Woo-Cumings, Meredith, ed. 1999. *The Developmental State*. Ithaca: Cornell University Press.

CHAPTER 4

The Real Plan: The Successful Struggle to Consolidate Economic Governance

This chapter will illustrate the ways in which Brazil consolidated economic governance, focusing on institutional changes it adopted in order to do so. This process involved numerous struggles for reform after the collapse of the previous development model; such said collapse led to hyperinflation. Despite many attempts to fight hyperinflation, it became clear over the years that the problems ran very deep indeed. The situation arose, more precisely, because some groups were able to shift the costs of their actions to society as a whole. It was not until the power of these actors was reduced, their opportunities for cost-shifting restricted, that policies to control hyperinflation showed significant and sustained results. The country then faced a new economic challenge when the stabilization process was threatened by yet another crisis. In response, authorities built a coalition supporting several institutional reforms that buttressed one another. This process and its outcome exemplifies the consolidation of economic governance through the formation of an institutional complementarity.

The changes implemented in Brazil to stop inflation went beyond monetary reform. Inflation control required a profound transformation of Brazil's political economy. Different actors, following their own paths, reformed institutions that became fundamental to stabilization. Reformers pursued their own individual struggles without considering the possible

A. Angel, *Consolidating Economic Governance in Latin America*, Governance, Development, and Social Inclusion in Latin America,
https://doi.org/10.1007/978-3-030-64522-9_4

systemic effects such institutional changes would produce. Subsequently, these effects played an important role in holding together the coalition that allowed for the control of inflation. This chapter uses the story of how Brazil controlled inflation in the first half of 1990s as a way into a theoretical argument about the consolidation of economic governance. It intends to show how independent institutional transformations became dependent on one another, ultimately preventing a return of hyperinflation. This mutual dependence among institutions constitutes an institutional complementarity. The chapter describes the political and economic conditions under which these institutional changes took place, though the *mise-en-scène* will not be exhaustive.

The institutional changes that will be analyzed are the privatization of Brazilian state-owned companies, commercial liberalization, and monetary and budgetary reforms. Privatization led to a better use of scarce resources, because state-owned companies demanded substantial public support. Far from their rent-capturing image (Niskanen 1971), bureaucrats themselves actually instigated the process of divestiture, because they saw how public resources sustained non-profitable businesses. At times these businesses sold products below their marginal cost, subsidizing their clients as a result. In this way, privatization ended the cost-externalizing strategy of some businesses that bought their inputs at below-market prices. While patronage also represented a political obstacle to surmount, this practice did not have significant inflationary effects.

In addition, there was a complex structure of protection that allowed local producers to transfer both their costs and their ad hoc profit margins to consumers. Without competition from external producers, locals could capture rents without any danger of losing their clients. Commercial liberalization prevented the continuation of this cost-externalizing strategy, as the improved conditions meant that external producers would now compete with local ones. Both policies, privatization, and trade liberalization barred the continuation of a strategy through which businesses' inefficiencies could be translated into higher prices. Such effects reinforce one another—they are complementary—and this makes stabilization possible and consolidates a new pattern of economic governance.

For a while, inflation was politically functional. Politicians raised expenses as a way of proving to their constituencies that they had clout over the government.[1] The revenues that would sustain them were not among politicians' concerns. However, the Treasury had a solution.[2] Given the high inflation, the way to "pay" for politicians' expenses was simply to delay payment, because their real value would erode with the ongoing hyperinflation (Bacha 1994, 9–10; Cardoso 2006, 141–142). The use of this strategy in the federal sphere and in bigger states had systemic effects, but it was also generalized within all governmental spheres. Thus, inflation was fostered through monetary emission; in its many iterations, it always had fiscal roots. Inflation was a problem with which Brazilians lived for several decades. Throughout this time, Brazil developed institutions to lighten its burden, mainly for a privileged sector of society. In part, inflation, within certain limits, was seen as a relatively inoffensive consequence of a process of development in which the state played a central role.[3] State intervention included ensuring a closed economy to protect new industries, direct state ownership of these industries, and the provision of subsidies.

State intervention in the economy sought to promote growth, which came to epitomize the objective of development. Policy instruments varied depending on the specific target. Heavy industries such as steel mills, mines, and utilities became the responsibility of the state because they had large sunk costs or strategic value. Meanwhile, market protection, subsidies, and soft loans, among other interventions, promoted private investments. The state became ubiquitous because of its direct involvement with productive activities, as well as with policy instruments that guaranteed a return. In the 1980s, however, when conditions changed dramatically, such deep and widespread intervention in the economy showed its weaknesses. The rising interest rates affecting the world economy ultimately made the pattern of intervention too onerous to sustain.

[1] Edmar Bacha. Interview by the author. Rio de Janeiro. February 21, 2014. Bacha is a founding partner and Head of the Instituto de Estudos em Política Econômica/Casa das Garças. He was President of the *Instituto Brasileiro de Geografia e Estatística*—IBGE (Brazilian Institute of Geography and Statistics) during the Cruzado Plan in 1986. Later he was nominated as President of different institutions during the Real Plan.

[2] Ferreira (2016) offers a discussion about the institutional evolution of the Treasury.

[3] Franco (1999, 219–222) evaluates critically the relationship between development and inflation.

Brazilians were familiar with high inflation, in part because it was considered relatively harmless. Nevertheless, some sectors (organized industries, labor, and the state itself) demanded protection from its effects, which clearly indicates that it was not innocuous. This protection came in the form of indexation,[4] which is the adjustment of a given price based on the previous inflation rate in order to recover the losses that it produced. However, when this is done at different paces depending on the price, a coordination problem occurs, because a price can also change in response to an exogenous shock, such as a bad harvest. Every single price in the economy will then vary in accordance with that price variation.

Indexation initially appeared under the first military government, that of Humberto Castelo-Branco (1964–1967). Controlling inflation and establishing a mechanism to deal with its consequences were among the problems that he faced (Simonsen 1970, 183),[5] and his institution of indexation established an enduring legacy. Although Brazilian legislation accounted for an automatic correction of asset values as of 1958, it was not until July 1964 that indexation made its first appearance with the enactment of Act 4357, which created the *Obrigações Reajustáveis do Tesouro Nacional*—ORTN (Adjustable Liabilities of the National Treasury). The value of this security was corrected in response to the observed inflation, creating an incentive for the public to buy it. It also allowed the state to finance public deficits through non-compulsory debt as well as through the indexation of tax revenues (Franco 2018, 116ff).[6]

However, it was primarily financial markets that would benefit from indexation, because many of their instruments were also indexed with shortening terms (Simonsen 1970, 188). Thus, indexation protected those few with access to financial products from inflation, or even allowed them to profit from it. Notably, the fact that indexation responded to some groups' demand for protection from the effects of inflation says a great deal about its political character. First of all, tax revenues were

[4] Indexation was used in salaries, exchange, taxes, financial contracts, and later in contracts in general (Franco 1999, 225). Indexation will be further discussed below.

[5] Following the historical statistics compiled by the IBGE (1990, 186), the difference between January 1964 (23.992) and January 1965 (41.335) was 17.343 percentage points (January 1967 = 100). The increase in 1964 would have been 72.28%.

[6] Although there were other measures introducing indexation in contracts, the above-mentioned examples make reference to the ways of financing state activities, debt, and taxes.

indexed while expenses were not; this protected state revenues. Some contracts were indexed *ex ante* whereas others were indexed *ex post*, which provided a different kind of protection depending on the asset possessed. This difference in the level of protection granted to different groups created collective action problems. As every group had an incentive to seek better protection than that granted to others, the actualization of numerous indexes rapidly accelerated.

Thus, the high rate of inflation in Brazil was a consequence of fiscal policies, monetary policies, and of the way in which particular markets adjusted to price increases: by increasing their own prices, often surpassing the official rate of inflation. Policies that fostered inflation therefore also created constituencies, which had powerful incentives to bet against any attempt to control it. Also, many of the factors that influenced inflation allowed those who benefited from it to avoid suffering any consequences for their actions. Paramount among these instruments of blame avoidance was indexation, because it allowed for price correction independent of the fundamentals of production processes or seasonal variations. As every price was attached to an index, when there was a price increase, that index was corrected, and with it the rest of the prices in the economy. In the end, high inflation seemed nobody's responsibility.

Generalized indexation was another element fueling inflation. This relationship was created through what came to be known as inertial inflation (Bresser-Pereira and Nakano 1987; Bresser-Pereira 2010), which refers to the automatic reproduction of inflation without any other fundamental change in the economy. Even when theoretical debates on the matter thrived, anti-inflationary policies ignored the hypothesis of inertial inflation, focusing instead on a traditional view of fiscal and monetary restraint. In the first half of 1980s, while the military was still in power, discussions about inertial inflation, both theoretical and practical, became common (Rego 1986; Williamson 1985). This serious consideration of the theory of inertial inflation was a consequence of the ineffectiveness of the programs implemented by the previous military government.

Indexation worked to correct the value of a given financial instrument, actualizing its real value following the losses caused by inflation. The degree of protection granted by indexation also depended on its periodicity. This meant that there was a direct relationship between the pace of correction and the effectiveness of the protection against inflationary depreciation. The alignment of incentives by significant actors—from the state to the banks, both state-owned and private, to those who could press for better indexation of their revenues and assets—led to the creation of several indexes. The possibility of being protected by a better index depended on the liquidity of the asset in question, because this is what would allow it to be transferred toward the best available correction.

These dynamics created a hierarchical structure in which only a few were capable of protecting their wealth, and fewer still were able to increase it. Some groups were able to partially protect their assets from inflation. The large majority of the population, namely those with fixed incomes such as salaries, suffered because indexation was only applied at the end of the month.[7] Salary earners did not fully recover the losses produced by inflation and, accordingly, they could not save through financial instruments or even through bank accounts, which could have protected them as well. Moreover, the absence of indexation on any instrument or contract on which somebody's income depended had direct consequences on the relative exchange value within the transaction. Therefore, indexation represented one of the power instruments through which the state distributed, in the end, the revenues of the inflationary tax.

Furthermore, the way in which the financial sector worked says a great deal about how it took advantage of inflation over the years. Indexation allowed banks to profit off of the permanent rollover of different financial instruments circulating in the Brazilian economy, effectively capturing the *seignoriage* tax. Private and state-owned banks were in distress. The long inflationary regime had allowed small banks to profit even if their operational margin was not significant. Even though banks represented the most prominent example of an institution taking advantage of indexation, every business with available resources could invest in indexed securities, allowing them to profit regardless of the profitability of their main commercial activity. State-owned banks rolled over the debt of their controllers (Jayme 1995), taking advantage of, among other things, the difference between the indexation of their revenues and their liabilities.

[7] The saying in Brazil was: "*Sobrou mês no fim do salário*" (There is plenty of month at the end of the salary).

There were eight stabilization plans after democratization in 1985 until 1992, as well as several previous attempts made by the authoritarian regime (Franco 2018, 466ff).[8] This long pattern of unsuccessful attempts created deep wounds in Brazilian society. However, the fact that these plans did not stop inflation as such does not mean that lessons were not drawn or that some legacies did not remain. Indeed, the various plans created both opportunities and constraints for different actors: they were faced with the choice of whether to work below the radar of the main anti-inflationary policies, passing through various political obstacles to do so; or, conversely, to join in the fight against inflation with the aim of capitalizing on the possible success of the current policy. The succession of the stabilization plans turned out to be a trial-and-error process over many years. Each plan focused on what policymakers considered to be the most important factor causing inflation.

However, after several years of living with inflation and the possibilities it offered for unloading the consequences of business decisions onto others, there was not just one single factor behind inflation, but many. The successive adjustments in the anti-inflationary policies from 1986 to 1992 showed what measures produced lasting results. This combination of policies became complementary when the possibility of inflation's return threatened a political downturn, forcing political actors to compromise so as to unite two unrelated policies. Privatization and liberalization each responded according to their own logic, without clearly or explicitly joining the fight against inflation. While there were some instances in which these policies were linked, for the most part they did not give any wiggle room to those in charge. When such different policies become complementary, economic governance is consolidated.

The next section will cover the privatization process and how it was related—or was not—to the fight against inflation.

[8] These plans were: Cruzado, *Cruzadinho* (Little Cruzado), Cruzado II, Bresser, *Arroz-com-feijão* (Rice-and-beans), *Verão* (Summer), Collor I, and Collor II. Sometimes the first two are considered as only one, with an adjustment.

4.1 Privatization

4.1.1 Development, Scarcity, and Reform

Throughout the twentieth century, the state remained a major player in the Brazilian economy, despite changing political and economic conditions. This was the case during the Vargas era with the creation (in 1941 and 1953, respectively) of both the *Companhia Siderúrgica Nacional*—CSN (National Steel Mills) and *Petrobrás* (Brazilian Petroleum). Even if the latter represented a complex negotiation with the army, among other sectors, economic nationalism was ever-present in the country (Wirth 1970). These negotiations represented the clash between nationalistic forces and groups embracing "economic liberalism," who tended to be more critical of the state's strong participation in the economy. This clash reappeared later on with the advent of the military regime in 1964. While the schism at that time was between populism and liberalism, soon, the economic and political reality would reignite the debate over the state's role in the economy once again.

The state's prominent role was in part due to the importance of foreign capital in fostering growth and national security (as defined by the military) in order to guarantee political stability (Bruneau and Faucher 1981, 1–2). State-owned enterprises concentrated on the production of raw materials and related activities, while foreign capital produced mainly consumer goods. The state's technocracy arbitrated this division through negotiations with both foreign capital and the military.[9] Foreign capital represented significant economic power, given the secondary position of the Brazilian market in the global economy, whereas the military represented political power, given its monopoly over repression (Faucher 1979, 755). The process of privatization had started officially under the military government of General João Figueiredo (1979–1985), with Decree 86.215, issued in 1981.[10] Initially the rationale for a privatization policy

[9] Paramount in the Brazilian technocracy was the *Banco Nacional de Desenvolvimento Econômico e Social*—BNDES (*National Development Bank*), whose role will be further discussed below.

[10] This decree created a special Commission composed of the Ministers of Planning, Finance, and Debureaucratization in charge of creating a list of businesses that could be sold to private interests. Its provisions were limited, as the president could decide if an enterprise was important for reasons of national security, because of state monopolies, in the interest of upholding basic social or economic infrastructure, or due to provisions allowing for national control of the development process.

was to respond to specific groups who saw privatization as part of an effort to change the regime, since the withdrawal of the state from the economy would also imply its "retreat" in the event of a regime change.[11] It was ultimately a group of bureaucrats from within the BNDES, however, that instigated the transformation of the state's role in the economy.

That said, even before the decision to privatize, there had already been a political mobilization of industrialists who called for a *Desestatização* (retreat of the state) from the economy. In their view, the excessive intervention of the state in economic matters was undermining the expansion of private capital. The campaign focused on the pre-eminence that foreign capital had acquired in the Brazilian capitalist landscape (Payne 1994, 62–63; Skidmore 1988, 201). The campaign was only supported by national businesses,[12] however, since the government had granted major contracts to foreign companies competing with Brazilian ones (Payne 1994). This limited support reveals the ambiguity of the industrialists' economic liberalism and suggests why they called for the retreat of the state instead of straightforward privatization.

By the early 1980s, after several decades in which the state played a key role in the Brazilian economy, the weaknesses caused by this model began to appear (Thorp 1998, 255). The state had accumulated equities in different industries that were not profitable.[13] These businesses had convertible loans with public banks such as the BNDES,[14] which were

[11] Therefore, privatization responded to such demands with the aim of controlling the pace of the retreat of the state while simultaneously granting symbolic concessions to those groups.

[12] Support for the campaign was based on a general support for representative government and the rule of law, and also because in a democratic regime business could better influence policy, in contrast to a situation in which bureaucrats favored foreign business (Skidmore 1988, 201).

[13] The industries in which these companies acted were copper and steel mills, mining, ferroalloys, cellulose, and machinery (Velasco 2010, 317).

[14] The founding of the Brazilian *Banco Nacional de Desenvolvimento Econômico*—BNDE in 1952 was remarkably late, given its importance as a development bank. It was first founded to finance infrastructure projects and other long-term investments that the Brazilian government wanted to promote, such as metals, chemicals, and cement, among others (Musacchio and Lazzarini 2014, 84–86). However, soon, during the government of Juscelino Kubitschek (1956–1961), it became the financial instrument for the ambitious National Development Plan (Evans 1995, 61). The adjective "Social" was added during the 1980s in order to highlight the new scope in the bank's activities relative to the development process (Schneider 1991b, 275 fn. 18).

then forced to assume their control and administration (Velasco 2010, 312). Bureaucrats at the BNDES realized their available resources were consumed by the administration of those controlled businesses (Fortes 1994). It is possible to see this problem as one of scarcity or alternatively as one of opportunity costs. The bank had to allocate financial resources to these enterprises without seeing any profits. In part, this was because companies were behind price adjustments, due to the practice of using public businesses' prices to control inflation. In an inflationary context, this meant that these companies were always in a deficit. Moreover, the BNDES had never intended to control such companies, but rather to support Brazilian industry through minority participations or credits (Musacchio and Lazzarini 2014, 97). By the 1980s, however, the situation in the Brazilian economy was completely different, and the successive crises had forced many companies into the bank's portfolio (Musacchio and Lazzarini 2014, 244).

These enterprises became a burden to the BNDES in terms of both human and financial resources. The bank's staff had to spend time managing very complex enterprises as well as supplying capital that would otherwise have been directed to more productive loans. This meant that scarce resources were being used to sustain unprofitable operations. The bank's leadership realized that it was in the best interests of the bank to sell those assets, which mainly represented liabilities.[15] The bank's control over these unprofitable companies, and its subsequent resource allocation, were inefficient both from a social point of view and an economic one. These companies dominated their respective markets. For instance, *Caraíba Metais* was the only copper metallurgy in the country, and *Sibra* was the biggest producer of ferroalloys at the time. *Aracruz Celulose* also had an important role in the cellulose market. Across the table, *Siderurgia Brasileira*—SIDERBRAS (Brazilian Steel Mills), the governmental steel holding, also had an interest in selling its failing subsidiaries[16] so as to

[15] However, a legitimate question would be whether the BNDES could decide on divestiture autonomously. During the transition to democracy, there was a high degree of continuity among the bureaucrats staffing the economic bureaucracy (Schneider 1991b, 230–233). Furthermore, financial profitability mattered to the bank because it had to pay for the use of the *Fundo de Amparo ao Trabalhador*—FAT (Worker's Protection Fund), which the bank administers and on which it pays interests (Bernardino 2005). Autonomy and profitability might add to the reasons that the BNDES made a political decision that politicians were not ready to make themselves.

[16] These were *Usiba* (Steel Mills of Bahía) and *Cofavi* (Vitória Iron and Steel).

guarantee the survival of the group as such.[17] Moreover, given BNDES's experience with the privatization of its own subsidiaries, SIDERBRAS designated the bank, through a subsidiary, as its privatization agent (Velasco 1997).[18]

The BNDES also had its own interest in the privatization of SIDERBRAS, because it had credits from those businesses. These credits could not be recovered in full because they had been guaranteed by the Treasury. Consequently, they could only be rolled out. The public nature of the BNDES, with the federal government as its only shareholder, implied that any credit against the Treasury was credit against its controller. In practice, those assets were really liabilities that the bank had to carry forward without any possibility of recovering them. Nevertheless, once the businesses were privatized, the possibility of transforming those liabilities into assets became real. This also applied to SIDERBRAS itself, as the bank also had credits against it. In other words, with the privatization of SIDERBRAS's subsidiaries the bank would recover the credits against the businesses, and would have a greater possibility of recovering what the holding owed, too.

In this way, then, all of these players sought to improve the efficiency of their available resources. However, this apparently win-win situation had also its detractors. They came from the private sector and were often those who took advantage of the difficulties of state-owned businesses. Also, authorities did not allow these businesses to increase their prices in order to control inflation, and the deficit was persistent as a result (Pinheiro and Giambiagi 2000, 18–19). Thus, their clients profited using the subsidies implicit in behind-the-schedule prices.[19] As a consequence of the privatization process, these actors asked the BNDES to formally suspend

[17] Licínio Velasco Jr. Interview by the author. Rio de Janeiro. February 24, 2014. Velasco Jr. was the Chief of the Department of Privatization Services of the BNDES in 1999. He entered the bank through one of its subsidiaries in the 1970s and made his career in the BNDES bureaucracy; he completed a Master's and a Ph.D. in Political Science at the *Instituto Universitário de Pesquisas do Rio de Janeiro*—IUPERJ (Institute for Advanced Research of Rio de Janeiro) in the 1990s and the early 2000s

[18] The relationship between BNDE(S) and steel goes back several decades (Schneider 1991b, 102–105).

[19] Subsidies were the main aim of low prices of state-owned enterprises. These also applied when state-owned companies were forced to buy from local suppliers even if their product was more expensive.

privatization (Velasco 1997, 10 fn. 4).[20] Many privatization auctions were also subject to temporary judiciary suspension until the BNDES contested such decisions (Velasco 1997, 15).

Support for the privatization process was additionally dependent on its importance for presidential political support from Congress. The government at the time lacked legitimacy as a result of José Sarney's (1985–1990) proximity to the military regime.[21] It was therefore forced to gather support by making concessions to different groups, which meant that privatizations were conducted at the margins of political negotiations seeking support for the government (Schneider 1991a, 28). However, once Congress agreed to increase the presidential period to five years, a change that had been Sarney's main political goal,[22] privatization could finally gain momentum, because it could no longer be used as a bargaining chip in the political game between the government and Congress. More specifically, the president could now offer explicit support, and privatization could be part of the main political agenda, which afforded it a prominence that the BNDES's bureaucrats had previously lacked. Nevertheless, the government's economic priority was inflation, which meant that privatization remained low on the government's political agenda, despite this new support (Velasco 2010, 313).

The low prioritization of privatization *vis-à-vis* other policies supports the idea that mid-level bureaucrats often model public policy, at least to some extent, according to their own priorities and within the limits of

[20] Wiring and rolling mills, the main clients of the copper metallurgy—*Caraíba Metais*—asked for such a suspension, which represented a not-so-veiled attempt to maintain the status quo.

[21] José Sarney was a member of *Aliança Renovadora Nacional*—ARENA (National Renovation Alliance), which supported the military regime. Following a long-standing tradition in Brazilian politics, Sarney defected from ARENA and joined the *Partido Democrático Social*—PDS (Democratic and Social Party), which was also pro-dictatorship, and then moved to the *Partido Movimento Democrático Brasileiro*—PMDB (Party of Brazilian Democratic Movement) in the last days of the military regime. Subsequently he became Vice-President under Tancredo Nêves through an indirect election held in 1985. However, as Nêves became severely ill and eventually died before taking office, it was Sarney who became the first President of the transition.

[22] The constitution of 1967 established a six-year term but Tancredo had promised a four-year term, so Sarney asked for five years (Schneider 1991a, 28).

the broader political game (Almeida 1999, 432).[23] As noted, privatization was somewhat removed from the main political struggles concerning the economy, namely inflation. The military government embraced privatization half-heartedly as a response to mounting political pressures. After the transition the new civilian president lacked legitimacy, and one of his attempts to gather political support was through public businesses. While privatization had to overcome some political resistance early on, this was minor when compared with the broader post-transitional political landscape. Privatization could only go as far as the government—which was in search of political support—allowed, confirming its secondary status at the time. Furthermore, the groups that opposed privatization policies could not contest them openly. Had they done so, it would have become evident that they were receiving hidden subsidies. Therefore, with no big constituency against it, and with only secondary importance among the incumbent's political priorities, privatization had considerable success during the Sarney administration.

At this time, privatization was not linked to the fight against inflation. In fact, the two policies were prioritized very differently in the Brazilian political system. However, the struggle described above represented a breakthrough in the process that would allow Brazilians to control inflation some years later. That institutional reform would insist that the state should relinquish responsibilities accumulated over the years, on behalf of some interested parties. This struggle was the first step in that process of reform, and it provided many useful lessons for those seeking to continue to develop such policies.

4.1.2 Collor Government: A New Priority

When Fernando Collor (1990–1992) took office, privatization assumed yet another dimension (Almeida 1996) with the creation of the *Programa Nacional de Desestatização*—PND (National Program for Privatization). The first economic measures taken by the new government demonstrated the relative importance that the new administration gave to downsizing the state.[24] This enthusiasm notwithstanding, political support

[23] This is reminiscent of the argument of the insulated technocratic elite that can push through market reforms even if they are not popular (Armijo and Faucher 2002).

[24] Among the economic measures taken by the new government, privatization ranked third in the list published after its inauguration (Faria 1990).

conditioned the privatization policy, because Collor did not have a clear mandate on liberal policies (Schneider 1992, 226).[25] Few in Congress were convinced of the adequacy of privatization (Schneider 1991a, 39–40), not even the *Partido da Social Democracia Brasileira*—PSDB (Brazilian Social Democracy Party), whose advisers had helped to delineate its necessary legal instruments.[26] Congress and the Judiciary approved Collor's policies during his first months in office, but since these did not produce quick results, political support soon evaporated (Pinheiro, Bonelli, and Schneider 2007, 79–80).

Despite the lack of support for Collor's initiatives, the results of the privatization processes during his administration are certainly quite impressive when compared with those of the previous governments (Table 4.1). Furthermore, "support" implies also the way in which society perceives governmental initiatives; it is not exclusively about Congressional approval. The privatization process of *Usinas Siderúrgicas de Minas Gerais*—USIMINAS (Steel Mills of Minas Gerais) serves as a good example of this phenomenon, for at least two reasons. First, it was profitable and second, its new selling model set a benchmark and helped to gather political support, partially because it showed that privatization was not only for loss-generating assets. Until then, almost all privatization processes had been for failed businesses that the state kept afloat. As a result, many demanded restructuration in order to continue with their selling processes. The atomization[27] of property as a selling mechanism was key to gathering the political support the government lacked.

The first privatizations conducted by the BNDES had a privileged buyer—or, at least, the property structure of the company had already been defined. In the case of USIMINAS, however, there was neither a prequalified buyer nor an expressive minimum bid, which allowed for a broader clientele. Also, the absence of a privileged bidder created an

[25] While his presidential campaign emphasized a position against the *Marajás* (Maharajas) of public agencies, once he was in office, the eliminated or transformed agencies lacked any political significance—with the exception of SIDERBRAS, which was already in crisis (*Globo* 1990).

[26] Gustavo H. B. Franco. Interview by the author. Rio de Janeiro, March 13, 2014. Franco was President of the Central Bank, head of its International Directorate, and Deputy Secretary of Economic Policy of the Ministry of Finance. He is now Chief Strategy Officer of Rio Bravo Investimentos.

[27] Schneider (1992, 234) translates the Portuguese word *pulverização* as "people's capitalism." "Atomization" is the preferred term.

Table 4.1 Privatization by Brazilian administrations. 1979–1992

Administration	*Number of Companies*	*Direct Revenues (Millions USD)*	*Transferred Debts (Millions USD)*	*Number of Employees*
João Batista Figueiredo (1979–1985)	20	188.51	n.d.	4864
José Sarney (1985–1990)*	18	548.3	620	22,707
Fernando Collor (1990–1992)†	18	3397.8	n.d.	43,469

n.d.: No data

*Velasco (1997, 9) offers different figures for the Sarney administration (Velasco Jr reports 17 companies with revenues of 549 million and debt transfers of 620 million; he is the only source for the latter figure. His sources are the report (1985–1989) of the *Conselho Federal de Desestatização* (Federal Council on Privatization) and the document, "*Privatização: A experiência da BNDESPAR no período 1987—89*" (Privatization: the experience of BNDESPAR. 1987–1989), analyzed through a process involving some criteria conciliation. Almeida (1996, 219) cites the Executive Secretariat of the Federal Council on Privatization for the same period. None of these sources was available to the author)

†Velasco (1997, 19) also offers different figures for the Collor administration. (He reports 16 companies with revenues of 3.9 billion. There are no sources for these figures.) Presumably, all monetary figures are in current dollars, as no sources indicate any actualization of their value following dollar inflation. This caveat, however, should not prevent comparison of the two periods because of their order of magnitude.

Source Own elaboration with data by Almeida (1996, 219)

incentive for numerous players to participate in the operation according to their resources. The distribution of USIMINAS's equity after the auction (Manzetti 1999, 174) also deactivated any opposition, because no group perceived the operation to be against its interests, as would have been the case if there had been a privileged player. This model was not thought of as a way to garner political support. It was clear, however, that those with stakes in the industries where privatized enterprises acted would resist the entry of a big competitor. The unrestricted bids were the basis for wide support of the process, since more actors became "owners," and those who did not foresaw the possibility of becoming owners in future processes.[28] Therefore, the political success of this strategy was twofold,

[28] These new owners included the savings trusts of public employees, notably that of *Banco do Brasil* employees with 15%; foundations belonging to other public enterprises, with 7.7%; and even public enterprises (*Companhia Vale do Rio Doce*—CVRD), with 15%,

as it prevented the rise of big opposition and attracted broad support to legitimize the process (Velasco 2010, 351–357).

Opposition to the privatization process came from two different groups: first, competitors, who would subsequently face an empowered owner when compared with state-owned businesses caught up in politics and not focusing on running a business; and second, unions, who benefited from the largesse that state managers could provide, and perceived that a transfer of the business to private hands would diminish their benefits. Nevertheless, the Collor government conducted privatization as it conducted every economic policy—that is, by isolating the decision team and privileging technocratic decision-making (Schneider 1992, 234–235). Importantly, economic reforms, including privatization, were closely associated with a comprehensive solution to the Brazilian fiscal crisis (Almeida 1996, 217).[29]

This association between marginal reforms and large-scale economic change had somewhat ambiguous effects on the possibility of crafting a supporting coalition for the government. On the one hand, the poor results of the ill-conceived stabilization plan, which did not stabilize the economy, created widespread mistrust of the government behind it. Because the public sector needed a thorough reorganization, which would be conducted throughout the 1990s, privatization could not produce the results necessary to earn the support that the government needed in the short term. On the other hand, it did help to create an unexpected support group through the compulsory acquisition of *Certificados de Privatização* (Certificates of Privatization), the value of which were determined based on the total assets of each financial company.[30] These

at the time. Their participation helped to neutralize claims that the state had retreated completely (Velasco 1999, 199 fn. 15).

[29] Kingstone (2000, 193) suggests that privatization and de-indexation were "key parts of the effort to stimulate competitiveness in the private sector." He argues that privatization sought to encourage investments and competitiveness instead of solving fiscal problems. However, this account ignores that, by legislation, revenue from privatization had to be used to pay public debts and, as discussed further below, many public bonds were accepted as "privatization currencies" or "privatization legal tenders."

[30] The package of Collor's economic reforms in the aftermath of his inauguration created these certificates. Forcing investors into compulsory debt to finance fiscal deficits represented a lasting tradition in Brazil, from which the ORTN, discussed above, was a departure (Simonsen 1970, 184–185).

certificates were securities that could only be used as legal tender in privatization processes, and they would lose one percentage point of its value every month after the first auction (Schneider 1992, 233).[31] Financial institutions had a strong incentive to get rid of these certificates (Velasco 1997, 27), as they were not as profitable as other available instruments. To minimize the possibility of losses as long as privatization processes continued, financial institutions formed yet another support group for privatization. The flexibility in the type and size of the bids undoubtedly also helped to attract more interested parties that would otherwise be indifferent to or even oppose the program.

This was the first time that the Brazilian government had tied several economic policies together.[32] The initiative, however, ultimately represented an obstacle to the political success of these policies. Partly because the motivation behind bundling policies in this way was to control hyperinflation, the lack of success in this case instigated a flood of disassociation strategies. The persistence of hyperinflation demanded that policymakers—generally mid-level but also second-ranking bureaucrats—adapt to the new political situation. This often involved silently continuing the policy while also taking advantage of the isolation created by the government in their effort to avoid the criticisms and scrutiny provoked by the fight against inflation. It is worth noting that if these policies had produced immediate results, they might also have provided the necessary support to continue.

Since privatization was strongly associated with the Collor government, once his impeachment process concluded and he departed,[33] it

[31] The Certificates of Privatization were one among many "privatization currencies" or "privatization legal tenders." Because the legislation stated that privatization revenue was earmarked to pay for public debts, different securities served as legal tender to pay for privatized businesses (Velasco 1997, 27). Every security was transformed into a new one, discounted by the Treasury, to use as legal tender in privatizations or to sell in the secondary market. There were also "rotten currencies," as the press called them: agrarian public debt of which no one was aware (Licínio Velasco Jr. Interview with the author. Rio de Janeiro. February 24, 2014).

[32] Collor's government tied the policies together against inflation with broader reforms such as privatization (Almeida 1999, 432). This represented a significant shift from the previous status of privatization in the public agenda. While this first effort was not successful, the complementarity between privatization and other reforms would later prove fundamental to stabilization, as will be further developed below.

[33] Collor was suspended from office on September 29, 1992, resigning officially on December 29, just before being found guilty by the Senate of "Responsibility Crime,"

was assumed that his successor, Itamar Franco (1992–1994), would stop the process. This course of action was expected for at least two reasons: first, because corruption scandals surrounding Collor cast doubt over his policies, and second, because of Itamar's own views about the role of the state in the economy.[34] Instead, however, he tried to slow down the pace of privatization, by ordering several re-evaluations of the companies to be privatized,[35] though these did not lead to any substantive changes in the price.[36] In general, the privatizations carried out by Itamar's government were of big businesses with symbolic importance, such as CSN. Also, some of the main privatizations during his term were done so against *Petrobrás*'s corporatist interests, as in the case of *Ultrafértil*. Despite successive attempts from opposition parties and unions to stop the process with judiciary action (Almeida 1999, 437–438), and although it was temporarily halted by the president following some corporatist agitation, privatization continued as planned under Itamar (Velasco 2010, 358).

In Congress, the opposition to privatization surfaced with a *Comissão Parlamentar Mista de Inquérito*—CPMI (Mixed Parliamentary Commission for Inquiry) for the whole privatization process (Lourenço, Ramos, and Medina 1994).[37] But although the opposition had seemed at first to hold the upper hand, the final account was favorable to the government. The CPMI had no practical effects on the inner workings of the PND (Velasco 2010, 358–359). The BNDES, which was in charge of the PND

i.e., administrative actions taken by a political agent that are contrary to the Constitution. This interregnum added more uncertainty to policymaking.

[34] The uncertainty of having those reforms aborted is expressed in the literature on both privatization (Manzetti 1999, 168; Velasco 1997, 7) and commercial liberalization (Bonelli and Pinheiro 2008, 100; Pinheiro, Bonelli, and Schneider 2007, 81). It makes reference to the ideas of Itamar Franco on the role of the state in the economy, but the main reason for instability was probably the strongly negative view of Collor's administration and its association with his corruption scandals.

[35] Each privatization process demanded an evaluation from two different consulting firms hired through special procurement. This was intended to prevent accusations of inside trading on the part of the privatized enterprises or the BNDES, the privatization agent. The re-evaluations ordered by Itamar Franco thus showed his reservations about the process.

[36] The biggest change was the composition of the tender used to make payments, now represented in current money and not only securities as with previous processes (Velasco 1997, 34).

[37] Its mandate was "to investigate issues related to and caused by the implementation of the National Program for Privatization – PND" (my translation).

throughout all of its stages, was able to keep the contested policy on track because many actors ended up backing privatization. These actors, while not being a formal coalition, favored privatization because they believed they could continue to win if they had already been winners, or could become winners in yet another privatization if they had not. The selling model that started with the USIMINAS auction allowed many players to get in on the game, uniting in these informal coalitions.

The opposition—that is, left-leaning parties, unions, and corporatists interests affiliated with the sold enterprises—was gradually defeated, and many subsequently became members of the supporting coalition. This defeat was also the result of public organizations participating actively as bidders in privatizations, weakening the case for the state's total retreat (Velasco 1999, 199 fn. 15). Moreover, unions affiliated with the *Força Sindical* (Union Force)[38] supported the PND after Act 8031 granted to public employees a percentage of the sold enterprises (Almeida 1999, 437). The explanation for the success of privatization is thus twofold: it deactivated powerful opponents and actually encouraged some of them to switch allegiances and participate in the process, and it also empowered key constituencies that would benefit from its continuation. In this way, atomization became an instrument for gathering political support.

During the Collor administration, privatization, along with other policies, was explicitly linked to the fight against inflation. While at this point the association between privatization and a solution to inflation did not produce lasting results, it is important to underline that this was the first move in such direction. Connecting privatization and the fight against inflation in this way was not successful because both policies suffered significant drawbacks. Even if inflation did not wane, privatization required a significant streamlining of the sold companies (Pinheiro, Bonelli, and Schneider 2007, 84), and, notably, the political support to implement it took some time to gather. The role of privatization in the fight against inflation would be crucial years later when an institutional complementarity appeared, even if the circumstances by this time were very different from those that defined Collor's tenure.

[38] *Força Sindical*, commonly referred to as *a Força* (the Force), is a post-Soviet-era union with different priorities than those traditionally associated with labor unions (Rodrigues and Cardoso 2009).

4.2 Trade Liberalization

4.2.1 First Phase

The relationship between Brazilian and international economies is complex. The large size of Brazil's market provides maneuvering space during international crises, because the economy can rely on consumption for the duration of each event.[39] Conversely, this condition tends to encourage a less prudent approach in the face of such crises. Such lack of caution is not only a function of market size, however. It also speaks to a nationalistic impulse shared by several groups within Brazilian society. This was certainly apparent during the crises of the 1970s: despite the worsening conditions after both oil shocks (1973 and 1979), military administrations continued to launch infrastructure and capital goods initiatives with external financing.[40] Authorities reacted to the restrictions following the 1981–1983 crisis, meanwhile, with significant devaluations (Kaufman 1988, 22).[41] These devaluations increased both inflation and commercial surpluses, simultaneously revealing a link between the external front and inflation in Brazil.[42] In addition, a current account deficit justified restrictive trade policies that prevented the entry of foreign-produced goods. In a context where inflation was becoming hyperinflation, the absence of foreign competition was yet another factor fueling an already out-of-control process.

Successive defaults on foreign obligations also became a concern. Later developments showed that foreign obligations were not in fact a fundamental factor driving Brazilian inflation, but in 1987 they were crucial.[43]

[39] This assumes that the international crisis does not affect consumption in Brazil. However, this is what happened around the world, including Brazil, as a consequence of the lockdowns during the pandemic of 2020.

[40] Lamounier and Moura (1986) analyze the response to the oil shocks of the 1970s and their consequences.

[41] Between 1981 and 1984, the accumulated devaluation of the Brazilian currency amounted to 1980% (CEPAL 2009, Appendix 5).

[42] An important actor in this realm was the International Monetary Fund—IMF, whose policies did not always address the complexity of Brazil's challenges. For a discussion of one such debate, see Bacha and Dornbusch (1983).

[43] Luiz Carlos Bresser-Pereira. Interview by the author. São Paulo. March 26, 2014. Bresser-Pereira is Emeritus Professor at the Getúlio Vargas Foundation in São Paulo. He was Finance Minister from April 29 to December 18, 1987, and Minister of Federal Administration (1995–1998).

The solution to the problem of foreign obligations provided by then-Minister Bresser-Pereira was their securitization (Bresser-Pereira 1999). With this move, he launched a multi-year process that would eventually finish with a bond exchange. At the time of this exchange, the foreign debt was no longer considered a factor preventing stabilization,[44] even in the midst of the Real Plan. In 1988, imports policy involved several instruments to isolate the Brazilian economy from foreign competition, including redundant tariffs, which had mostly been kept in place since 1957[45]; additional taxes on exchange and for the use of ports; non-tariff barriers, such as importation lists, previous importation authorization, and quotas; and 42 special tax-reduction regimes (Kume, Piani, and Souza 2003, 10–11).

The complexity of these policies explains in part the slow pace of change. Tariffs were unified without substantial changes to the protections already in place, given their redundancy with non-tariff barriers (Kume, Piani, and Souza 2003, 13). This process was negotiated within the *Comisão de Política Aduaneira* (Customs Policy Commission), where government, agriculture, and industry were all represented. Even if this strategy had helped Brazil in the past, however, its formulation might have reflected the Commission members' interests more than the broader society's (Baumann, Rivero, and Zavattiero 1997, 559). Tariffs were just another policy instrument used to regulate Brazilian international trade (Almeida 1996, 229 fn. 13). Nevertheless, tariff unification implied a rationalization of protection inasmuch as it aligned the tariff structure with the relevant differential between internal and external prices (Kume, Piani, and Souza 2003, 11).

[44] Andre Lara Resende. Interview by the author. São Paulo. March 25, 2014. Resende is an Adjunct Senior Research Scholar at Columbia University and founding partner of the Instituto de Estudos em Política Econômica/Casa das Garças. He taught economics at PUC-RJ, was a member of the board of directors of the Brazilian Central Bank, and was President of BNDES.

[45] For details, see Kume, Piani, and Souza (2003, 20–22, Table 1).

4.2.2 Actual Opening

Fernando Collor had some of the traits of a typical populist Latin American leader, even if he did not entirely conform to the model.[46] During his presidential campaign, he founded his own party, which would not survive the next election; he sold himself as an outsider (Martins 1993, 31–32); and he tried to communicate directly with the masses, selling an image of himself as a handsome playboy. One of his phrases, "*Nossos carros são verdadeiras carroças*" (Our cars are really carts), signaled, sympathetically, the backwardness of Brazilian industry under its continued protection from international competition. This protection had been present since the beginning of industrialization. But Collor's government implemented a new commercial policy.[47] The global trend toward a liberalized economy created a viable environment in which to discuss commercial liberalization. South America, particularly what would become the Southern Common Market—Mercosur,[48] was seen in light of Brazilian foreign policy; in other words, it was considered within Brazil's natural zone of influence (Malamud 2011, 6). Furthermore, a controlled liberalization within a defined region was ideal leverage against the kind of liberalization sought by the United States (Cason 2011, 53). Consequently, Mercosur was well situated to start trade liberalization; this path would be reinforced by changes in the tariff structure that created a common external tariff for the bloc. However, since the common external tariff was not implemented until years later, Brazilian authorities decided to reduce barriers autonomously (Kume 1996, 2–3).

Businesses, meanwhile, were divided in debates around commercial liberalization. Non-tradable sectors were indifferent to liberalization and Mercosur. Multinational corporations with substantial operations in Brazil favored the process because they had the scale to profit from both liberalization and integration. However, many of these companies also opposed the process because their investments relied on a protected Brazilian market (Cason 2011, 53–54). Brazilian companies reproduced that pattern. That is, bigger companies could take advantage of their scale to enter into Argentinean markets, whereas many middle-sized companies

[46] For a discussion about Latin American populism, see Weyland (2001), and for its relation with neoliberalism, see Weyland (2003).

[47] Frisch and Franco (1993, 27–32) provide an account of this.

[48] Established by the *Tratado de* [Treaty of] *Asunción* (1991).

that relied on tariff barriers struggled with the process and had little or no political leverage to change it.

The negotiation of commercial liberalization followed corporatist lines. Because business is organized by industry and region, it is difficult to aggregate demands coherently. And, due to the absence of national representative voices, every business interest—whether regional, sectoral, or both—has an incentive to lobby independently, which inevitably hampers the returns of any collective effort (Kingstone 2004, 168–170). In this context, firms responded differently to the challenges of liberalization. In some industries, mergers and acquisitions prevailed; in others, it was preferable to see producers transform into importers of the same good. In any case, businesses did not rely exclusively on lobbying to prevent changes from taking place, and Brazilian producers endured a significant transformation throughout the 1990s (Kingstone 2004, 171).

The Ministry of Economy, Budget, and Planning, which was in charge of commercial liberalization, centralized decision-making for this and other policies (Baumann, Rivero, and Zavattiero 1997, 559).[49] Partially because the Ministry of Foreign Affairs had already been working on commercial negotiations with Argentina, it was among the groups that supported the trade liberalization policies implemented by Collor's government (Bonelli and Pinheiro 2008, 98).[50] Moreover, Mercosur, as a model for Brazilian liberalization, was highly presidential—that is, it depended heavily on the will of individual presidents, which highlights the top-down character of liberalization within the context of the regional integration effort (Cason 2011, 51).

Collor's reforms were conceived as a set, to be implemented more or less simultaneously. The end of hyperinflation gave cohesion to the package, with the core policies of the reform directed toward this goal. These core policies included the freezing of financial assets and prices. Policies of secondary priority but attached to the general reform nonetheless were privatization and commercial liberalization (Carneiro 1991, 157–159). However, the lack of results in reducing inflation and Collor's populist political strategy isolated the president and his government. Even though they had initially been bundled with other economic measures,

[49] Kingstone (2004, 166) mentions that the Collor government excluded business from policy deliberations concerning trade liberalization, among other policies.

[50] Puntigliano (2008) discusses the traditions of Brazilian foreign policy affecting the diplomatic corps.

commercial reform and privatization were relegated to the background of political discussions, because price freezes, wage freezes, and the confiscation of financial assets included in the Collor I plan used up all the attention of political actors at the time (Albuquerque 1993, 151).

Commercial reform consisted of sudden ground-breaking changes, similar to other policies of the Collor administration. These policies involved not only a change in the level of instruments, such as lower tariffs, but also a change in the instruments themselves, as the exchange rate became more important. The explicit goal of these policy changes was productive transformation while maintaining a price differential (Kume, Piani, and Souza 2003, 13–14). Despite the apparent generalized change, some specific criteria were required to implement the program, mainly to prevent the rise of opposition. The first phase involved a more substantial drop in tariffs to capital and intermediate goods than in tariffs on consumer goods. There were two reasons for this choice: first, a smaller drop in tariffs on consumer goods would prevent imported products from flooding the internal market (Kume, Piani, and Souza 2003, 15), and second, it would promote increased productivity among national producers (Longo 1997, 38–39).

This differential between tariffs for intermediate versus consumer goods also reflects coalition-building efforts, i.e., not alienating possible political support. Beyond the economic rationale, which involves the balance of payments, the schedule of tariff reduction was also designed to prevent opposition to the policy from the competitive internal producers (Bonelli and Pinheiro 2008; Kume, Piani, and Souza 2003). Furthermore, the tariff reduction schedule reflected the clout of certain firms.[51] Tariff reductions by industry gave firms, especially large ones, the possibility of bargaining for exemption from the schedules and for different fiscal treatment (Armijo and Faucher 2002, 25). Thus, the accommodation of the tariff schedule responded to both political and economic imperatives, and either can account for the changes that were implemented.

Nevertheless, the interested sectors did not resist liberalization, partially because businesses were also dealing with the recession caused by the Collor Plan. Additionally, the policy lacked credibility, and so few in the business community thought that liberalization would actually happen

[51] The automotive industry enjoyed the maximum effective protection between 1987 and 1998 (Kume, Piani, and Souza 2003, 30ff).

(Bonelli and Pinheiro 2008, 99). In general, the liberalization policy was conducted pragmatically. For example, the schedule of tariff reduction was accelerated when it became clear that Itamar Franco (who maintained nationalist positions in several policy areas) would replace Collor, in an effort to prevent a reversal of the entire process (Bonelli and Pinheiro 2008, 100). Although commercial liberalization had been among the top priorities of Collor's administration it soon descended to low-priority status, as the unfolding of anti-inflationary measures and their disastrous consequences became of prime concern. This secondary status allowed liberalization to continue, both because the government perceived it as less important and because many economic actors had to deal with a recession simultaneously. This "low-politics" character of liberalization was short-lived, however, and the introduction of the new currency in 1994, and its subsequent appreciation, implied that liberalization had now taken center stage because of its role in stabilization.

Bonelli and Pinheiro (2008, 101–102) identify four factors that improved liberalization's chances of success. First, its initial impact was lost amid the effects of the recession caused by the Collor Plan; second, the public supported liberalization because it allowed them to consume goods to which they did not previously have access; third, the tariffs were under the exclusive authority of the Executive branch, preventing the interference of Congress or the Courts; and fourth, the claims of powerful groups were attended to pragmatically, without reducing the average tariff but by increasing its variance. Decision-makers clearly enjoyed a wide margin of arbitration, as they responded in an ad hoc manner to the lobbies against liberalization, but the result was a reduced level of protection nonetheless.

Although the political struggles surrounding commercial liberalization were complicated given the different stakes for various different groups, it is clear that they were of low intensity when compared the struggles to implement other policies, especially those targeting inflation. It is noteworthy that the reforms that showed some success during Sarney's and Collor's respective tenures, especially the latter's, were those outside of the core political debates. Privatization only advanced during Sarney's tenure, to the extent that it did not interfere with his coalition-building efforts. During Collor's tenure, commercial liberalization showed significant progress when it was detached from the main political game of his inflationary policies and the controversies around the impeachment that would end his mandate. The next section will discuss the policies that were specifically designed to fight inflation.

4.3 Anti-Inflationary Plans

4.3.1 First Organized Attempts

In the early 1980s, there was intense discussion, mainly in the Economics Department of the Catholic University of Rio de Janeiro—PUC/RJ, about possible solutions to the general indexation of the economy.[52] Part of the explanation for Brazilian inflation was that indexation had created a cascade effect on prices. Price adjustments tried to recover the losses caused by inflation, but in the process prices increased even more. Cascade effects became even more pronounced in the last phase of the military regime as severe measures were implemented without any effect on inflation. Indeed, beyond the fiscal problems apparent to many observers, inflation had an inertial component that thwarted any changes, allowing it to continue on its own (Bresser-Pereira and Nakano 1984).

Two positions were prominent in the debates at PUC/RJ.[53] The first proposed a shock capable of forcing everyone to coordinate their actions to solve the problem of collective action that underpinned price indexation (Lopes 1984). The second considered other solutions, such as a general indexation of the economy so as to align expectations to a single index (or inflation-free currency), in order to subsequently de-index the economy (Arida 1983; Arida and Lara-Resende 1985; Bresser-Pereira and Nakano 1984, 76ff; Lara-Resende 1984). These solutions addressed the inertia that seemed to characterize Brazilian inflation and that was, presumably, the reason for the ineffectiveness of the stabilization programs implemented at the end of the military regime.

After the indirect election of a civilian government in 1985, a new economic policy was anticipated, despite the compromises offered to authoritarian elites by the President-elect, Tancredo Nêves. However, following Nêves's premature death, Vice-President José Sarney took

[52] Franco (2018, 466ff) provides a detailed account of pre-Real anti-inflationary plans, from both economic and legal points of view.

[53] The larger debate was between those who preferred a gradualist approach to solving inflation while the economy continued to grow (the *gradualistas* or gradualists) and those who argued that inflation should be stopped through a shock treatment. Simonsen (1970) is a classic on this theme.

office, and gradually changed the economic team built by the president-elect.[54] Soon, a new anti-inflationary plan designed to respond to inertial inflation appeared. The Cruzado Plan and its amendments, *Cruzadinho* (Little Cruzado) and Cruzado II, concentrated on indexation and price management throughout 1986.[55] The Plan was to consist of both a fiscal adjustment and a subsidiary price freeze. Once the price freeze was instituted, however, it created the impression that inflation was suddenly a matter of the past. Because prices seemed to be under control, the promised fiscal adjustment never materialized; politicians wanted to capitalize electorally on the plan's early success without further changes. Therefore, the price freeze became its trademark. Inflation returned after less than a year.[56]

The next plan, named the Bresser Plan after the minister who created it, dealt with foreign debt and tried to manage a price freeze in a more orderly way. This plan included a fiscal adjustment, which did not have political support. A difference between the Bresser Plan and its predecessor was that the Bresser Plan did not intend to bring inflation to zero but merely to control it, keeping it at a lower, more manageable level (Bresser-Pereira 1988). There are two possible reasons for this. First, Bresser-Pereira recognized the unfeasibility of controlling inflation without encountering the same problems as the Cruzado Plan; second, policymakers were by now aware of the difficulty of credibly controlling inflation in the long run without a serious fiscal adjustment. Given the

[54] Transitional dynamics led Néves to nominate a cabinet of compromise, with some of its members representing interests linked to the authoritarian government; after his passing, however, Sarney did not feel bounded by these compromises. The changes he made represented a departure from economic teams imbricated with the authoritarian regime and their interpretation of Brazilian inflation.

[55] Its launch date was February 28, 1986, to start on March 1, surprising economic agents. It was thought that an unexpected shock would halt inflation. Further adjustments were made on July 24 and November 22. The latter was exactly one week after the general elections.

[56] Modiano (1989, 357–365) offers details of the Cruzado Plan and its subsequent adjustments from an academic economist point of view, while Sardenberg (1987) provides a journalistic version. Modiano (1987) and Carneiro (1987) provide detailed contemporary analyses.

impossibility of the latter, the plan simply tried to use another index, along with a price freeze (Bresser-Pereira 1993).[57]

It is important to mention the role of the PMDB. The party supported President Sarney, but many members did not entirely trust him—despite the fact that he, too, was a member. Many politicians wanted to maintain the price freeze implemented by the Cruzado Plan so that they could capitalize on its initial success. To PMDB politicians, however, there was no connection between fighting inflation and sacrificing patronage resources. This was also the case during Bresser-Pereira's tenure as Minister of Finance, as he also lacked the political support to make a fiscal adjustment. The lack of collaboration among politicians can also partially be explained by the emergence of a new set of elites who were finally participating in the distribution of resources after the military government had kept them at bay for twenty years. One might infer that these elites were merely stating, at last, their long-repressed demands.

The actions and decisions of the Collor government (1990–1992) would also profoundly affect future plans. The stabilization plans implemented by Collor's administration, popularly known as Collor I and Collor II,[58] consisted of drastic measures involving severe monetary restriction—in other words, asset confiscation. Among the suspected causes of inflation was the large internal public debt, which circulated in the form of bonds corrected by indexation and traded in the secondary market on a daily basis. In the first days of Collor's government, these assets were no longer tradable and had to remain in the Central Bank's custody for eighteen months. Although the assets remained out of reach, inflation did not decrease, however. This was in part because of discretionary exceptions to the confiscation (Carneiro 1991, 161), but mainly

[57] There were two more stabilization plans during Sarney's government. First, there was *Feijão-com-Arroz* (Beans-with-rice)—a reference to the simplicity of the recipe—which consisted of a tighter monetary policy, expenses reduction, and better indexation. Second, there was the *Verão* (Summer) Plan, which consisted of a new monetary reform and a combination of measures, like those of *Feijão-com-Arroz*, as well as more heterodox ones that aimed to eliminate existing indexes that were creating inertial inflation. However, while this plan lasted throughout 1989, it was quietly abandoned and the government merely administered hyperinflation until the new government took office in March 15, 1990 (Modiano 1989, 375–381). These stabilization plans are not presented in detail because they did not have significant legacies in terms of policy-learning and were generally perceived as simply the administration of hyperinflation.

[58] See note 8 for the succession of anti-inflationary plans.

because public debt as such was not *the* cause of inflation. The Collor administration had implemented the confiscation specifically to control inflation.[59] Secondary measures in this plan were commercial liberalization and privatization. At first, these policies were considered to be as important as asset confiscation in controlling inflation. However, after the failure of anti-inflationary measures, the association between these policies and inflation waned, at least until a new government was elected. They continued to be implemented despite the political upheaval caused by Collor's impeachment; notably, their dissociation from core anti-inflationary policies allowed them to advance further.

Given the central importance of inflation in the Brazilian economy, these policies constituted the main political debate. For both political and economic (theoretical) reasons, the fight against inflation compelled political actors to mobilize substantial resources to secure their positions. The political salience of inflation was amplified by the uncertainty surrounding the possible upcoming stabilization plan and the potential for big losses, which often implied betting against its success. While many plans proposed a thorough reform of the state, advances on this front depended on the extent to which the reform could be isolated from the core political game. This isolation can be seen, for example, in the move toward privatization under Sarney's government, and in the efforts at liberalization under Collor's government. These secondary political struggles succeeded in the mid-term because they represented incremental changes.

Substantive results appeared only after years of such incremental changes. The returns produced by privatization and commercial liberalization could not be accumulated because they could still be countered and their effects could be neutralized; in other words, inflation still created opportunities for those who could take advantage of it. Throughout successive stabilization plans, teams of economic authorities concentrated solely on inflation, thus relegating other significant policies to the background. While many teams were aware of the necessity of implementing the non-core policies in order for stabilization to succeed, this ultimately

[59] It represented a major political cost for the government because it sowed resentment among some sectors of society and empowered the opposition that would eventually lead Collor's impeachment process.

proved impossible. They were impeded by coalition-building compromises, or simply because it was not clear in the eyes of politicians that these changes were actually necessary.

Many stabilization plans were based partially on the idea that people should be surprised to break the pattern of inflationary spirals created by indexation. However, people can be fooled once, maybe twice, but not indefinitely. Surprise worked with the price freeze of the Cruzado Plan in 1986, but it was less effective in subsequent freezes. What is more, as both the authorities and the citizenry learned new lessons about what to expect with each new stabilization plan, the potential for success of these plans grew increasingly complicated. People began to anticipate the changes, and every time a new plan was on the horizon, they prepared for the next freeze, dismantling, as they did so, the logic behind the plan. And yet, nevertheless, those who were not able to adapt to the freezes accumulated loses.

4.3.2 The Time of the Real

The measures that would later be part of the Real Plan were conceived after these failures. Every change that would directly affect the population was designed in order to manage expectations and prevent defensive strategies or violent disruptions to the economy. But it was not obvious how such disruptions could be avoided, given the political uncertainty at the time, with a recent impeachment and no signs of controlling inflation. Between September 1992 and April 1993, there were three Ministers of Finance. The persistence of inflation exacerbated uncertainty (Fig. 4.1). In May 1993, President Itamar Franco nominated the Minister of Foreign Affairs, Fernando Henrique Cardoso, as Minister of Finance.[60]

The political uncertainty in which this plan took shape and was implemented cannot be underestimated.[61] Cardoso had to fight on several fronts. Some were preliminary. First, political actors needed to transform the way they used the budget. Second, the financial relationship between the federal government and the states had to change, because

[60] His nomination signaled the support of significant parts of the Brazilian political system, both partisan and non-partisan.

[61] It brings to mind a description of critical junctures: "a situation in which the structural (that is, economic, cultural, ideological, organizational) influences on political action are significantly relaxed for a relatively short period" (Capoccia and Kelemen 2007, 343).

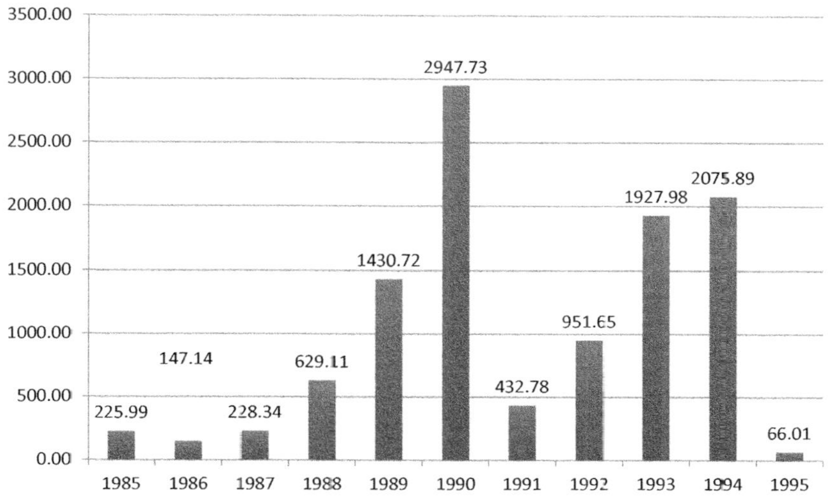

Fig. 4.1 Inflation. Consumer prices. 1985–1995. Percentage (*Source* Own elaboration with data from IBRD [2016])

the states did not pay what they owed to the federal government. Moreover, the government's budget did not reflect their real expenses at this time. It was merely a collection of the initiatives of various politicians who wanted to show their political clout over the government without acknowledging their real value. By delaying these expenses, the federal government allowed their inflation-corrected value to corrode, decreasing its relative importance. Economic authorities wanted to change this.[62]

Expenses should decrease by 20% in exchange for the possibility of effectively expending without inflationary corrosion. Since stabilization could be achieved in this case without political consequences (as in, without negatively affecting electoral success), politicians authorized the general cut.[63] The political significance of this approval cannot be underestimated. It required convincing politicians that even if expenses were

[62] In Congress, there was also a *Comissão Parlamentar de Inquérito*—CPI (Parliamentary Commission for Inquiry) investigating corruption surrounding the congressional budget definition, known as the scandal of the Budget Dwarfs because of the short stature of the presumably benefiting congressmen.

[63] Edmar Bacha. Interview by the author. Rio de Janeiro. February 21, 2014.

cut in nominal terms, the remaining resources would be effectively spent. The cut expenses were redirected to a fund called *Fundo Social de Emergência*—FSE (Social Emergency Fund). But there were also drawbacks to this move. Economic authorities' initial intentions were also to include the states' earmarked constitutional fund, a plan that was not approved by Congress and had to change. The governors mobilized their political resources in Congress to prevent a cut in the states' earmarked expenses[64]; therefore, the cuts were approved without taking these into account (Cardoso 2006, 153). The other option would have been a complete rejection of the measure, which would have weakened the economic feasibility of the new plan, not to mention the political position of Cardoso and his team. Conversely, an unrestricted approval would have represented an even bigger control of federal expenses given the size of the constitutional fund relative to the federal government's revenue.

On their end, the states were struggling to solve a fiscal crisis despite their constitutional prerogatives. Brazilian federalist politics at the time were considered a zero-sum game in which the states tried to keep the upper hand over the federal government (Jayme 1995). The preliminary phases of stabilization were no exception, partially because the transition involved a series of concessions from the federal government to the elected governors. They acted as though they were not a part of the public sector or as though stabilization would not affect their fiscal stance (Afonso 1996, 34)—something that proved true a few years later.

As the preliminary reforms were carried out, nominations in key posts within the economic bureaucracy brought together the people who had implemented the Cruzado Plan. This had important implications throughout the Brazilian political system. The main political consequence of a price freeze is the election of the party in power, not to mention the increased popularity of the authority who declares it. That was certainly the case with the Cruzado Plan. When politicians perceived that the same team was once again assembled, they anticipated that a new price freeze was coming. However, the team had learned their lesson. Once you implement a price freeze there is nothing else to offer.[65] Your hands are

[64] Abrucio (1994) discusses the importance of governors within the Brazilian political system.

[65] The price freeze during the Cruzado Plan created the false expectation that no further actions were required to control inflation, e.g., fiscal adjustment, liberalization, etc. Their absence was crucial to its failure.

tied.[66] An understanding of the inertial component of inflation remained at the core of this new attempt to control it, but the problem was approached using different principles this time. It was essential to take advantage of the Brazilian habit of indexing contracts, offering them a general index that they could trust while the "old" currency corroded with inflation. This was a different approach from Cruzado's experience. In fact, there was a consensus about the need to avoid a price freeze and instead taking advantage of the indexation of contracts. Also, this time around every change was announced prior to implementation, so as to gain the public trust (Bacha 2012, 139–141) that had been lost after numerous economic plans.

It was at this time that the *Unidade Real de Valor*—URV (Real Value Unit) was born.[67] The URV allowed for the indexation of contracts on a voluntary basis, offering simultaneously a rule for conversion to the corroded currency and an exchange rate. The rules surrounding the URV were complex because they encompassed the whole monetary regime and the ways in which people used the currency. Currency has a number of functions, within modern societies. It preserves value, it is an accounting unit, and it is an instrument of payment. Under hyperinflation, Brazilian currencies had lost the first two functions to financial instruments and different indexes respectively. The URV was meant to recover the lost functions of the currency—though the last function, currency as a mode of payment, remained the province of the *cruzeiro real*, the circulating currency at the time. In other words, contracts were indexed in URV, but retail prices had to be expressed in *cruzeiros reais*.

Besides these monetary complexities, there were also political ones. The plan needed to find support in Congress, because the *Medida Provisória* (Preliminary Measure)[68] that had created the URV would eventually have to be transformed into law, and to do this the consent, or at least the acquiescence, of the PSDB—of which the members of the economic team were a part—was required.[69] President Itamar

[66] Edmar Bacha. Interview by the author. Rio de Janeiro. February 21, 2014.

[67] This paragraph relies on Franco (1995).

[68] Special presidential decree. It remains valid for three months and Congress has to approve it to become an Act, otherwise it has to be reinstituted to remain valid.

[69] On the PSDB, see Roma (2002).

Franco wanted a price freeze because it would increase his popularity; however, the respect he showed throughout the process toward Fernando Henrique Cardoso during his tenure as Minister of Finance was paramount to the success of the whole enterprise.[70] Itamar supported Cardoso and his team even when their proposals seemed counterintuitive. And the situation was similar with the PSDB politicians. Given the uncertainty and the complexity of the stabilization program, the tentative timing for its completion was November 1994—in other words, after the elections. What the economic team asked of politicians was that they risk electoral defeat if something were to go wrong. Politicians granted their support according to the way in which tasks were divided within the party: politicians were in charge of political guidance, technocrats were in charge of technocratic guidance (Bacha 2012, 141; Cardoso 2006, 184). The trust between politicians and technocrats had been built over the course of many political campaigns.[71]

The complexity of this plan, legal and otherwise, might obscure the political scenario. But Cardoso's potential presidential campaign sheds some light on the situation. Given the lasting challenge of Brazilian inflation, the electoral potential of someone who could control it was overwhelming. It seemed as though Cardoso could well be that person. But uncertainty remained high, and in the preliminary stages of the plan it was difficult to assess how viable his bid for the presidency would actually be. Every time a new measure was announced during the Real Plan Cardoso was exposed to the media, with very high political stakes. If the measures were successful, his chances at the presidency would increase; if they failed, evidently, his campaign would become decreasingly viable.

This media exposure was crucial, however, as communication with the public was a priority in this plan. Previous stabilization plans had relied heavily on the element of surprise, which caused profound economic disturbances. Therefore, the strategy was to announce with due anticipation each and every change affecting actors' expectations. This feature granted the transparency that had been lacking in preceding plans. However, it also had the political consequence of increasing the electoral

[70] In my interviews with them, both Edmar Bacha and André Lara Resende refer to the paramount importance of Cardoso for the success of the plan. His prestige garnered the respect and support from the president and the political system, as well as intellectual respect from the members of his team.

[71] Edmar Bacha. Interview by the author. Rio de Janeiro. February 21, 2014.

chances of those responsible for such announcements. In other words, on the economic side, transparency allowed for adaptation to a new environment while preserving existing commitments. On the political side, it fostered confidence in the authorities and increased recognition of the person responsible for such openness—and as a result, increased that person's chances of winning the presidential election. After the enactment of the Real Plan at the end of February 1994, two important developments occurred. First, the population embraced the URV and many contracts were converted to this index; and second, following his resignation as Minister of Finance in April, Cardoso was going to become the presidential candidate.[72] A change in the schedule moved the monetary reform—when the URV would become the Real—from October to July 1, 1994. Transparency was maintained, and an official announcement was made before this change took place (Franco 2018, 574). Such transparency and anticipation made the Real Plan fundamentally different from previous stabilization plans.

Once the monetary reform was completed, economic authorities worried about sustaining the stabilization without losing the ground already gained. The external environment was unfriendly. During the second half of the 1990s, several international financial crises took place (Mexico 1994, South-East Asia 1997, and Russia 1998), leaving the Brazilian economy in distress. This hostile environment pressured authorities to make adjustments in economic policy. Some of these will be discussed below. Stabilization as such—which is to say, slow price changes or none at all—can be achieved through specific measures as the Cruzado Plan showed during the 1980s. The difficult part is to maintain the pace of price change. In Brazil, this involved important changes, including a deepening of both privatization and liberalization.

4.4 Consolidating Reforms

One of the lessons of the Cruzado Plan was that stabilization, understood as a reduced pace of price change, could be achieved with the right measures at the right time. More difficult, however, was maintaining this reduced pace in the long run. The fact that inflation can be temporarily improved but that stabilization measures are not sustainable reveals its

[72]The Complementary Act No. 64 establishes that a person cannot be a presidential candidate if he or she has been a minister in the six months preceding the election date.

politico-economic complexity. Institutional changes in other arenas were absent while the Cruzado Plan was implemented, making a sustained stabilization very difficult to achieve. This was the case for at least two reasons. First, there were no significant changes in the fiscal or international trade realms, which meant that long-standing cost-externalizing strategies were held up; second, political actors did not perceive any political costs for their inaction. Institutional complementarity appears when one institution needs the presence of other institutions in order to work effectively. In the context of the Real Plan, this happened when one institutional reform supports other institutions in a way that without working together, both institutions would be void. This consolidation required political compromises within a coalition gathered around a common interpretation of a looming crisis. Just such a situation was created by the possible return of inflation, which would have had significant political consequences. The actors involved feared that a return of inflation would cause them to lose political power, and so they took the necessary actions to prevent such an outcome.

At the end of Itamar's government, all the non-constitutionally protected businesses were privatized, demonstrating the overall success of privatization (Pinheiro, Bonelli, and Schneider 2007, 84). During Cardoso's administration, there was also a close association between privatization and inflation control. Cardoso's administration, however, had a different character: less discourse-driven and more pragmatic. They responded to the economic challenges in at least two venues: banks owned by state governments, and the telecommunications sector, a constitutionally protected monopoly. The first was a part of redefinition of federal relationships (Amann and Baer 2000, 1816); the second was related to a general trend toward the privatization of public utilities and petrochemicals (Amann and Baer 2000, 1812), with debt relief in mind. To relax budgetary restrictions, state treasuries allowed their banks to roll over bond-denominated debts. An indicator of the Real Plan's success in de-indexing the economy was the banking crisis that occurred after its implementation. Many state-owned banks were privatized in exchange for a new repayment schedule for the states' debts to the federal government; once indexation, which had become a life support system for these banks, ceased to exist, their controllers were forced to face their real deficits (Beck, Crivelli, and Summerhill 2005). This was done through the *Programa de Incentivo à Redução do Setor Público Estadual na Atividade Bancária*—PROES (Incentive Program to Reduce State Banking Activities).[73]

With this program, state governments participated actively, albeit constrained by circumstances, in the stabilization effort for the first time. As mentioned above, when the FSE was created, they had opposed a partial cut to their constitutional transfers. With this move, they allowed the non-cooperative federalist arrangement that had begun in 1974 to persist. One way that state treasuries played this game was by using their banks to finance the government's activities (Jayme 1995), thus capturing part of the inflationary tax through indexation. Following stabilization, however, this strategy was not available anymore. They had to sell their banks in order to refinance their bond-denominated debts with the federal government—with subsidized rates, nonetheless (Beck, Crivelli, and Summerhill 2005, 9–11).

In 1994, when the Real was introduced, the international arena became deeply attached to the consolidation of stabilization. In the first phase of the program, a further reduction in tariffs helped to control the price increases that had been caused by higher demand in the aftermath of stabilization. In time, however, tariff reduction was no longer the only instrument used to liberalize or to control prices; the exchange rate was more effective. After the monetary reform, an appreciated exchange rate helped to stabilize prices, because it promoted competition through cheaper imports.[74] Thus, liberalization was implemented using a combination of instruments: tariffs and exchange rate. Economic authorities kept the latter appreciated precisely because it was identified as central to the stabilization effort[75]—although another interpretation of this early appreciation (Fig. 4.2) is that markets trusted the monetary reform (Franco 1999). Economic authorities[76] debated the exchange

[73] The *Programa de Estímulo à Reestruturação e ao Fortalecimento do Sistema Financeiro Nacional*—PROER (Stimulus Program to Restructuring and Strengthening of the National Financial System) was created to handle the bankruptcy of private banks.

[74] This competition changed the productive structure of the country significantly. It involved many industries, though not all (Barros and Goldenstein 2000, 12).

[75] Edmar Bacha. Interview by the author. Rio de Janeiro. February 21, 2014.

[76] Economic authorities changed over the years, mainly because people asked for voluntary resignation. Key posts remained the same, however. People who had already participated, for instance, as Director of the Central Bank could become President of the

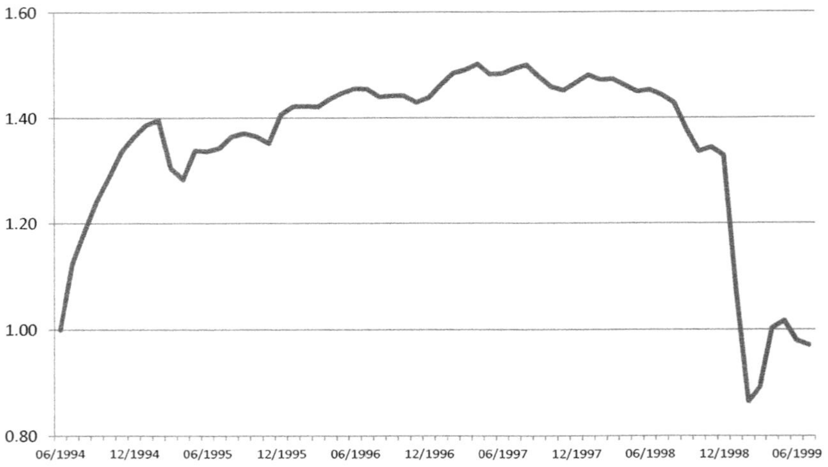

Fig. 4.2 Exchange Rate Index (IPCA). (For details of the *Índice de Preços ao Consumidor Amplo*—IPCA (Broad Consumer Price Index), see IBGE (2015, 4–6).) 1994–1999 (*Source* Elaborated by the author with data from Brasil [2020])

policy extensively during the first Cardoso government (1995–1998), hampering the implementation of changes. Under the difficult conditions faced by the country (Cardoso 2006, 2014), this led to even more contentious discussions.

Debates about the exchange rate focused on when to alter its level, what the best instrument would be to pursue such a policy, and what measures would most effectively prevent market actors from betting against this change.[77] The first of these debates took place in early 1995, amid uncertainty surrounding the Mexican crisis, which would arise again later, too. Three groups of technocrats developed proposals about how to implement these changes. First, José Serra, Minister of Planning, defended a sudden shift to a lower rate (i.e., maxi-devaluation); second,

same institution. Broadly speaking the economic authorities consisted of the Ministry of Finance, Ministry of Planning, the President and some Directors of the Central Bank, the President of the BNDES, and other members of the government acting as counselors. They were all commanded by the President when a political decision was unavoidable.

[77] Cardoso (2006, 377–398, 406–413) describes these debates at various moments of his first government (1995–1998).

Pérsio Arida, President of the Central Bank and some of its directors, defended a wide exchange band where the central bank would intervene in the market only to tame the riskier investors (i.e., market dominated intervention); and third, Pedro Malan, Minister of Finance, and Gustavo Franco, director of the international area of the Central Bank, defended a narrow exchange band with heavier intervention by the central bank, which would induce a controlled devaluation (Cardoso 2006, 339–345).

The successive crises challenging Brazilian financial stability were numerous in the second half of 1990s. They were present both internally and externally. If external crises represented the biggest threat to stabilization, prompting questions about whether to change the exchange policy, support in the domestic arena was also critical. Many thought that a return to hyperinflation was a real possibility, leading some to bet against the program, particularly in the case of the exchange rate (Cardoso 2016, 369ff). Even if a return to a 1980s-like scenario, with its numerous failed stabilization plans, was not on the horizon—which speaks to the success of the Real Plan in several arenas—the threat of the plan's failure was ever-present in light of the challenges coming from the external front. Stabilization was considered a work in progress and also susceptible to failure, and in this way, to be sure, the situation in the 1990s was reminiscent of the critical moments lived throughout the 1980s.

Every step in the right direction was key to cementing the success of stabilization. Substantial changes were required to launch the privatization of the telecommunications industry, since it was under a constitutional monopoly. However, unlike the CSN, *Embratel*, the main public provider, did not provoke the same level of debate around its possible privatization. The privatization of the *Telebrás* system[78] was delayed after the introduction of the Real, because of the necessary legal reforms.[79] There were incentives for both national and foreign companies to participate in the privatization bids as associates (Velasco 2005, 60). As a result, the tasks could be divided: Brazilian companies (banks, pension funds,

[78] *Telebrás* was the holding, operating one company per state.

[79] These included the removal of its strategic character (8th Constitutional Amendment) in August 1995, its correspondent legal development (Act 9295), which created a regulatory agency in July 1996, and finally (Act 9472), in July 1997, market regulations and general guidelines for the privatization of public enterprises acting in the telecommunications sector (Velasco 2005, 56–59).

communication and industrial companies) pooled their respective capital and expertise, while a foreign operator brought its business know-how and hard currency to bear (Velasco 2005, 66).

The revenue from privatization helped to maintain a stable exchange rate. The literature agrees on the moment when privatization revenue became important to stabilization, but researchers interpret the reasons for this in different ways. Some suggest that the importance of the absolute values emphasizes the macroeconomic relevance of privatization revenue after 1996 (Modiano 2000, 325); others emphasize its importance in the response to the Asian crisis of 1997, as it allowed the entry of substantive resources protecting the economy from instability (Pinheiro and Giambiagi 2000, 33); and others still argue that the influx of foreign direct investment helped to finance the current account deficit (Pinheiro 1999, 166), which stabilized the exchange rate.

These accounts present two different channels through which privatization revenues were important to stabilization. The first, referring to the size of the transfers to public coffers, is linked to a fiscal stance[80]—that is, it helped to control fiscal deficits. The other arguments highlight the importance of foreign currency in keeping the exchange rate as an anchor of stabilization. Depending on how authorities conceive of such interventions, the two accounts are not contradictory. Moreover, they both underline that privatization was paramount to stabilization. Revenue derived from privatization helped with the fiscal deficit,[81] even if it was earned only once (Pastore 1997, 32–33). And once the Real was in place, the exchange rate became essential to keeping prices down.[82] Economic authorities were also aware of the importance of external transfers from privatizations, as in the case of telecommunications, to control the exchange rate (Pinheiro 1999; Pinheiro and Giambiagi 2000).

Given the very close association between the government and stabilization, the success of both the politicians and their policies was intertwined. While external uncertainties threatened stabilization, in the domestic

[80] From 1996 to 1998 the revenues from privatization amounted to more than 35 billion USD, with 22.6 billion alone in 1996 (Manzetti 1999, 171–172).

[81] The total revenue of the privatization of the *Telebrás* system were BRL 22.05 billion at the end of July 1998. Foreign resources were equivalent to BRL 15.8 billion (USD 13.6 billion) or 60% of the total (Dalmazo 2000, 211). Manzetti (1999, 217) puts the amount as 75% of USD 19 billion, which is 14.25 billion.

[82] Edmar Bacha. Interview by the author. Rio de Janeiro. February 21, 2014.

arena, the relevant issue for many actors was the survival of the government and its allies. The possibility of the President's re-election provided another key incentive for these actors to support both the government and the necessary measures to fight inflation. Had high inflation returned, the government's supporters would have had to concede defeat to the opposition. Furthermore, had the opposition defeated the government on key projects, such as the privatization of important companies or re-election reform, the government's political force would have been questioned, and with it, the continuation of the stabilization program. These links were evident throughout 1997 when key reforms were discussed in Congress as the Asian financial crisis unraveled. Indeed, congressmen who supported both the government (Brasil 1997a, 15832, 1997b, 02969, 02972) and the opposition (Brasil 1997b, 02961, 02966) were fully aware of the connection between the successes of the President's re-election and the privatization reforms, and that of stabilization itself.

There were therefore several interlocking reforms supported by a broad coalition who saw that these reforms' survival depended on their mutual success. They were not simultaneous, but all of them occurred within a relatively short time. Re-election and privatization reforms took place in the first half of 1997, while the financial crises threatening the Real peaked in the second half of that year. Thus, these institutional reforms became complementary, because their mutual consolidation substantially reduced the possibility of passing the costs of private actions onto society—for instance, in the case of the failed speculation on the currency on the wake of the Asian crisis (Cardoso 2016, 369ff). Re-election and privatization reforms gave credibility to the government and allowed for an influx of foreign currency later on. We can argue that at this point, economic governance was consolidated; however, the real test of such consolidation would not come until later.

The existence of a broad coalition for reform does not mean that there were not losers. A significant point of tension involving other actors within the political economy concerned fiscal balance. This issue was contentious on the external front because the interest rate was connected both with the possibility of attracting capital—thus preventing speculation with the currency—and with the debts of subnational governments and their own fiscal balance. Furthermore, a more restrictive fiscal policy would allow more latitude to economic authorities because it would eliminate inflationary expenses and allow them to prevent an inflationary return. Therefore, an instrument that was attached to the core stabilization effort had implications throughout the economy, and generated controversies with other political actors.

Some industries, such as the auto industry, were protected because of their political clout. In general, however, the concerns affecting business leaders were linked to Brazilian systemic costs (mainly labor costs) combined with commercial liberalization (Kingstone 1999, 208). In response, the government increased tariffs in sectors where dumping was rampant and offered special credit lines to firms affected by commercial liberalization. Pragmatism on both sides guaranteed a sound relationship between business and government. However, a cleavage within the business community prevented it from taking more consistent action to explore the possibilities of liberalization. On the one side, multinational corporations and the financial industry benefited from the possibilities of an open economy. On the other, producers focused on the internal market, or aligned to old corporatist lines and ISI standards, were hit hard. This division allowed the government to respond to the most pressing issues without derailing the adjustment process (Kingstone 1999, 224–227).

By the end of 1997, Brazil's overvalued currency allowed for the entry of foreign products, while at the same time, an increase in tariffs protected industries from those products—even after a renewed use of non-tariff barriers (Kume, Piani, and Souza 2003, 18)—and helped to mitigate the accumulation of current account deficits (Kume, Piani, and Souza 2003, 32). The contrast between the ease with which particularistic instruments such as tariffs and non-tariff barriers to trade can be changed and the intense debates around modifications to the exchange rate is quite remarkable. One possible explanation for this is that certain groups were able to press the authorities for protection while disregarding the rationale of the policy in question, or the consequences of its adoption (Barros and Goldenstein 2000, 16). In essence, the exchange rate was exposed to too many different actors, including the international financial system. Speculation with the currency would have been disastrous for stabilization. Although the exchange rate represents the price of international trade, it did not have a constituency defending a precise change. Instead, multiple constituencies defended contradictory modifications adapted to their own necessities.

After years of debate, in January 1999, the exchange policy was finally altered. The President nominated a new President of the Central Bank,

Francisco Lopes, who suggested establishing an endogenous diagonal exchange band, which seemed to provide both space for the market and control for authorities without increasing interest rates (Cardoso 2006, 406ff). The mechanism did not work as intended, however, and this triggered yet another change in the presidency of the Central Bank. The new president, Armínio Fraga, proposed inflation targeting, primary surplus, and floating change as key policy instruments that could prevent the return of inflation. Three factors explain the successful avoidance of a deeper exchange crisis at this point: the special treatment of international actors, the structure of socioeconomic interests, and the absence of veto players (Faucher and Armijo 2004). Vested interests were not able to discretionally externalize their costs. Inflation did not return to its former levels.

4.5 Conclusions

The consolidation of economic governance in Brazil was a long process involving many institutional changes. These institutional changes, including trade liberalization, privatization, and monetary and fiscal reforms, each built on the effectiveness of the others, leading to a new pattern of economic governance. This outcome took years to materialize and needed a strong coalition that would grant support to the whole set of reforms. At the beginning of the reform process, this was hardly the case. Each institutional reform advanced mostly independent from the others and in response to the collapse of the previous model, which resulted in hyperinflation. In such a model the state had several responsibilities, which allowed some groups to pass on the costs of their actions to the rest of society. While the reforms gradually limited the ability of these groups to continue with such a strategy, they still allowed some space for it to persist. Truly shutting down this cost-shifting tactic required more complex political action than a collection of groups advancing their reforms independently.

Later on, new crises appeared on the horizon, reminding politico-economic actors that hyperinflation could return. They had to mobilize all the political resources at their disposal to confront such a possibility, and so they coalesced to advance various reforms that buttressed one another: they became complementary. This complementarity prevented some actors from continuing their cost-shifting strategies. The reforms strengthened the government that had brought inflation down to reasonable levels, because there was a close association between the stability of the government and the feasibility of defeating hyperinflation. Therefore, when political actors supported a given reform, they were really defending the president, and, because this was the surest way to defeat hyperinflation, it was also the best way of defending their interests. Politicians and organized interests were vocal when providing this support, and the population at large also was aware of the connection between politics and the fight against inflation, which explains the swift re-election of Cardoso in 1998. Although the language of economic governance is that of economics, its true character is only apparent through political means.

The successful consolidation of economic governance requires the continuous support of involved actors. The Brazilian case shows that even after major institutional reforms were carried out, laying the foundations for stabilization to succeed, it was still necessary for actors to continue in the struggle, because otherwise they would be defeated. In their initial stages, institutional reforms are susceptible to political pressures that try to prevent them from consolidating in a way that would later be even harder to overcome. The struggles in and around the Brazilian economy are a reminder of just how fragile institutional arrangements can be in their early phases. Even if there is a powerful incentive to launch institutional transformations, these must be supported by larger political processes in which conflicts must be overcome, in order finally to deliver the returns society expects.

The completion of reforms, which made them complementary, signals the consolidation of economic governance. Economic governance was consolidated when actors could no longer pass on the costs of their actions to others, though this was only achieved after several attempts. There were several exchange crises in the late 1990s and early 2000s, even after the consolidation of reforms, that continued to threaten the new institutional arrangements. However, since they were already consolidated, they were able to withstand these threats and prevent the return of hyperinflation. Although we can assert that economic governance consolidated at a particular moment—that is, throughout 1997—it is clear that the actors who were involved in the process did not necessarily perceive it that way. Despite the challenges that these crises represented, by the late 1990s, various actors were already abiding by the policies of institutional reforms and paying the price of their actions. Society at large recognized that something had indeed changed because the government behind those changes was re-elected in 1998. In fact, four years later, the opposition candidate, Luíz Inácio Lula da Silva, had to publicly declare that he would not backtrack the set of institutional reforms discussed here (Silva 2002) to make his bid for the presidency viable (Morais and Saad-Filho 2005, 9–10). Economic governance is, above all, a political outcome.

References

Abrucio, Fernando Luiz. 1994. "Os Barões da Federação." *Lua Nova* 12 (33): 165–190. https://doi.org/10.1590/s0102-64451994000200012.

Afonso, José Roberto Rodrigues. 1996. "Descentralizar e Depois Estabilizar: A Complexa Experiência Brasileira." *Revista do BNDES* 3 (5): 31–62.

Albuquerque, José Augusto Guilhon. 1993. "Unfinished Reforms." In *Brazil and the Challenge of Economic Reform*, edited by Werner Baer and Joseph S. Tulchin, 149–154. Washington: The Woodrow Wilson Center Press.

Almeida, Maria Hermínia Tavares de. 1996. "Pragmatismo por Necessidade: os Rumos da Reforma Econômica no Brasil." *DADOS Revista de Ciências Sociais* 39 (2): 213–234.

Almeida, Maria Hermínia Tavares de. 1999. "Negociando a Reforma: A Privatização de Empresas Públicas no Brasil." *DADOS Revista de Ciências Sociais* 42 (3): 421–451. https://doi.org/10.1590/s0011-52581999000300002.

Amann, Edmund, and Werner Baer. 2000. "The Illusion of Stability: The Brazilian Economy Under Cardoso." *World Development* 28 (10): 1805–1819. https://doi.org/10.1016/s0305-750x(00)00058-9.

Arida, Persio. 1983. "Neutralizar a Inflação, uma Idéia Promissora." In *Economia em Perspectiva*. São Paulo: Conselho Regional de Economia-SP.

Arida, Persio, and André Lara-Resende. 1985. "Inertial Inflation and Monetary Reform: Brazil." In *Inflation and Indexation. Argentina, Brazil, and Israel*, edited by John Williamson, 27–55. Washington: Institute for International Economics.

Armijo, Leslie Elliott, and Philippe Faucher. 2002. "'We Have a Consensus': Explaining Political Support for Market Reforms in Latin America." *Latin American Politics and Society* 44 (2): 1–40. https://doi.org/10.2307/3177093.

Bacha, Edmar. 1994. "O Fisco e a Inflação: Uma Interpretação do Caso Brasileiro." *Revista de Economia Política* 14 (1(53)): 5–17.

Bacha, Edmar. 2012. "O Plano Real: Uma avaliação." In *Belíndia 2.0. Fábulas e Ensaios Sobre o País dos Contrastes*, edited by Edmar Bacha, 135–175. Rio de Janeiro: Civilização Brasileira. Original edition, 2003.

Bacha, Edmar, and Rudiger Dornbusch. 1983. "The IMF and the Prospects for Adjustment in Brazil." In *Prospects for Adjustment in Argentina, Brazil, and Mexico: Responding to the Debt Crisis*, edited by John Williamson, 31–50. Washington: Institute for International Economics.

Barros, José Roberto Mendoça de, and Lídia Goldenstein. 2000. "O Real e a aliança inflacionária." In *O Brasil e os Desafios da Globalização*, edited by Pedro da Motta Veiga, 11–19. Rio de Janeiro: Relume-Dumará.

Baumann, Renato, Josefina Rivero, and Yohana Zavattiero. 1997. "As Tarifas de Importação no Plano Real." *Pesquisa e Planejamento Econômico* 27 (3): 541–586.

Beck, Thorsten, Juan Miguel Crivelli, and William Summerhill. 2005. State Bank Transformation in Brazil—Choices and Consequences. In *Policy Research Working Papers*, edited by World-Bank. Washington.

Bernardino, Ana Paula da Silva. 2005. "Fontes de Recursos e Atuação do BNDES sob uma Perspectiva Histórica." *Revista do BNDES* 12 (23): 53–72.

Bonelli, Regis, and Armando Castelar Pinheiro. 2008. "Abertura e Crescimento Econômico no Brasil." In *Brasil Globalizado. O Brasil em um Mundo Surpreendente*, edited by Octavio de Barros and Fabio Giambiagi, 89–124. Rio de Janeiro: Elsevier.

Brasil, Departamento Econômico. Banco Central do. 2020. "Índice da taxa de câmbio efetiva real (IPCA)" [Spreadsheet]. Banco Central do Brasil, Last Modified August, 22 2018, accessed July 16, 2020. https://www3.bcb.gov.br/sgspub/localizarseries/localizarSeries.do?method=prepararTelaLocalizarSeries.

Brasil, República Federativa do. 1997a. "Ata da 91ª Sessão, da Câmara dos Deputados, Da 3ª Sessão Legislativa, Da 50ª Legislatura, em 11 de Junho de 1997." *Diário da Câmara dos Deputados*, June 12, 1997, 15832–15836.

Brasil, República Federativa do. 1997b. "Discussão, em primeiro turno, da Proposta de Emenda à Constituição nº 1-B, de 1995, que dá nova redação ao § 5º do art.14 da Constituição Federal." *Diário da Câmara dos Deputados*, January 29, 1997, 2953–3002.

Bresser-Pereira, Luiz Carlos, and Yoshiaki Nakano. 1987. *The Theory of Inertial Inflation: The Foundation of Economic Reform in Brazil and Argentina*. Boulder: Lynne Rienner Publishers. Original edition, 1984.

Bresser-Pereira, Luiz Carlos. 1988. "Os Dois Congelamentos de Preços no Brasil." *Revista de Economia Política* 8 (4): 48–66.

Bresser-Pereira, Luiz Carlos. 1993. "Brazil." In *The Political Economy of Policy Reform*, edited by John Williamson, 333–354. Washington: Institute for International Economics.

Bresser-Pereira, Luiz Carlos. 1999. "A Turning Point in the Debt Crisis: Brazil, the US Treasury and the World Bank." *Revista de Economia Política* 19 (2): 103–130.

Bresser-Pereira, Luiz Carlos. 2010. "Depoimento. A Descoberta da Inflação Inercial." *Revista de Economia Contemporânea* 14 (1): 167–192. https://doi.org/10.1590/s1415-98482010000100008.

Bresser-Pereira, Luiz Carlos, and Yoshiaki Nakano. 1984. *Inflação e Recessão*. São Paulo: Editora Brasiliense.

Bruneau, Thomas C., and Philippe Faucher. 1981. "Introduction." In *Authoritarian Capitalism. Brazil's Contemporary Economic and Political Development*, edited by Thomas C. Bruneau and Philippe Faucher, 1–9. Boulder: Westview Press.

Capoccia, Giovanni, and R. Daniel Kelemen. 2007. "The Study of Critical Junctures: Theory, Narrative, and Counterfactuals in Historical Institutionalism." *World Politics* 59 (2): 341–369. https://doi.org/10.1017/s0043887100020852.

Cardoso, Fernando Henrique. 2006. *A Arte da Política. A História que Vivi*. Rio de Janeiro: Civilização Brasileira.

Cardoso, Fernando Henrique. 2014. "Estamos Lenientes com a Inflação". In *Istoé Dinheiro*, edited by Luís Artur Nogueira. São Paulo: Três Editorial.

Cardoso, Fernando Henrique. 2016. *Diários da Presidência. 1997–1998*. 4 vols. Vol. 2. São Paulo: Companhia das Letras.

Carneiro, Dionisio Dias. 1987. "El Plan Cruzado: Una Temprana Evaluación Después de Diez Meses." *El Trimestre Económico* 54 (Número Especial: Planes Antinflacionarios): 251–274. https://doi.org/10.2307/23397293.

Carneiro, Dionisio Dias. 1991. "Los Primeros Tres Meses del Plan Collor." In *Elecciones y Política Económica en América Latina*, edited by Guillermo Rozenwurcel, 149–193. Buenos Aires: Editorial Tesis. Grupo Editorial Norma.

Cason, Jeffrey W. 2011. *The Political Economy of Integration: The Experience of Mercosur*. Abingdon: Routledge.

CEPAL, Comisión Económica para América Latina y el Caribe. 2009. *América Latina y el Caribe: Series Históricas de Estadísticas Económicas 1950–2008, Publicaciones Periódicas, Revistas y Boletines*. Santiago: CEPAL. Cuadernos Estadísticos de la CEPAL.

Dalmazo, Renato Antônio. 2000. "Os Atores, os Interesses e as Mediações Cruciais na Privatização da Telebrás." *Ensaios FEE* 21 (1): 193–232.

Evans, Peter. 1995. *Embedded Autonomy: States and Industrial Transformation*. Princeton: Princeton University Press.

Faria, Silvia. 1990. "Collor congela preços e corta consumo." *O Globo*, March 17, 8.

Faucher, Philippe. 1979. "Croissance et répression, la double logique de l'État dépendant: le cas du Brésil." *Revue canadienne de science politique* 12 (4): 747–774. https://doi.org/10.2307/3230204.

Faucher, Philippe, and Leslie Elliott Armijo. 2004. "Crises Cambiais e Estrutura Decisória: A Política de Recuperação Econômica na Argentina e no Brasil." *DADOS Revista de Ciências Sociais* 47 (2): 297–334. https://doi.org/10.1590/s0011-52582004000200004.

Ferreira, Alcides. 2016. "Origens e Evolução da Secretaria do Tesouro Nacional." In *A Crise Fiscal e Monetária Brasileira*, edited by Edmar Bacha, 99–116. Rio de Janeiro: Civilização Brasileira.

Fortes, Márcio. 1994. "Integração competitiva e privatização." *Folha de S.Paulo*, August 20.

Franco, Gustavo H. B. 2018. *A Moeda e a Lei. Uma História Monetária Brasileira. 1933–2013*. 2 ed. Rio de Janeiro: Zahar. Original edition, 2017.

Franco, Gustavo H. B. 1995. "O Plano Real e a URV Fundamentos da Reforma Monetária Brasileira de 1993–94." In *O Plano Real e Outros Ensaios*, edited by Gustavo H. B. Franco, 27–78. Rio de Janeiro: Francisco Alves.

Franco, Gustavo H. B. 1999. *O Desafio Brasileiro. Ensaios sobre Desenvolvimento, Globalização e Moeda*. São Paulo: Editora 34.

Frisch, Winston, and Gustavo H. B. Franco. 1993. "The Political Economy of Trade and Industrial Policy Reform in Brazil in the 1990s." In *Serie Reformas de Política Pública*, edited by ECLAC. Santiago.

Globo. 1990. "Governo extingue IAA, IBC e mais 22 órgãos." March 17, 18.

IBGE, Instituto Brasileiro de Geografia e Estatística. 1990. *Estatísticas Históricas do Brasil. Séries Econômicas, Demográficas e Sociais de 1550 a 1988*. 2a. ed. Vol. 3, *Séries Estatísticas Retrospectivas*. Rio de Janeiro: IBGE.

IBGE, Instituto Brasileiro de Geografia e Estatística. 2015. Indicadores IBGE. Sistema Nacional de Índices de Preços ao Consumidor IPCA INPC. IBGE.

IBRD, The World Bank. 2016. "Inflation, Consumer Prices (annual %)" [Spreadsheet]. World-Bank, accessed December 12, 2016. http://data.worldbank.org/indicator/FP.CPI.TOTL.ZG?end=1993&locations=MX&start=1964.

Jayme, Frederico Gonzaga, Jr. 1995. "Crise Fiscal, Federalismo e Endividamento Estadual." *Nova Economia* 5 (2): 81–115.

Kaufman, Robert R. 1988. *The Politics of Debt in Argentina, Brazil, and Mexico: Economic Stabilization in the 1980s, Research Series*. Berkeley: Institute of International Studies. University of California.

Kingstone, Peter R. 1999. *Crafting Coalitions for Reform: Business Preferences, Political Institutions, and Neoliberal Reform in Brazil*. University Park: Pennsylvania State University Press.

Kingstone, Peter R. 2000. "Muddling Through Gridlock: Economic Policy Performance, Business Responses, and Democratic Sustainability." In *Democratic Brazil: Actors, Institutions, and Processes*, edited by Peter R. Kingstone and Timothy J. Power, 185–203. Pittsburgh: University of Pittsburgh Press.

Kingstone, Peter R. 2004. "Industrialists and Liberalization." In *Reforming Brazil*, edited by Mauricio A. Font and Anthony Peter Spanakos, 161–176. Lanham: Lexington Books.

Kume, Honorio. 1996. "A Política de Importação no Plano Real e a Estrutura de Proteção Efetiva." In *Texto para Discussão*, edited by Instituto de Pesquisa Econômica Aplicada - IPEA. Rio de Janeiro, RJ.

Kume, Honorio, Guida Piani, and Carlos Frederico Bráz de Souza. 2003. "A Política Brasileira de Importação no Período 1987–1998: Descrição e Avaliação." In *A Abertura Comercial Brasileira nos Anos 1990. Impactos sobre Emprego e Salário*, edited by Carlos Henrique Corseuil and Honorio Kume, 9–37. Rio de Janeiro: Ministério do Trabalho e do Emprego/IPEA.

Lamounier, Bolivar, and Alkimar R. Moura. 1986. "Economic Policy and Political Opening in Brazil." In *Latin American Political Economy: Financial Crisis and Political Change*, edited by Jonathan Hartlyn and Samuel A. Morley, 165–196. Boston: Westview Press.

Lara-Resende, André. 1984. "A Moeda Indexada: Uma Proposta para Eliminar a Inflação Inercial." In *Texto para Discussão*, edited by Departamento de Economia PUC/RJ. Rio de Janeiro.

Longo, Carlos Alberto. 1997. "The State and the Liberalization of the Brazilian Economy." In *The Brazilian Economy: Structure and Performance in Recent Decades*, edited by Maria J. F. Willumsen and Eduardo Giannetti da Fonseca, 25–44. Miami: North-South Center Press/University of Miami.

Lopes, Francisco Lafaiete. 1984. "Só um Choque Heterodoxo Pode Derrubar a Inflação." In *Economia em Perspectiva*. São Paulo: Conselho Regional de Economia-SP.

Lourenço, José, Paulo Ramos, and Rubem Medina. 1994. Relatório Final da Comissão Parlamentar Mista de Inquérito. Criada através do Requerimento N° 002, de 1993-CN "Destinada a Investigar Fatos Decorrentes da Execução do Programa Nacional de Desestatização." In *Diário do Congresso Nacional*. Brasília: Congresso Nacional.

Malamud, Andrés. 2011. "A Leader Without Followers? The Growing Divergence Between the Regional and Global Performance of Brazilian Foreign Policy." *Latin American Politics and Society* 53 (3): 1–24. https://doi.org/10.1111/j.1548-2456.2011.00123.x.

Manzetti, Luigi. 1999. *Privatization South American Style*. Oxford: Oxford University Press.

Martins, Luciano. 1993. "Three Dimensions of the Crisis: A Political Analysis." In *Brazil and the Challenge of Economic Reform*, edited by Werner Baer and Joseph S. Tulchin, 31–37. Washington: The Woodrow Wilson Center Press.

Modiano, Eduardo. 1987. "El Plan Cruzado: Bases Teóricas y Limitaciones Prácticas." *El Trimestre Económico* 54 (Número Especial: Planes Antinflacionarios): 223–250. https://doi.org/10.2307/23397292.

Modiano, Eduardo. 1989. "A Ópera dos Três Cruzados: 1985–1989." In *A Ordem do Progresso. Cem Anos de Política Econômica Republicana 1889–1989*, edited by Marcelo de Paiva Abreu, 347–387. Rio de Janeiro: Editora Campus.

Modiano, Eduardo. 2000. "Um Balanço da Privatização nos Anos 90." In *A Privatização no Brasil. O Caso dos Serviços de Utilidade Pública*, edited by Armando Castelar Pinheiro and Kiichiro Fukasaku, 321–327. Rio de Janeiro: BNDES/OCDE.

Morais, Lecio, and Alfredo Saad-Filho. 2005. "Lula and the Continuity of Neoliberalism in Brazil: Strategic Choice, Economic Imperative or Political Schizophrenia?" *Historical Materialism* 13 (1): 3–32. https://doi.org/10.1163/1569206053620924.

Musacchio, Aldo, and Sergio G. Lazzarini. 2014. *Reinventing State Capitalism: Leviathan in Business, Brazil and Beyond*. Cambridge, MA: Harvard University Press.

Niskanen, William A. 1971. *Bureaucracy and Representative Government*. Chicago: Aldine Atherton.

Pastore, Affonso Celso. 1997. Senhoriagem e Inflação: O Caso Brasileiro. In *Texto para Discussão*, edited by Centro de Estudos de Reforma do Estado/FGV. Rio de Janeiro.

Payne, Leigh A. 1994. *Brazilian Industrialists and Democratic Change*. Baltimore: Johns Hopkins University Press.

Pinheiro, Armando Castelar. 1999. "Privatização no Brasil: Por quê? Até onde? Até quando?" In *A Economia Brasileira nos Anos 90*, edited by Fabio Giambiagi and Maurício Mesquita Moreira, 147–182. Rio de Janeiro: BNDES.

Pinheiro, Armando Castelar, Regis Bonelli, and Ben Ross Schneider. 2007. "Pragmatism and Market Reforms in Brazil." In *Understanding Market Reforms in Brazil: Similar Reforms, Diverse Constituencies, Varied Results*, edited by José María Fanelli, 73–93. Houndmills and Basingstoke: Palgrave Macmillan.

Pinheiro, Armando Castelar, and Fabio Giambiagi. 2000. "Os Antecedentes Macroeconômicos e a Estrutura Institucional na Privatização no Brasil." In *A Privatização no Brasil. O Caso dos Serviços de Utilidade Pública*, edited by Armando Castelar Pinheiro and Kiichiro Fukasaku, 13–43. Rio de Janeiro: BNDES/OCDE.

Puntigliano, Andrés Rivarola. 2008. "'Going Global': An Organizational Study of Brazilian Foreign Policy." *Revista Brasileira de Política Internacional* 51 (1): 28–52. https://doi.org/10.1590/s0034-73292008000100002.

Rego, José M., ed. 1986. *Inflação Inercial, Teorias sobre Inflação e o Plano Cruzado*. Rio de Janeiro: Paz e Terra.

Rodrigues, Leôncio Martins, and Adalberto Moreira Cardoso. 2009. "Força Sindical: Uma Análise Sociopolítica." In Rio de Janeiro: Centro Edelstein. PDF, accessed July 3, 2015. http://books.scielo.org/id/qmncm.

Roma, Celso. 2002. "A Institucionalização do PSDB entre 1988 e 1999." *Revista Brasileira de Ciências Sociais* 17 (49): 71–92. https://doi.org/10.1590/s0102-69092002000200006.

Sardenberg, Carlos Alberto. 1987. *Aventura e Agonia: Nos Bastidores do Cruzado*. São Paulo: Companhia das Letras.

Schneider, Ben Ross. 1991a. "A Política de Privatização no Brasil e no México nos Anos 80: Variações em Torno de um Tema Estatista." *DADOS Revista de Ciências Sociais* 34 (1): 21–51.

Schneider, Ben Ross. 1991b. *Politics Within the State: Elite Bureaucrats and Industrial Policy in Authoritarian Brazil*. Pittsburgh: University of Pittsburgh Press.

Schneider, Ben Ross. 1992. "Privatization in the Collor Government: Triumph of Liberalism or Collapse of the Developmental State?" In *The Right and Democracy in Latin America*, edited by Douglas A. Chalmers, Maria do Carmo Campello de Souza, and Atilio A. Boron, 225–238. New York: Praeger.

Silva, Luíz Inácio Lula da. 2002. "Leia íntegra da carta de Lula para acalmar o mercado financeiro." *Folha de S.Paulo*, June 24. https://www1.folha.uol.com.br/folha/brasil/ult96u33908.shtml.

Simonsen, Mario Henrique. 1970. *Inflação: Gradualismo X Tratamento de Choque*. Rio de Janeiro: APEC Editôra.

Skidmore, Thomas E. 1988. *The Politics of Military Rule in Brazil, 1964–85*. New York: Oxford University Press.

Thorp, Rosemary. 1998. *Progress, Poverty and Exclusion: An Economic History of Latin America in the 20th Century*. Washington and Baltimore: IADB/Johns Hopkins University Press.

Velasco, Licínio, Jr. 1997. "A Economia Política das Políticas Públicas: Fatores que Favoreceram as Privatizações no Período 1985/94." In *Textos para Discussão*, edited by BNDES. Rio de Janeiro.

Velasco, Licínio, Jr. 1999. "Privatização: Mitos e Falsas Percepções." In *A Economia Brasileira nos Anos 90*, edited by Fabio Giambiagi and Maurício Mesquita Moreira, 183–215. Rio de Janeiro: BNDES.

Velasco, Licínio, Jr. 2005. "Políticas Reformistas no Presidencialismo de Coalizão Brasileiro." In *Textos para Discussão*, edited by BNDES. Rio de Janeiro.

Velasco, Licínio, Jr. 2010. "A Privatização no Sistema BNDES." *Revista do BNDES* 33: 307–382.

Weyland, Kurt. 2001. "Clarifying a Contested Concept: Populism in the Study of Latin American Politics." *Comparative Politics* 34 (1): 1–22. https://doi.org/10.2307/422412.

Weyland, Kurt. 2003. "Neopopulism and Neoliberalism in Latin America: How Much Affinity?" *Third World Quarterly* 24 (6): 1095–1115. https://doi.org/10.1080/01436590310001630080.
Williamson, John, ed. 1985. *Inflation and Indexation: Argentina, Brazil, and Israel*. Washington: Institute for International Economics.
Wirth, John D. 1970. *The Politics of Brazilian Development*. Stanford: Stanford University Press.

CHAPTER 5

The Chilean Pension System: Contentious Economic Governance

Chile has been portrayed time and time again as a case where liberalizing reforms demonstrated a clear sense of purpose and unity. The military government (1973–1990) justified its actions as a response to the socialist government of Salvador Allende (1970–1973). Subsequent democratically elected governments (1990–2010) had to tread carefully, as the threat of a regression to authoritarianism loomed constantly on the horizon. This complex political heritage—and the possibility of a return either to socialism or authoritarianism—made the policymaking process painstakingly incremental, and has prevented the consolidation of economic governance. Throughout the process of institutional evolution, conflicting interpretations of new crises led to uncertainty surrounding the constitution of the institutional complementarity around which economic governance could consolidate. Building coalitions around key reforms was hard under such conditions. To consider this phenomenon in more detail, the following chapter analyzes reforms to the individual-accounts-based pension system and the financial system.

In post-transition Chile, debates arose between those who defend the legacy of the authoritarian regime and those who wish to challenge it. For example, some consider the new pension system a prime example of the military government's lasting and positive achievements. Because of its special status among the legacies of the military government, the pension

A. Angel, *Consolidating Economic Governance in Latin America*, Governance, Development, and Social Inclusion in Latin America, https://doi.org/10.1007/978-3-030-64522-9_5

system has generally inspired ideological debates. Low pensions that do not meet people's expectations reinforce the antipathy toward the system. These do not preserve living standards—though the previous system had not preserved them either, so the reforms did not represent any departure in this regard. Essentially, the pension system has always suffered politically due to both its origins and its outcomes, which numerous reforms have endeavored to improve. Considering the origins of the system, subsequent adjustments sought a balance between the perceived red lines of the military regime and a more progressive agenda. However, neither the threat of a return to military rule nor the risk of implementing an irresponsible economic policy led the country to a collapse, so that subsequent reforms to both pensions and financial systems would require a politically motivated intervention to ensure their survival as was the case in the 1980s. Until the mid-1990s, the two systems grew increasingly integrated. Had these efforts toward integration failed, the democratically elected government would have fulfilled the prophecy foretold by military government supporters[1]—who would have had to recognize that their cherished policy had significant flaws.

The first democratically elected government in twenty years had to prove that a sound economic policy was compatible with democracy. Growth was high in this period, compared to the average annual rate between 1960 and 2010 (Ffrench-Davis 2014, 30). A return of the military regime remained a possibility during the first half of the 1990s, since Augusto Pinochet was still Commander of the Armed Forces. Capital markets were increasingly important as a source of funding for companies, and most of their resources came from the pension system (Stallings 2006, 159–161). As a result, in the mid-1990s, complementarity between the pension system and the financial system was on the path toward consolidation. The financial crisis in Southeast Asia in 1997–1998 derailed this process, however. At the same time, it became clear that neither a return to authoritarian rule nor flagrant mistakes of economic policy were on the

[1] Business leaders argued that the opposition would return to the policies implemented by Allende. An economic team composed of Christian Democrats and Socialists would foster a social situation that, by their own account, was characterized by social protest, fiscal deficits, and overwhelming demands. It was likely these demands—that is, revisiting privatization processes, from which they had profited dearly—that dominated their concerns (Gárate 2012, 361). International financial circles also mistrusted the new center-left economic policies (Cavallo 1998, 57).

horizon. As the military's clout waned, the questions surrounding their reforms intensified.

Chile's capital markets were affected deeply by the financial crisis in South-East Asia, which instigated a withdrawal of resources from emerging economies.[2] Meanwhile, the limits of the new pension system were revealed. While some evidence suggests that the continuous accumulation of resources in the pension system contributed to the deepening of the financial system (Schmidt-Hebbel 1997, 1998), it is not clear why this trend did not continue. The consolidation of economic governance depends on a common interpretation of new crises among political actors. In Chile, such consensus did not exist: the ongoing political debate over the military government prevented a unified interpretation of the potential threat, and this clearly hindered the consolidation of economic governance.[3]

This chapter discusses the process through which the pension system and the financial system in Chile became increasingly dependent on each other, until political debates began to question their fundamental principles. It is neither a history of the pension system nor a history of the financial system, even if their institutional evolution is important for understanding the theoretical argument about economic governance. More specifically, the gradual consolidation of democracy, within the limits of the influence exercised by the military, prevented the continuation of a process that would lead to the consolidation of institutional complementarities. Nevertheless, supporters of the military government and democratically elected officials pursued similar paths; the pension system held symbolic importance for both of them. The chapter will develop an analysis of the theoretical implications of this relationship.

Several existing accounts explore the importance of the pension reform to the Chilean economy. For instance, Schmidt-Hebbel (1997, 1998) is enthusiastic about the way in which the reform deepened capital markets. A later contribution by Corbo and Schmidt-Hebbel (2003) became the touchstone reference on this subject because it places the pension reform at the very center of the Chilean economy's growth. But while a deep financial system might be a necessary condition to maximize growth,

[2] Simultaneously, the Chilean peso (CLP) started to depreciate in real terms after a long trend of appreciation (Banco Central de Chile 2020).

[3] Because not every change to the institutions studied here is relevant for the argument, their presentation is not exhaustive.

it is not sufficient either. Other less elaborate accounts emphasize the creation of side markets (Bustamante 2006), and others still acknowledge the contribution of the pension system to the housing market (Larraín 2006, 99).

Authorities have focused mainly on keeping regulations surrounding the pension system up-to-date, adapting them to market practices and failures identified along the way. The system's structure was not substantially modified between its inception in 1981 and 2008, when a scheme providing a minimum pension for the poorest 60% of the population was created.[4] While such modifications clearly represent a significant change, many actors believed that the opportunity for a bigger transformation had been lost. The different perceptions of this reform reveal the balancing act that the state has been playing with respect to pensions ever since the return of democracy.

On one side, implementing policies that follow the best economic advice that the political juncture allows, while, on the other, hoping that the expected outcomes of those policies would help to build a social consensus over those policies. Nevertheless, the difficulties those policies had always had in expanding its support beyond its initial constituencies reflect the gulf between a technocratic view of economic governance and a view based on the political support those institutional reforms can muster. In the former, institutional reforms alone are constitutive of economic governance; in the latter, institutional reforms, which are complementary to one another, need strong and broad coalitions of actors that accept to limit their discretion with which they had previously acted.

5.1 Pension System Reform

The Chilean social security system was established in 1924 along corporatist lines (Arellano 1985b, 28). Each sector had its own *Caja*[5] and was able to grant workers the right to a pension. Not surprisingly, when the Great Depression occurred, the authorities used social security resources

[4] It created a scheme providing a minimum pension for the poorest 60% of the population within the "solidarity pillar" (Larrañaga, Huepe, and Rodríguez 2015). Other pillars are the contributive pillar, which is the system studied in the present work, and the voluntary pillar.

[5] In Spanish, this refers to the organization that keeps money on interest. In this case, the *Caja* would act as the fund's administrator.

to stimulate economic recovery. Lack of resources was not a problem in subsequent years. Corporatism would prove a heavier burden given the diversity of conditions that had to be met to access pensions as well as benefits (Hepp 1980, 15–18). The parameters on which pensions usually depend (e.g., age, time of contribution, monthly contribution) varied substantially. The three main *Cajas* were the *Servicio de Seguro Social*—SSS (Social Security Service), for blue-collar workers; the *Caja de Previsión de Empleados Particulares*—EMPART (Retirement Cooperative of Private Employees), for white-collar workers; and the *Caja Nacional de Empleados Públicos y Periodistas*—CANAEMPU (National Retirement Cooperative of Public Employees and Journalists). Banking employees, Central Bank employees, and other categories of workers also had their own retirement regimes.

This variation in pension regimes was already perceived as problematic in the 1950s—as indeed was the whole social security regime. To this effect, a report was commissioned to the *Comisión de Reforma de la Seguridad Social* (Commission on the Reform of Social Security) or Prat Commission (Prat 1964).[6] Its proposed solution for pensions was the creation of a general regime through a universal Pay-As-You-Go—PAYG regime.[7] Although this constituted a departure from the system's corporatist origins, its use of a Defined-Benefits-PAYG scheme was in line with international practices.[8] In the 1950s, these regimes were the standard in Latin America and in Western Europe (McGillivray 2006, 232–233).

The oddest pension regime was that of equestrian workers. This category represented neither a substantial number of workers, nor a defined

[6] The Commission was created in 1959 and was chaired by Jorge Prat, a respected politician (Chumacero et al. 2007, 126) who was presumably a deal broker. Gárate (2012, 185, 239) asserts that Prat belonged to a profoundly antidemocratic current in Chilean politics.

[7] These systems are based on intergenerational transfers. As current workers contribute to the system, the resources they provide are used to pay the pensions of the preceding generation on the spot, i.e., "pay as you go."

[8] A Defined-Benefits system offers the workers contributing to it a given income regardless of their contributions provided they fulfill some conditions. In contrast, a Defined-Contribution system establishes a periodical contribution to workers but offers no guarantee as to how much the retirement income will be. In the former, financial and actuarial risks are the responsibility of the fund administrators, in the latter, the burden of the actuarial risks is on each worker as the fund's administrators do not offer any guarantee concerning retirement incomes.

sector of production. And although many regimes were generous, their regime was the most generous—for example, some equestrian workers could retire after contributing for only ten years (Hepp 1980, 15). Other regimes granted benefits according to the income of the last year of work (Hepp 1980, 18), instead of the income of a working life. The conditions to obtain a pension and its corresponding benefits fostered actuarial disequilibria (Hepp 1980, 12).[9] *Cajas* often made investments that broke the principle of long-term inter-temporal return. Many of them granted benefits to the workers at the same time that they contributed funds to the system—for example, through subsidized loans or privative retailers.[10] When Salvador Allende was elected in 1970, the Chilean economy was already caught up in problematic trends, and these were only exacerbated by his policies. However, the pension system did not change significantly during his government.

When the military took power in 1973, it was evident that they were divided over these general trends.[11] The majority of officers believed, in line with the views of an earlier dictator and constitutional president, Carlos Ibáñez del Campo (1927–1931 and 1952–1958, respectively), that the state should have a strong presence in the economy, even if the officers themselves did not necessarily have their own economic project. Higher positions were filled by economists close to the Christian Democracy, who implemented gradualist privatization and anti-inflationary policies. The implementation of these policies shows that many economists fundamentally agreed with the economic model that was applied, within some limits, between the 1930s and the 1960s. Indeed, the bulk of the high officialdom supported this consensus, because they had made their careers precisely when Ibáñez del Campo was implementing the policies. This congenial state of affairs did not last for long, however.

[9] The actuarial balance of a pension regime is the difference between the present value of its liabilities, i.e., pensions to be paid, and the present value of its revenues, i.e., contributions plus financial returns received until the maturity of its liabilities (ILO-FACTS 1998, 2; Plamondon et al. 2002, 483).

[10] Joaquín Vial. Interview with the author. Santiago. August 5, 2014. Vial is Deputy Governor of the Chilean Central Bank. He has been the Chief Economist of the Global Trends Unit of the Economic Research Department at BBVA (a bank) and was Chief Macroeconomic Adviser to the Minister of Finance (1992–1994) and Head (1997–2000) of the *Dirección Nacional de Presupuesto*—Diprés (National Budget Directorate).

[11] The next paragraphs rely on Gárate (2012).

As inflation persisted even after a year of gradualist policies, and the prospects for 1975 seemed strikingly similar to those of 1973, a group of officers led by Augusto Pinochet as Commander of the Army and José Merino as Commander of the Navy decided to break with the past. They offered the group of liberal economists, who had initially been relegated to second-ranking posts, the opportunity to put their own preferred policies in place.[12] Thus, after 1975, several radical liberalizing policies were implemented, despite the ongoing opposition of officers who still believed in the previous arrangement. In the specific case of the pension system, meanwhile, the continuing debate over the role of the state prevented an earlier reform of the *cajas*-based system from occurring at this time.

On one side of this debate, a group of technocrats who worked with Miguel Kast, Deputy Director of the *Oficina de Planificación Nacional*—ODEPLAN (National Planning Bureau),[13] sought to break from the past by creating a system based on market principles. On the other side, mainly active members of the Army, led by Air Force Commander General Gustavo Leigh, believed that the state should not relinquish control of the resources that were administered by the *cajas* and that, at the time, were headed by army officers. The first side saw the complexities of the system and its disparities as a consequence of rent-seeking behavior,[14] while the second saw the provision of social benefits as a source of legitimacy for the state.[15] These statist officers, General Leigh chief among them, were

[12] They came to be known as the "Chicago Boys," because they had graduated in economics from the University of Chicago during the 1950s and 1960s. When they returned to Chile, they became industrialists or heads of banks, until they became the technocratic core of the military regime. Valdés (1995) and Silva (2009, 143ff) provide details about the Chicago Boys and their relationship with the military regime.

[13] ODEPLAN was created during the government of Eduardo Frei Montalva (1965–1970) to assist the president in the complex process of planning the country's development. Although it was created in 1967, it had been operational since the beginning of Frei's government (Silva 2009, 123). Gárate (2012, 215–221) discusses the relation between ODEPLAN and the different generations of Chicago Boys.

[14] Hepp (1980, 1) lists as the first symptom of the crisis of the pension system that there "does not exist a direct relation between the level of contribution from affiliated workers throughout their lives and the benefits, in form of pensions, they receive" (Author translation).

[15] Chief among these complexities was the proliferation of regimes, both in terms of organizations, e.g., *cajas*, and in the conditions to obtain benefits. Even if the existence of many *cajas* is not problematic per se, this trait was considered an incentive to seek benefits without bearing the corresponding costs.

gradually isolated, first because many retired, and second because their attitudes were deemed incongruous with due military obedience.[16] This situation allowed Pinochet to consolidate his power within the military.

The way was thus paved for the market-based proposal to be transformed into law. The organizing principle of the system proposed by Kast and his team was not entirely new, given that capitalization was already in use as a complement to mandatory systems (Arellano 2007, 3). However, the attempt to put it at the center of the system was certainly a novel initiative. In this context, doubts about the convenience of such a change were reasonable. Given the risks, both political and economic, Kast and his team chose a path of close oversight.[17] Officials generally considered rent-seeking behavior to be the reason for the problems of the system. Within this framework, the main problem was the lack of correspondence between the costs borne by each individual actor and the actual benefits received (República de Chile 1980, 4). Even after incremental reforms were enacted to prevent these problems,[18] officials were not convinced that they would not reappear, since the incentives of the PAYG system were still in place.[19]

[16]This was certainly the case for General Leigh, who, after an interview in the *Corriere della Sera* in which he severely criticized the government, was removed by the military junta in 1978 (Gárate 2012, 242 fn. 45).

[17]Alfonso Serrano Spoerer. Interview with the author. Santiago. August 20, 2014. Serrano was the Under-Secretary of Social Protection from 1976 to 1985, making him an important member of the team in charge of shepherding the reform from conception to completion. He was later nominated (in 1985) as Vice-President of the Central Bank and, after the reform granting independence to the institution, in 1989, he was chosen to be a Member of the Board of Directors.

[18]Among these were the leveling of the minimum pensions for blue-collar and white-collar workers with Decree-Act 255 of January 1974; non-minimum pensions were adjusted to the purchasing power they had at the moment of retirement with Decree-Act 2444 of September 1978. Finally, with Decree-Act 2448 of February 1979, mandatory requirements were established: e.g., time of contribution (35 years) and different age requirements for women and men, adjustment of pensions following the Consumer Price Index—CPIn—and the substitution of pursuer-pensions with an adjustment of the last income following the CPIn, instead of receiving all the benefits of the active worker (Hepp 1980, 5–8).

[19]The system incentivized rent-seeking and free-riding behaviors. Rent-seeking refers to the action of deriving a rent that does not correspond to the fair price of a good or service in the market (Krueger 1974). Free-rider behavior refers to an action whereby an agent that takes advantage of a public good to which he does not contribute, while also making it impossible to stop him from doing so. Mas-Colell, Whinston, and Green (1995),

Under the old system, a significant number of actors received benefits systematically higher than the costs they bore (Hepp 1980). Thus, according to Miguel Kast and his team, the best solution was to create the strongest relation possible between the costs and the benefits for each actor.[20] The idea was to establish a system based on different foundations. The benefits that each worker would receive at the end of his work life should be perfectly aligned with the contributions made during his work life. Individual savings accounts offered this kind of alignment, since the funds to finance future pensions would come exclusively from these accounts and, in principle, would not involve any other contribution from society as a whole. The new proposal created a strong link between the individual contributions—or the costs—and the pensions obtained—the benefits. Private managers, organized as *Administradoras de Fondos de Pensiones*—AFP (Pension Fund Administrators), would administer the individual accounts with a clear separation between the savings and the managers. Thus, in the event that one of these entities went bankrupt, their savings could only be transferred to other AFPs. This, of course, would protect savers.

At the time, arguments about the advantages of market-based reforms were influential, including the arguments about the incentives for each worker to make contributions to the new system. Since individual accounts were the only source to finance pensions, each worker would have the incentive to contribute to his fund. This was in sharp opposition to the old system, where pensions were financed through state contributions (Hepp 1980, 6). These incentives transformed workers into a new class of capitalists ready to participate in the market (Gárate 2012, 269); AFPs could now compete for their contributions. The leadership of Miguel Kast and his team was later embraced by the Labor Minister José Piñera,[21] who would become the main promoter of the

specifically chapter 11, provide a precise definition of free-riding and its microeconomic implications. Free-riding has also been studied within the framework of collective action (Olson 1965; Ostrom 1990). In the Chilean pension system, rent-seeking occurred when a group of workers tried to enact a generous pension regime well above the prevalent conditions of other regimes. The free-rider problem came about when a group of workers enjoyed the benefits of a social security regime as a public good without making the corresponding contributions.

[20] Alfonso Serrano Spoerer. Interview with the author. Santiago. August 20, 2014.

[21] Alfonso Serrano Spoerer. Interview with the author. Santiago. August 20, 2014.

defined-contribution individual-accounts system at the international level (Weyland 2006).

Some authorities, mainly the military, feared that these mandatory savings could be diverted from their intended use.[22] This was especially salient given that the profit maximization of private administrators—AFPs—would be one of the new system's main organizational features. Authorities feared that profit maximization would lead administrators to take advantage of deposits to boost businesses instead of benefiting savers. Moreover, there was also a concern that these funds would be poorly managed, or used to support side businesses of the fund' administrators.[23] The emergence of a new organizational pattern within a mandatory system—that is, profit-making administrators—was a groundbreaking change.

This change determined the structure of the system, since authorities needed reassurance that administrators would not take advantage of savings. From the institutional design to the regulations governing the new scheme, a strict regulatory framework was required in order to get the reform approved. Regulations covering the assets in which AFPs could invest funds meticulously defined several quantitative limits for the composition of their portfolio. At first, AFPs could invest exclusively in fixed-income instruments, such as bonds issued by the Central Bank, the Treasury, certain corporate bonds, or bank deposits (Berstein and Chumacero 2003, 3). These were considered the safest investments in the Chilean market. As discussed above, since one of the fears of the reformers was that administrators could capitalize on their own businesses with workers' savings, related investments were not authorized.[24]

The *Superintendencia de Administradoras de Fondos de Pensiones*—SAFP (Superintendency of Pension Fund Administrators) was created as

[22] Promoters said the new system would provide financing for activities in need of a significant amount of resources, such as infrastructure and housing (Piñera 1988a, 317); however, others, like Myers (1988), suggested that the interest of Chilean officials in the possibility of spillovers from the new pension system should be moderate because a pension system, obviously, is intended to pay pensions.

[23] Alfonso Serrano Spoerer. Interview with the author. Santiago. August 20, 2014.

[24] Berstein and Chumacero (2003) and Iglesias-Palau (2009, 17–18) point out that a fraction of the funds could be invested into companies belonging to the same group that owned the AFP; however, neither of them provide a date when this change might have taken place. It probably took place in the 1980s (ca. 1985), since Pérez (1988, 226) refers to this possibility too.

a regulatory body to which AFPs had to report monthly on their portfolios. While regulation was strict, the main feature of the new scheme was market discipline, as it would create incentives leading to a Pareto-optimal solution. Regulations therefore focused on ways to improve market performance, such as the entry of new competitors, the possibility of changing funds for affiliates, and risk assessment, among others.[25] At first, the system was overregulated to avoid criticisms about putting retirement funds in the hands of AFPs. Another consideration was the requirement of responding to workers' long-term needs. While the latter situation is understandable given the implicit governmental warranty on acquired pension rights, it is also clear that the intention was to avoid repeating past mistakes while taking the lowest possible risk. But this tension is difficult to resolve.[26] While some past mistakes, like breaking the inter-temporal logic of long-term savings with contemporary benefits—such as cheap loans to the members of the *cajas*—were easy to avoid, others proved harder to overcome. Returns on low-risk investments were low, and therefore the accumulation of resources was slow, affecting the resources available to calculate an individual's pension.

And yet it was not clear how competition was to be enforced if investments were going to be restricted to public bonds or bank deposits. Moreover, the concentration of market power within financial markets, which derived from the accumulation of contributions made only to a few, created doubts about the competition that would exist (Arellano 1982, 120). The conditions that had to be met to create an AFP were strict, reinforcing barriers to entry. The risk of an oligopoly and the market power its members would subsequently hold was real; indeed, two big economic groups created two respective AFPs, which amounted to almost 40% (4 of 11) of the supply. The tension between efforts to maximize profits on behalf of workers and strict control to reduce risk was present from the beginning. Investment possibilities were restricted in order to gather public support, considering the novelty of the system.

[25] Examples of changes in such dimensions include: Act 18255 of June 1983, Act 18398 of January 1985, Act 18646 of August 1987, Act 18964 of March 1990, Act 19301 of March 1994, and Act 19389 of May 1995.

[26] Jaime Ruíz-Tagle. Interview with the author. Santiago. July 30, 2014. Ruíz-Tagle is a sociologist; he was Director of the Labor Economics Program, Head of the Office of Forecasting Studies at the Ministry of Planning, and has been involved in social security issues since the 1980s.

During the Chilean financial crisis of the early 1980s, the first AFPs created by big economic groups were bankrupted along with their controllers, but without losing savings.[27] This was the result of a design feature of the system in which the funds (pooled resources) were separated *de jure* from their administrators. In the case of bankruptcy, the idea was that the AFP would disappear while the funds would be transferred to another AFP, thus safeguarding workers' interests. The financial crisis revealed some serious flaws with this feature, however: for instance, it required deep fiscal commitments, which were partly responsible for the deteriorated fiscal balance (Arellano 1988, 136; Uthoff 2001).[28] Regulatory authorities have always managed to prevent a total loss of savings altogether. But this move was not without its costs in the long run: low risks produce low returns, which in turn caps the resources available to finance pensions. Replacement rates never actually reach 100%, but in Chile, they are consistently low, regardless of where the worker is in the scale of income distribution (Sojo 2014, 33). Nevertheless, the absence of lost contributions because of bankruptcy vindicates authorities' strict regulatory framework.

After the reform was enacted, there was a transitional period for its implementation. This period allowed workers who wanted to remain in the old system to do so, and allowed each worker to decide on the best scenario for them. This apparently flexible situation notwithstanding, however, many workers had no choice but to join the system. One of the conditions established by the new pension system was a smaller monthly contribution to the retirement fund. The result of this smaller contribution was an 11% increase in a worker's available income (Ruíz-Tagle 2001, 9). It is important to remember the context in which the choice about whether to join the new system was made: Chile was in a recession, which implied a growth rate of −14% in 1982–1983 (Ffrench-Davis 2014, 48), as well as a high unemployment rate, around 20% (Ffrench-Davis 2014, 305). Clearly, many workers decided to change because of the favorable short-term conditions, without necessarily taking into full consideration the long-term consequences. Making an informed decision between the two systems by weighing all relevant variables was simply impossible given

[27] Alfonso Serrano Spoerer. Interview with the author. Santiago. August 20, 2014.

[28] The fiscal equilibrium policy was abandoned for a more pragmatic approach because of the financial crisis and the subsequent economic downturn.

the complex layers of commissions and hidden costs—even if promoters argued at the time that only a low level of financial literacy was needed to understand the new system (Piñera 1988b, 327).

Deeply divisive debates around the reform continued even after its implementation, largely as a result of its origins. Supporters of the individual-accounts system, apart from those who had direct interests, such as the owners of the AFPs, were mainly people who were close to the military regime. Criticism, in turn, came mainly—though not exclusively—from public employees who had lost some privileges with the reform.[29] In addition, following the pattern of several other Chilean post-transitional debates, critics were legion in social organizations opposing the military regime. Authorities have tried to referee these debates by reforming the system in place while also improving the workers' actual situation. As will be discussed further below, the *Concertación* did not challenge all the legacies of the military regime.[30] Indeed, their leaders considered that every reform in economic policy had to preserve growth (Arellano 2012; Ominami 2013).

In the late 1990s, the reforms were scrutinized closely. First, a complex regulatory structure was put in place, with the aim of controlling the investment of the resources owned by workers. Second, there was vigorous debate surrounding the substantial amount of resources that had accumulated because few pensions had to be paid and yet contributions maintained a steady pace. Supporters of the reforms argued that these resources meant an increase in the aggregated savings of the country (Schmidt-Hebbel 1997). Critics, on the other hand, argued, since at least the late 1980s, that it did not represent an increase in aggregated savings, but rather a transfer of assets between the state and the private sector (Arellano 1988; Arenas-de-Mesa 2000, 53–55). As the main investment was public bonds, there were indeed no new resources saved, but the state became increasingly indebted.[31]

[29] Joaquín Vial. Interview with the author. Santiago. August 5, 2014.

[30] The coalition of parties opposing the military regime has won all the elections but two since the democratization in 1990. The main parties are the Christian Democrats (DC), the Party for Democracy (PPD), the Radical Social-Democrat Party (PRSD), and the Socialist Party (PS). Later on, Michelle Bachelet, in the campaign for her second term (2014–2018), proposed a new name for the coalition, the New Majority, which incorporates, among other social movements, the Communist Party.

[31] The terms of that debate illustrate to what extent this was an obscure subject for the majority of Chilean workers. This continues to be the case (Berstein et al. 2009,

Later in the 1990s, limitations started to be more evident.[32] Competition among AFPs was supposed to encourage efficiency, service provision, profitability, and so on. But the returns of the system were disappointing nonetheless (Carrasco 2001, 948–949), and regulation is said to be one of the causes. For example, one important regulation was the averages that the AFPs had to respect, which caused herd behavior and subsequently diminished the competition incentives within the market.[33] Averages were useful insofar as losses were rare. But by leveling the playing field, at least to a certain extent, they meant that consumers (workers) could not choose among providers that were distinguished by significant differences. The main price charged by AFPs was a two-tiered fee, a fixed fraction and another fraction proportional to the balance, which in turn had low price-demand elasticity, thus transposing competition to another arena. As a result, the AFPs increased their sales force, which impacted the number of transfers and reduced the system's efficiency, since the costs were higher within essentially the same market. Workers also experienced this decrease in efficiency, as they saw their yields diminish (Berstein and Micco 2002). In an effort to mitigate the problems, authorities limited transfers from one AFP to another, which slightly relieved the pressure surrounding prices.

Following an ongoing pattern of relaxing the narrow provisions of the AFPs' investment regime, a reform was introduced in 2002 allowing them to offer a plurality of portfolios. The "multi-fund reform," as it was called, pretended to diversify the risks borne by each worker, depending on his or her preferences. The multi-fund structure consisted of five different portfolios with distinctive risk levels. The rationale for this reform was to maximize the returns of workers' savings, according to their life cycle. Salaries from first employments are low compared to later ones; however, those will be more significant to the calculation of the pension, as they will have produced returns over a longer period of time. Before the multi-fund reform, the risk was a flat average, which affected young contributors

161–164). Ignorance about how the system works was mentioned as one of its main weaknesses by both Alfonso Serrano Spoerer and Joaquín Vial.

[32] Subsequent paragraphs rely heavily on Uthoff (2001, 236–238).

[33] If the profitability of a given fund falls short of the industry average, the AFP must use its own resources on the compulsory deposit to compensate its affiliates. Therefore, the incentive is to avoid such patrimonial drawback.

more; they could afford higher risks, since they would have more time to recover potential transitory loses (Ruíz-Tagle 2013, 499).

The reform also allowed AFPs to diversify their risks. Not surprisingly, however, each fund within the multi-fund scheme was regulated according to the same strategy that had been used with old funds—that is, using an industry average as a benchmark. Thus, the multi-fund reform reproduced the old model on a broader level. While the rationale behind the reform was sound—risk diversification depending on the life cycle—the time required for it to produce noteworthy results was well beyond any reasonable timeframe for a successful political evaluation. Furthermore, retiring Chileans had to contend with numerous problems that only increased uneasiness surrounding the system. As critics point out, the system did not guarantee the living standards of pensioners. This resulted in a growing discontent, and complications started to surface as more people decided to keep working even after they had reached the age of retirement.[34] There was discord around the fact that so far, the system had not paid any complete pensions, because many pensioners in recent years had been entitled to Recognition Bonds.[35] Those who pointed to the accumulated resources of the pension system were challenged by those who argued that contributions to the social security system should pay for pensions rather than increasing the available resources for companies to grow.[36]

[34] The evidence for this point remains anecdotal. In addition, in September 2019 there was a legal challenge to the entire pension system based precisely on the property rights over the accumulated resources (CNN-Chile 2019). The Appellate Court of Antofagasta on its decision of a Recourse of Protection (Rol N° 2797-2019) accepted the challenge where the claimant argued that her last income before retirement was CLP 1,200,000, while her pension was only CLP 185,000. Such discrepancy led her to ask for the totality of her balance held by the AFP on the basis of her property rights over such resources because she needed them to pay her mortgage, which she could not otherwise continue to service. The Appellate Court asked the Constitutional Court to rule on the matter, who ruled later in December of that year that the property rights over the balance of each pension accounts are limited and therefore could not be used to other ends different than paying pensions. However, in July 2020 the Chamber of Deputies, in response to the crisis the pandemic created, changed the Constitution authorizing the withdrawal of up to 10% of the individual accounts in a time window of one year after the reform (Superintendencia de Pensiones - República de Chile 2020).

[35] The Recognition Bond is a one-time deposit made by the state to the pension account of each worker who contributed to the former system.

[36] Gonzalo Cid. Interview with the author. Santiago. August 1, 2014. Cid was Head of the Pension Studies Directorate within the Chilean Ministry of Labor (2014–2018).

Nevertheless, the reforms enacted during the 2000s were indeed intended to improve the performance of the system. In 2002, the multi-fund reform was meant to improve returns on investments. The 2008 reform had a broader scope, as it created a subsystem that guaranteed a minimal pension for the poorest 60% of the population, but the commission in charge of evaluating proposals was supposed to focus on improving personal savings accounts, not replacing them (Iglesias-Palau 2009, 55). Indeed, this motivation accounts for the scope of that reform, as it hoped to enhance the performance of the system, even for those who might have stayed out of it. The 2008 reform also introduced a bid for new entrants, as yet another way to reduce costs and improve performance.

Despite all of these good intentions, however, other interests benefitted from the system beyond simply the fund administrators, who of course had expected to profit. Not the least, many workers are now accustomed to knowing how much their pensions will grow, and are not prepared to give up this certainty. In an effort to accommodate key interests and avoiding further confrontation, the transformation of the system has occurred through incremental changes, mainly in the regulatory sphere, but also in its general architecture, as in the two reforms proposed during Michelle Bachelet's administrations, in 2008 and 2014.[37] While criticisms remain with regard to its scope,[38] the 2008 reform is considered quite important and the discussions leading to its enactment are considered groundbreaking in a democratic context, since previous reforms of this magnitude occurred only under military rule (Arenas-de-Mesa 2010; Marcel 2012). The pension system will continue to be on the agenda because it is a politically salient subject.

Before that, he was the Head of the Pension Unit of *Centro de Estudios Nacionales de Desarrollo Alternativo*—CENDA (Center for National Studies on Alternative Development), a Chilean think-tank at the left of the political spectrum. CENDA is part of what is known in Chile as the extra-parliamentarian left, which seeks through its policy propositions a replacement of the Chilean democracy-market model, and therefore does not participate in the marketplace of ideas on Chilean policy and is not recognized as legitimate by other think-tanks (Gárate 2012, 476).

[37] The latter was never enacted (Borzutzky 2019).

[38] Carlos Ominami. Interview with the author. Santiago. August 12, 2014. Ominami was Minister of the Economy (1990–1992) during the government of Patricio Aylwin and was elected Senator in 1993 and reelected until 2009. He participated in the transition team from the military government to the democratically elected government.

5.2 Financial System Reform

The main feature of the Chilean financial system in the middle of the twentieth century was the struggle against inflation. Policymakers also delved into industrialization and external restrictions. These were all related, because the fluctuation in the prices of exports caused shortages of hard currency, which increased inflation (Fajardo 2015). However, domestic policy also contributed to inflationary problems. In practice, the Central Bank funded both the public sector, through direct transfers to the Treasury, and commercial banks, through a complex scheme of compulsory deposits and rediscounted instruments. This was a functional arrangement for both the state and several sectors of society; the members of the Bank's Board of Directors reflected these sectors, including bankers, workers, and members of Congress.

The public sector was the main user of credit, financing a chronic fiscal deficit using the inflationary tax. The creation of a Unitary Fiscal Account in the Bank of the State, through which all public institutions had to administer their resources, only further increased the Treasury's grasp on financial resources (Ffrench-Davis 1973, 131). The public sector was also a key factor in the segmentation of financial markets, despite the efforts represented by the merger of several retail operations of public institutions into the Bank of the State in 1953. Banking regulations were differentiated according to region in Santiago and Valparaiso, and throughout the rest of Chile. On the other side of the question of segmentation, however, was the fact that the banking industry was fairly concentrated, with two big private banks accounting for the bulk of credit operations in the private sector.

Legal reserves financed the operations of big enterprises that had access to credit—which other actors, such as small enterprises, did not have. Public development banks were important for industrial activity, agriculture, and housing; each of these sectors had a dedicated institution. Private banking focused on lending to big companies, although high inflation represented a serious challenge given the possibility of negative real interest rates. This was a consequence of the legal limit on interest rates, which had been intended to help borrowers, by offering low interest rates (Fontaine 1996, 23). The authorities in charge of different sectorial banks allocated the remaining credit (Fontaine 1996, 24). Because inflation was higher than interest rates, people with access to credit were subsidized and savers lost in real terms.

With high inflation, there were not enough ways to preserve the value of assets. Holding foreign currency was also unavailable. In the early 1960s, Chileans who held non-declared assets abroad had the opportunity to repatriate them. Authorities allowed such assets to be held in dollar-denominated accounts in Chilean banks (Ffrench-Davis 1973, 129–130). However, this proved to be a weaker incentive than tightly controlled interest rates. Except for foreign trade, commercial operations in American dollars were strictly forbidden, fostering a peer-to-peer credit market in which companies were the main creditors of their clients (Fontaine 1996, 24).

The issuance of inflation-protected bonds aimed at developing long- and medium-term financing for affordable housing and agricultural loans established indexation. This was also, in part, a response to the crowding out of most borrowers. Some privileged employees enjoyed access to mortgages and loans that were effectively subsidized by the social security system, which was the main provider of such loans. Indexation was supposed to protect savers and, ultimately, to encourage the accumulation of assets, but it could only go so far; since real interest rates were not high enough, savings did not increase (Jud 1978, 69–90). When mortgage operations were introduced by the Bank of the State following its creation in 1953, they became increasingly important for the circulation of the economy's savings, without necessarily implying significant changes.

Savings and loan associations, together forming the *Sistema Nacional de Ahorro y Préstamo*—SINAP (National System of Savings and Loans), were authorized to offer mortgages, because commercial banks lost the authorization to operate this market. In 1964, these associations were also authorized to take deposits from the public. These deposits offered higher liquidity than other instruments in the financial system, increasing deposits in the SINAP more than six-fold in five years. In fact, the SINAP represented almost 20% of all deposits in 1970 (Valdés 1993, 408–410). Between 1930 and 1970, the government increasingly became not only the regulator of the financial system, but its main player.

Between 1970 and 1973, the government virtually crowded out private institutions. Through takeovers of commercial banks, the government nationalized the banking sector, using different instruments to allocate resources depending on the established priorities (Valdés 1993, 411). In

1970, the *Corporación de Fomento de la Producción*—CORFO (Production Development Corporation),[39] a development bank, represented almost three quarters (73%) of the total credit of the economy (Valdés 1993, 410–411) and was the preferred instrument for the nationalization of commercial banks (Held 1990, 176–177). This represented one aspect of the state's increasingly important role in productive activities. Being responsible for a bigger portion of production, it also controlled this sector's financial means. The nationalization of almost the entire banking system during Allende's government represented a departure from traditional Chilean policies—that is, from tightly controlled credit allocation by the Central Bank. But during the 1970s, in less than a decade, the Chilean financial system would swing from this extreme to one where credit allocation was decided entirely by market mechanisms.

After it took power, the military government quickly privatized the previously nationalized banks, as well as other nationalized companies.[40] However, consistent with its role in other arenas, the state continued to participate in the financial industry through a retail bank, the Bank of the State, and a downsized CORFO.[41] Further changes in the financial system reversed the policies of the deposed government, lifting caps in legal interest rates and ending market segmentation. Through competition among providers, the market shaped the Chilean financial system after liberalization in 1974–1975. That said, despite the expansion of competition, regulations to control and manage risks continued to be the same. These regulations and financial provisions—available in the event of an increase in non-performing loans—were conditioned to an over-controlled banking system, while actual practices suddenly became those of a free market.

This lack of correspondence between practices and regulations imposed risks on financial intermediation, and economic agents responded with

[39] The state had been increasing its presence in the economy ever since the Great Depression with organizations such as CORFO, which served as a holding for several state-owned enterprises (Lüders 1993, 138–144). Mainly through CORFO, the Allende administration nationalized 500 medium- and large-sized firms (Chumacero et al. 2007, 97).

[40] Schamis (1992) provides a broad political perspective on privatization in the Chilean and international contexts.

[41] The state retained ownership in strategic sectors, namely mining, with *Corporación del Cobre de Chile*—CODELCO, the national copper mining company, and the *Empresa Nacional de Petróleo*—ENAP, the national oil company (Lüders 1993, 149).

confusion and lack of coordination (de-la-Cuadra and Valdés 1992). Financial liberalization also had unintended consequences for state's finances. The government had to backtrack many of its changes to the financial markets, such as quantitative credit controls and part of the market fragmentation. As well, a drastic decrease in inflation and in the price of copper affected the government's finances. In an inflationary economy where indexation is fairly well developed, as Chile's was in the 1970s (Jud 1978), inflation is the government's main source of revenue.[42] Since the state had controlled the financial system for several years, its finances depended in part on these instruments, which had disappeared with liberalization.

Also, given the liberalization of credit, consumers were eager to take out loans so that they could access consumer goods that had not been available before.[43] The swift change from tight controls to their near-complete withdrawal reveals the support for market reforms, both on the part of state officials and that of market operators. The former took a hands-off approach, however, and the latter did not properly evaluate the risks of the loans granted. Authorities had planned to promote the financial intermediation market through privatization and the end of market fragmentation. Because the financial system regulation was implemented through a wide range of instruments, there was a lack of coordination among them, and this complicated the liberalization process. The first stages of liberalization, between 1974 and 1977, revealed that some measures had not been part of a carefully thought-out plan; instead, many changes were muddled through as challenges surfaced.

If enthusiasm about market reforms was widespread among authorities and market operators alike, lack of experience with an unregulated environment was also universal. Regulators, bankers, and the general public all made serious mistakes during the deregulating process that exacerbated the intrinsic risks associated with banking. The bankruptcy of *Banco Osorno y La Unión*, a middle-sized bank, and the way in which it was handled by the authorities, was a landmark event in the course

[42] Indexation prevents the deleterious consequences in terms of revenue of the Oliveira-Tanzi effect. This effect appears when the real value of the collected tax disappears between the moment in which the tax is incurred and the moment it is paid. Bacha (1994) discusses how inflation can be central to governmental finances, albeit focused on the Brazilian hyperinflation of the 1980s and 1990s.

[43] This paragraph relies on Valdés (1993, 412–420).

of the Chilean banking crisis.[44] However, other events in those years also signaled serious problems in the financial system (Barandiarán and Hernández 1999, 8; de-la-Cuadra and Valdés 1992, 46–67; Harberger 1985, 453–454; Larraín 1989, 10). Besides the concerns in the domestic financial market, by the end of the decade, a fixed exchange rate had added yet another factor of instability to the balance sheets of several banks and other financial institutions.

In June 1979, the government committed to a fixed exchange rate. However, neither interest rates nor inflation aligned with international levels, which exacerbated Chilean external disequilibria. Interest rates were affected by the US Federal Reserve policy against inflation. Companies at the time paid real interest rates, ranging from 11 to 57% on 30-day loans (Chumacero et al. 2007, 122). The external disequilibria, forced the government to depreciate the peso in June 1982, which started a long trend of currency depreciation (Carrasco 2001, 403–407). Because many companies, including banks, were heavily leveraged in dollars, the devaluation hit them especially hard.[45] Moreover, related loans were prominent in bank portfolios, and such loans became difficult to execute (de-la-Cuadra and Valdés 1992, 41–45; Edwards and Edwards 1987, 60–62). By 1981–1982, the crisis was serious enough to require a full intervention.

Authorities debated about the best course of action to pursue. The first possibility was to let banks go bankrupt, which would have involved political costs, given the lost deposits. The second possibility was for the state to take over the banks as lender of last resort, and to absorb the cost of bailing out the failed banks. The third possibility was a compromise in which the state would intervene the banks, but make the shareholders and taxpayers pay for the intervention. This option did not receive a consensus among authorities. The events surrounding the banking crisis had significant political consequences. Politically, the banking crisis put an end to

[44] This bail-out operation signaled an implicit unlimited warranty over deposits by the government. This, in turn, led actors to engage in riskier practices.

[45] Quantitative restrictions to external indebtedness of commercial banks were gradually lifted between 1975 and 1979, without fundamentally changing the exchange regulations that had been in place since the early 1960s. However, between June 1979 and April 1980, these were lifted completely without changing the destination of such operations, that is, foreign trade loans or domestic dollar-denominated loans. Therefore, access to foreign currency was artificially restricted, giving the banks some rents over these assets, which were taken advantage of by their controllers through related loans, giving them in turn a lower interest rate (Fontaine 1996, 66).

the hegemony of the liberal economists who had taken over economic policy in 1975. Santiago de Castro, Minister of Finance and one of the leaders of that group, lost his post to Hernán Büchi, who was a milder liberal economist; he brought a more pragmatic approach to economic policy.

It is interesting to observe how the balance of power, as well as the dominant economic point of view, changed over a short period of time. The bailout of the *Banco Osorno y la Unión* in the late 1970s was comprehensive because authorities thought that this type of bankruptcy would deal a blow to the reforms that were underway at the time. It was seen as a compromise between the free-market policies and the intervention that was needed to save those policies.[46] Nevertheless, because such interventions were among the main causes of the banking crisis in early 1980s,[47] and in part due to the pressure on the government to change, there was a shift in the attitude of the economic team. During the 1980s crisis itself, the choice to bail out the banks while making shareholders and managers pay for some of the burden of the crisis represented a more complex compromise. It implied a thorough intervention in the banking system through which the state took over the management, meaning that a shift had occurred from a non-interventionist vision toward a more pragmatic one.

This intervention implied the takeover of several large financial institutions and the forced liquidation of various small ones; a third group was neither taken over nor liquidated, but received public support (Fontaine 1996, 56). This represented a departure from the official policy[48] and led

[46] This move seemed to be an easy compromise, since other liberalizing reforms, such as trade liberalization, were being implemented simultaneously. Thus, avoiding the bankruptcy, through a thorough intervention in the middle of a broader liberalizing process, was a small price to pay to save policies that were high among policymakers' priorities. Valdés (1993, 422–427) offers details concerning the bankruptcy of the *Banco Osorno y la Unión* and of other financial institutions.

[47] The bailout created a moral hazard, because actors considered that there was no limit in the guarantee provided by economic authorities of savings in the financial system, thus leading numerous actors to take bigger risks. The weak position in which financial companies were in the early 1980s was among the reasons for the banking crisis.

[48] The government implemented other changes in economic policy, including a less radical view about the role of the state in the economy (Ffrench-Davis 2014, 210–213). Silva (1996) and Schurman (1996) discuss how the Chilean state played an important role in strengthening sectors and supporting entrepreneurs.

to the creation of what came to be known as the "odd sector." These banks were privately owned in legal terms, but the government nominated the managers that administered them (Chumacero et al. 2007, 131). The government also took other actions to resolve the financial crisis, including the nationalization of foreign debt, the rescheduling of several loans, and the provision of a subsidized exchange rate for indebted companies. All of these interventions represented substantial costs, in both financial and human resources, for the state and the Central Bank (de-la-Cuadra and Valdés 1992).

The decision to save the banks also had implications outside the financial sector. When the pension system was launched, some of the investments were channeled through the banking system. If several banks had filed for bankruptcy during the crisis, the pension reform would have been aborted (Chumacero et al. 2007, 124). This would have implied yet another political cost, when the country had already been hit by recession. The situation allowed space for political dissent from actors who capitalized on the economic slowdown to mobilize the population against the military regime (Silva 2009, 166). While traditional accounts of the association between the new pension regime and the financial sector emphasize its importance for the Chilean economy, the first instance of this relationship was in fact fundamentally political.

Because the liberalization process created significant problems for the economy, it raised questions about the proper sequence in which reforms should be implemented (Fontaine 1996, 83–85). But more than just that, this situation reveals how economic policies affect one another. Beyond technical connections among policy spheres, including the idea of a proper way to liberalize, the main concern is political: solving the crises required a great number of political compromises, and so did liberalization. Whether the economic costs of one reform path were higher than those of another was less important than the overall political costs. Thus, the relationship between the banking and the pension systems shows how failure to save the financial system and, by extension, the pension system could have led to insurmountable obstacles for the military's political project.

In the worst moment of the crisis, January 1983, a major intervention in a substantial part of the financial system was required. At this point, authorities modified the banking law and related regulations.[49] They reinforced the authority of the *Superintendencia de Bancos e Instituciones Financieras*—SBIF (Superintendency of Banks and Financial Institutions) so that it could handle similar crises while reducing possible future costs to the state. A combination of interbank negotiations and prudential regulations was formalized so as to limit state intervention. But the Banking Act of 1986 (No 18576 of November 27, 1986) granted extensive powers to the SBIF, allowing it to render public the relevant information of its supervised institutions, among other competencies (Ramírez and Rosende 1992). Despite efforts to reassure agents about the soundness of the financial system, in 1986, the outlook was less than promising (Edwards and Edwards 1987, 207).

In the mid-1980s, there was a new initiative to privatize recently bailed-out banks. This time, it was characterized in part by "popular capitalism," which involved the extension of governmental soft loans (Chumacero et al. 2007, 123). In subsequent years, the financial sector deepened and a securities market was created. Such developments were markedly influenced by the crisis. For instance, a bank-based financial system was stabilized (Ramírez and Rosende 1992, 213–216), even as, simultaneously, different types of securities became available, marking a movement toward a capital-market financial system. Since the companies listed in the local stock exchange (*Bolsa de Comercio de Santiago*) were only those large enterprises that would have been able to finance their operations through traditional credits, capital markets focused on public bonds. However, the rise of corporate and mortgage bonds also represented a modest increase from 1.5 to 4.5% of GDP in corporate bonds during the second half of the 1980s (Stallings 2006, 158; Table 6.3).

The new democratic authorities in this period demonstrated their commitment to upholding a sound economic policy. Liberalizing the capital account involved a series of considerations. First, in the early 1990s, the presence of institutional investors, mainly AFPs, in the domestic capital markets grew steadily; second, faster economic growth

[49] In June 1982, the government allowed a devaluation of the Chilean Peso by 14% and subsequently its flotation in July, thus creating an exchange crisis. With the banking crisis reaching its peak in January 1983, alongside the major intervention in the system, Chile found itself with "twin crises." The term "twin crises" is used when a banking crisis takes place at the same time as a balance of payments crisis (Diaz-Alejandro 1985; Kaminsky and Reinhart 1999).

demanded an increase in long-term securities, even though domestic capital markets were not prepared for the amount of available resources that would be required.[50] Changes in the financial market regulation were necessary to cope with these trends. Authorities were fully aware of the importance of taking new measures in order to better organize capital markets; this would also support Chile's increasing presence within the world economy (Foxley 1991, 17). Moreover, given the Chilean government's desire to return to voluntary international debt markets, policy measures in line with the opening of the capital account were also necessary (Foxley 1992, 52).

In principle, portfolio diversification was a wise approach for institutional investors such as AFPs. However, due to the appreciation of the Chilean peso, there was little incentive for this course of action, as it would likely generate losses. This was the case until 1997, when the AFPs had only invested 0.5% of their resources abroad (Ffrench-Davis 2014, 358–359). That said, the amount of resources handled by AFPs had increased steadily, so that even such a modest fraction could well represent macro-economically significant resources. Therefore, even if the authorization to invest in foreign markets seemed to be in order, it turned out to be only a small escape valve at the time of implementation.

Since then, several efforts have been made to improve the performance of capital markets, with different reforms aiming to deepen it and to improve accessibility and stability.[51] Moreover, general stability and risk management in the traditional banking system continue to be a top priority for authorities, which only further illustrates the profound scars left by the financial crises of the late 1970s and early 1980s. Meanwhile, risk management has evolved toward prudential regulation, implying marginal increases in the risk of financial institutions.

The development of the financial sector and the creation of institutional investors, of which AFPs are the most significant, happened simultaneously. A causal argument exists in both directions. Whether the financial sector flourished *because of* the presence of institutional investors, or whether institutional investors flourished *because of* the development of the financial sector, remains unclear. In any case, the

[50] In the late 1980s, the market was starting to saturate with the volume of resources managed by the AFPs (Pérez 1988).

[51] Acts 19768 and 19769 enacted on October 24, 2001, 20190 enacted in June 5, 2007, 20448 enacted on August 16, 2010, and 21130 enacted on January 12, 2019.

Chilean financial sector is still largely bank-based, since businesses depend mostly on bank loans to finance their operations (Biron, Córdova, and Lemus 2019, 5). Capital markets continue to be restricted to the biggest companies in the country, partly because of the administrative costs involved in participating. This situation exists, in some ways, because banking sector reforms were driven mainly by the consequences of the events of the early 1980s. These were successful in organizing and stabilizing financial intermediation while, at the same time, making a transition toward prudential regulation.[52] These successive reforms of capital markets also opened a space for a more systematic use of the available resources in the hands of institutional investors.

Financial regulation in Chile is not detached from broader international trends. Even an indigenous banking crisis, and the preoccupations it might have produced, would not have been enough to isolate the regulatory behavior of Chilean authorities. Further regulations have taken into account international regulatory frameworks (Matte 2017, 48). For instance, the new General Banking Act, enacted in 2019, strengthened supervisory institutions, banking solvency standards, and provisions for crisis resolution (Berstein and Marcel 2019, 29–32). After over four decades of the financial crisis, financial regulation has kept up with new challenges by implementing incremental reforms that each addressed a different regulatory issue.

5.3 Continuous Struggle and Unease

The connection between the financial system and the pension system has been a matter of debate for some time. There are many questions about how actors evaluate both the reforms themselves and their consequences. This section of the chapter will focus on the moments when the connection between the two systems helped to consolidate economic governance. As in the cases discussed in previous chapters, here, the creation of complementary institutions fosters a stronger connection between the two systems. In Chile, however, a key part of the mechanism of complementarity identified earlier—that is, a common interpretation of critical situations—has been difficult to achieve. In a polarized polity, what constitutes a crisis depends on the political position of the actor.

[52] For details on prudential regulation and its variants, see Brunnermeier et al. (2009).

Below, in chronological order, I present the development of this impasse, describe the context within which policy actors made their choices, and consider how these initial decisions inspired subsequent reforms.

In this case, institutional complementarity would exist if the resources accumulated in the individual-accounts pension system were used to deepen the Chilean capital markets. In return, deep capital markets would allow for the pension system to offer pensions that preserve, to a reasonable extent, the living standards of the retirees. Given the thorough transformations that such reforms would imply and the vested interests that they would question, a consolidation of economic governance would engender politico-economic stability insofar as complementary institutions would not be contested. However, the successive reforms to Chilean pensions indicate the ongoing dissatisfaction of many actors with the results of the pension system, which has prevented the consolidation of a new pattern of economic governance more broadly. This issue points to the political, as opposed to the technocratic, dimension of economic governance insofar as the system, despite numerous reforms implemented over the years, has been repeatedly questioned.

Given the traumatic events that occurred in Chile throughout the 1970s and early 1980s, a mutual interpretation of new critical situations was elusive, and as noted above, this affected the consolidation of economic governance.[53] The early connection between the financial system and the pension system is a precedent for the phenomena explained here. At the time of the pension reform, there were not enough financial instruments in which to invest the monthly contributions of affiliated workers, but bank deposits were one of the authorized options. These resulted in significant resources within the financial system, amounting to 7.7% of Chilean financial assets at the end of 1982 (Arellano 1985a, 734). For the AFPs, bank deposits represented 73.39% of their assets at the end of 1982, just before the banking intervention (Table 5.1). When authorities decided to intervene in the financial system, the significant pension resources that would be lost if bank deposits disappeared with bankruptcy were among their key considerations (Chumacero et al. 2007, 124). After 1980, it was relatively clear that Pinochet would

[53] The list of complex policy legacies is a long one. In the political realm, it includes socialist and bureaucratic-authoritarian governments. In the economic realm, it includes widespread expropriation in the 1970s and an economic crisis that contracted GDP by almost 15% in 1982.

Table 5.1 Assets diversification of AFPs. 1981–1988 (%)

	Public institutions				*Private companies*			
	Central Bank	*Treasury*	*Other*	*Total*	*Financial institutions*	*Enterprises*	*Available assets*	*Total*
1981	95.53	2.43	0.00	97.96	0.00	2.04	0.00	100
1982	4.27	21.73	0.00	26.01	73.39	0.60	0.00	100
1983	14.07	30.40	0.00	44.47	53.37	2.17	0.00	100
1984	16.50	25.56	0.00	42.06	55.65	1.81	0.48	100
1985	20.29	22.14	0.00	42.44	55.97	1.11	0.48	100
1986	25.98	20.49	0.16	46.64	48.66	4.59	0.12	100
1987	29.71	11.60	0.05	41.36	49.44	8.82	0.38	100
1988	29.99	5.40	0.03	35.41	50.06	14.49	0.04	100

Percentages calculated as of December 31 of each year
Source Own elaboration with data from Carrasco (2001, 947–948)

remain in power for at least nine more years, which meant that the loss of pension resources would not affect the government as it would have in a democratic regime. However, aborting a pension reform on which they had invested considerable time and political capital would have ruined the reputation of a government that considered itself a modernizer.

By 1988, there were already some concerns over the consequences of the increasing resources administered by the AFPs. These concerns arose because once the system was in place, the severe regulations around how AFPs could invest had only gradually been lifted. Since the domestic market was already saturated, the financial risk associated with inappropriate asset diversification increased. One approach to risk diversification was to allow AFPs to invest abroad. This process, however, raised several conflicts, because it was not clear for some observers why the diversification should be exclusively external, or how this policy would affect workers' retirement. Nevertheless, if nothing was done, there would be other important risks in the mid-term. The domestic financial market was not able to supply enough instruments to meet the demand of the AFPs, and so there was a heightened risk that prices could increase artificially (Pérez 1988, 217). A price correction would, evidently, affect workers—although at that moment the situation was not yet critical. However, significant problems could appear within a timeframe of three to eleven years (Pérez 1988, 241). While one solution would be to allow the AFPs to invest in foreign markets, Chile still needed resources to pay back its external debt.[54]

In October 1988, the country held a plebiscite with the aim of reaffirming Pinochet's mandate, as established in the Constitution written by the regime in 1980.[55] For the regime, it was simply to be another rubber-stamping instance, like the plebiscites of 1978 and 1980, meant to extend the military government for another eight years. However, against all expectations, the plebiscite resulted in a landslide victory for the "No" side, putting an end to the military government. Throughout the negotiations concerning the transition, both through institutional and informal channels, the military and their allies propagated the view that their counterparts represented a danger to the country, because of their intention to return to policies resembling Allende's. The military government therefore enacted a series of "Tying Acts" (*Leyes de Amarre*), mainly involving civilian-military relations, which institutionalized authoritarian enclaves (Garretón 1989, 51–63), and somehow, surprisingly, also granted independence to the Central Bank.[56]

The main reason that authoritarian elites shielded their cherished policies from any possible reform was, of course, to avoid any changes that the opposition might institute once in power. This was certainly the case with the independence of the Central Bank, the only economic law included within the Tying Acts (Boylan 2001). The absence of any mention of the pension system or the financial system in these provisions can be attributed to at least two factors: first, the perceived institutional consolidation of the two policy arenas by the authoritarian elites, and second,

[54] José Pablo Arellano. Interview with the author. Santiago. August 8, 2014. Arellano was Head of Diprés (National Budget Directorate) (1990–1996) and Minister of Education (1996–2000). He was a prominent member of the *Corporación de Investigaciones Económicas para América Latina*—CIEPLAN (Corporation of Economic Research for Latin America) from its foundation in 1976 onwards, where he has served in several senior positions.

[55] This paragraph relies heavily on Valenzuela (1997).

[56] These acts regulated: (1) The suspension of possible inquiries by the Chamber of Deputies of any military or public servant of the military government; (2) A freeze of the civil service, which restrained the available nominations for the incoming president to 400, from a peak of 30,000; (3) Central Bank independence; (4) A law about municipalities, in which Pinochet would nominate council members responsible for subsequent mayoral nominations; (5) Regulation of the Judiciary, allowing for the nomination of a favorable Supreme Court; (6) Civilian-military relations; and (7) An electoral law establishing the binomial system (Valenzuela 1997, 35–37).

their mild importance, in the eyes of the opposition, in determining civilian-military relations or the organization of the Judiciary. Between the plebiscite of October 1988 and the inauguration of Patricio Aylwin in March 1990, a heavily charged discourse dominated political debates, indicating that the military might well return to power if they considered it necessary (Valenzuela 1997, 32–34).

Even before it became clear that the military would no longer remain in power, the opposition started to use the same kind of language as the government's technocrats. This was actually a way to stand up to the government, because it meant that the opposition's language could not be dismissed as non-technical, but rather accepted as equivalent to the government's own discourse (Silva 2009, 167ff).[57] However, the opposition's main priority was the consolidation of suitable conditions for the successful transition to democracy, such as strong civilian-military relations and the protection of human rights. In the context of a transition that was highly contentious, if not violent, it was important to choose one's battles carefully. But as a result, the whole heritage of the authoritarian regime, including the new pension system, was barely questioned at all.

Indeed, reforms were considered a topic that should be broached only with great caution. To the leadership of the opposition,[58] the experience of Raúl Alfonsín in Argentina was to be avoided at all costs. His remarkable political reforms did not prevent the catastrophic mismanagement of the economy, which in turn had consequences for the government that followed. The lesson, then, was to conduct political reforms with the above-mentioned priorities while leaving the economy to keep working as best it could; this, the opposition hoped, would prevent supporters of the authoritarian regime from arguing for or attempting a reversal of the political transition.[59] To be sure, the opposition—which would later form

[57] This was the strategy of CIEPLAN from the mid-1970s; since its members' academic credentials were impeccable, and very similar to those of technocrats at the time, they could not be dismissed (Kinney 1997, 237). In the last years of the military government, this continued to be the case. Puryear (1994) analyzes the role of intellectuals in the opposition to the military government and subsequent transition to democracy.

[58] While only Carlos Ominami, Minister of Economy (1990–1992) of the Alwyn government (1990–1994), was interviewed by the author, he consistently referred to the opposition as a group during the interview.

[59] Carlos Ominami. Interview with the author. Santiago. August 12, 2014.

the *Concertación*—was critical of many reforms enacted by the authoritarian government, but they were also conscious of the need to keep most of them in the name of democratic consolidation.

During the transition to democratic rule, whenever a policy contrary to their priorities (loosely defined) was suggested, the military threatened to intervene. Despite the fact that not every threat from the deep core of the military regime was taken seriously (Valenzuela 1997, 34–35), it was clear that policymaking had to be conducted carefully, and reforms had to be subordinate to the survival of the transition. Not only were many aspects of the authoritarian regime's legacy left unquestioned, then, but some were actually enhanced, in an effort not to create any political reasons for military intervention. These reasons could stem from political issues, such as the privatization of banks, or from economic issues, such as the liberalization of the capital account. In any event, radically different views about the political situation during the transition meant that any common interpretation of critical situations would be elusive, and the possibility of consolidating economic governance would thus remain distant. Authoritarian elites thought that a return to the 1970s was imminent, and the democratic forces wanted to avoid a confrontation that could justify, in authoritarians' view, a new intervention.

By the time the military government was defeated, the pension system had accumulated significant resources that were saturating the domestic financial market. As mentioned earlier, one solution to this saturation was to open the capital account and authorize AFPs to invest abroad. As the first democratic government settled in, the threat of a reversal to authoritarian rule was moderate, and policy changes had to both preserve macroeconomic stability and foster growth. Opening the capital account in the first two years of the democratic government involved many considerations, including the benefits of returning to international debt markets and the need to prepare the country for a strong entry into the world economy (Foxley 1991, 17; 1992, 52). There was also the question of whether to allow AFPs to invest abroad, in order to diversify their portfolios. Thus, in the face of a credible menace to political-economic stability, agents pushed for a reform that would foster complementarity among institutions.

Gradually, a consensus emerged among Chilean elites about the general direction that economic policy should take. Growth with equity was the official strategy. It allowed for some continuity with the economic policy of the authoritarian regime, focusing on growth, while simultaneously emphasizing an area in which the regime had clearly underperformed. In other words, social policies, which were considered the main instrument for increasing equity, changed significantly, but they were always carefully subordinated to policies allowing for the maintenance of growth. Authorities preferred instruments that would not create inefficiencies affecting growth; the scope of social policies had to be in line with what public finances could handle, and also had to have some assurance of macroeconomic stability, as a way to guarantee their persistence in the long term (Arellano 2012, 11).

Two particular traits concerning the pension system and the Chilean economy materialized in the first half of the 1990s. From a political perspective, the new pension system was not questioned because it was broadly considered a positive legacy of the dictatorship, and thus had to be carefully handled. Moreover, as there were more pressing challenges and the available information about the general operation of the system was limited at best, since it had only been recently enacted, it was not considered an important subject.[60] From an economic perspective, the costs were carried out through a significant fiscal effort, in which the public sector increased its savings in order to pay off the debts that had been contracted years before (Bennett, Schmidt-Hebbel, and Soto 1999, 49). National statistics do not include data specifically focused on the transitional period between the PAYG system and the new system, but the official responsible for the budget was conscious of the transfers that fiscal surpluses implied, given the composition of the debt.[61]

In subsequent years, the political salience of these two traits would shift strikingly. Whereas the fiscal cost of the transition started to decrease,[62] political debate about the system intensified. By the end of the 1990s, there was far more evidence about the failures than the successes of the system, because the accumulated individual savings had not met expectations. Conversely, the democratic transition was more consolidated than many had predicted, as Pinochet was no longer Chief Commander of the army (1998) and the *Concertación* had, as presidential candidate, a member of the Socialist Party, Ricardo Lagos. These conditions

[60] Carlos Ominami. Interview with the author. Santiago. August 12, 2014.

[61] José Pablo Arellano. Interview with the author. Santiago. August 8, 2014.

[62] Joaquín Vial. Interview with the author. Santiago. August 5, 2014.

allowed for a broader discussion about the system that would eventually materialize through a series of reforms that took place in the 2000s.

Those in favor of the new pension system argued that it would hold increased aggregate savings (Schmidt-Hebbel 1997), following the position taken by then Minister of Labor José Piñera when the system started (Piñera 1988a). This implies that, presumably, the resources accumulated by the AFPs over the years were available for economic agents to use, which would turn AFPs one of the engines of Chilean growth (Corbo and Schmidt-Hebbel 2003). This fact, however, should be taken with a grain of salt: even if such resources were now available, they had not come from nowhere. In fact, while funds administered by the AFPs grew in the first years of the system, some other sectors—such as the public sector—saw their available resources diminish (Arellano 1988, 137).

In the mid-1990s, several critical events took place. After the end of the first term of the *Concertación* in 1994, the disastrous scenarios predicted by the military authorities at the end of their reign failed to materialize. Instead, the *Concertación* implemented an economic policy that respected the basic lines established during the second half of the military regime, that is, market economy only intervened pragmatically when necessary. After several years, during which neither economic nor political chaos took place, the clout of the hard-liners waned along with the plausibility of their predictions. In the economic arena, the Southeast Asian financial crisis (1996–1997) increased the risk aversion of financial markets, thus bringing to a halt the consolidation of Chilean capital markets. Given the scale and impact of the crises not only in Southeast Asia but also in Mexico (1994–1995), Chilean economic authorities tried to regulate the influx of foreign capital to the domestic market. Meanwhile, the pension system was openly criticized in the wake of the sales war among AFPs, forcing authorities to intervene.[63] The deepest concerns about political-economic stability were now absent and there was no longer any direct political threat, but partly for this very reason—because of this firmer democratic structure—political questions about the

[63] In the mid-1990s, AFPs competed for new clients based on transfers of already affiliated workers, hence the increase in their sales force. However, this increased the costs of the AFPs and therefore decreased the return of workers' funds. Because this was a result of a loophole in the regulation authorizing unlimited transfers among AFPs, the response of the authorities was to restrict the possibility of transfers to very specific situations and to impose a series of relatively strict conditions (Berstein 2010, 136–137).

reforms began to arise. The supposed path leading to the interconnection between the pension system and the financial system, which in the eyes of supporters would fit the definition of an institutional complementarity, was no longer straightforward.

A notable implication of the regulation of the pension system is that every flaw is considered a market failure.[64] This is a result of the way in which the system has been understood—that is, as a market, which means that any problem it presents is a consequence of market failure. This approach, of course, did not prevent the appearance of new failures from time to time, and these were all subsequently tackled with new reforms. Following this reasoning, regulation can be considered a system of recurrent attempts to address market failures. Severe crises involving the loss of retirement savings or the misuse of funds were prevented. However, regulations consistently revealed the limits of the system and of the regulations themselves, since every new regulation would create unintended consequences requiring new regulations. Indeed, even when market solutions appeared to address the shortcomings of the system—for example, new providers to increase competition and decrease prices—the industry still opposed them fiercely (Borzutzky 2019, 221). The technocratic solutions that would improve the performance of the system are not accepted across the board—actors in both sides of the political spectrum have questioned them—signaling that these responses alone do not consolidate economic governance.

The interwoven operations of the AFPs and the financial market also started to show its limits by the middle of the 1990s. Institutional investors, which include AFPs, insurance companies, and mutual funds, were an important source of demand for corporate bonds and other kinds of long-term securities. The maturity of these instruments extended continuously, to the point that twenty-year maturities had become common by the middle of the 1990s (Cifuentes, Desormeaux, and González 2002, 96). The Central Bank was instrumental in this modification, as it issued bonds in both domestic and international markets in order to create a country benchmark, even if Chile had a long tradition

[64] Mas-Colell, Whinston, and Green (1995, 350) define market failures as "situations in which some of the assumptions of the welfare theorems do *not* hold and in which, as a consequence, market equilibria cannot be relied on to yield Pareto optimum outcomes" (italics in the original). That is, they are situations in which the market allocation of resources does not lead to the most efficient outcome, hence market *failure*.

of fiscal surplus. Such progress notwithstanding, this market was incapable of promoting a broad deepening of financial markets that would include smaller firms. Subsequent reforms did not significantly transform this situation.

The argument that a connection between the resources handled by AFPs and the development of capital markets creates a virtuous circle has been recurrent (Bril-Mascarenhas and Maillet 2019, 106–107). And developing a related argument about the existence of an institutional complementarity in this same setting is certainly tempting. But the measures intended to allow AFPs to invest their resources in foreign markets at the beginning of 1990s did not mean that the interested parties automatically took advantage of them. Similarly, capital market reforms created new investment opportunities for institutional investors—mainly AFPs, though not exclusively. In the late 1990s, the Asian crisis had an important effect on the market capitalization of Chilean stocks, and a debate quickly arose about exactly what had happened.[65] While the terms of that debate are beyond the scope of this discussion, it is clear that a steady provision of finances through AFPs does not guarantee that these resources will be used in productive activities.

Moreover, subsequent reforms that were intended to foster a closer link between the pension system and the financial system failed to interweave them effectively. The multi-fund reform of 2002 had the potential to deepen Chilean capital markets, since significant resources could have been invested with a diversified risk profile: the principal instrument of the reform intended to increase workers' retirement funds. However, the capital market peaked in the mid-1990s (Cifuentes, Desormeaux, and González 2002, 88–89), just before the Asian crisis, indicating that even although the multi-fund reform had certainly affected risk diversification, its impact was not enough to deepen the market further.[66]

[65] Cifuentes, Desormeaux, and González (2002) offer a detailed discussion of the causes of the market shrinkage in the mid-1990s.

[66] Braun and Briones (2008, 158–159) provide an explanation for the virtual oligopsony in the market for corporate bonds where AFPs and insurance companies account for 80–90% of the outstanding corporate bonds. Both AFPs and insurance companies are legally bound to buy securities rated above the BBB level, restricting the pool of successful issuers in the bond market. This insight also offers a possible explanation for the lack of consolidation of a deeper capital market despite the increasing availability (~70% GDP in November 2016) of resources administered by AFPs (Superintendencia de Pensiones - República de Chile 2016, 1). By definition, non-risky investments must be a small

Notably, neither economic nor political instability hung on the horizon, as had been the case in previous reforms, despite some political pressure to improve the functioning of the pension system in favor of the workers.

Another dimension that continues to be contentious in Chilean politics is the regulatory regime, since many actors question its parameters and the way in which it protects workers' interests. The group of AFPs has been able to prevent any major changes in the regulatory environment. Indeed, the manifestation of the industry's instrumental power has been key in maintaining favorable regulations, even in the face of the continuous discontent that the system elicits (Bril-Mascarenhas and Maillet 2019). Continuing the trend of attempting to solve market failures through regulation, the 2008 reform tackled an oligopoly through an inversed auction.[67] Since barriers to entry were high, this reform stated that the winner of the inversed auction would bring together all new entrants into the system for a two-year period, in an attempt to lower the system's average fee. Every two years, there would be a new auction to keep the fee down. However, there was an important caveat to this instrument. The system would soon arrive at a threshold, at which point it would start to pay pensions to the people who had been contributing since its inception. In order to pay these pensions, new costs would be added to the production function of the AFPs, thus reducing their profit margins. As a result, as long as the prices remained at a low threshold, the only way to profit would be by downgrading the quality of the AFPs' services.[68]

The 2008 and 2014 reforms to the pension system reveal how the complexity of gathering stable coalitions affects the consolidation of economic governance (Borzutzky 2019). Both reforms tried to enhance the individual accounts-based system, not to replace it. An attempt to replace it would have been political suicide for the two Bachelet governments (2006–2010, 2014–2018), since the system is considered one of

share of the whole pool of possible investments; therefore, AFPs would have a difficult time deepening capital markets so as to invest in smaller businesses, which are riskier. Otherwise, their investments would continue to be concentrated in the bigger, and less risky, companies.

[67] The inversed auction implies that the bidder with the lowest price will win the auction. In this case, the AFP offering the lowest fee will win the auction.

[68] Joaquín Vial. Interview with the author. Santiago. August 5, 2014.

the positive legacies of the military regime. Thus, in Chile, it is politically impossible to completely replace the individual accounts system. Yet incremental reforms also disappointed sectors that wanted to see the system replaced completely. This lack of consensus over the contours of the pension system contrasts with the more consolidated perspective that economic policy should focus on growth with equity.

The growth-with-equity strategy satisficed a broad part of Chilean society because it was devised as a compromise at a time when its elements were cast as contradictory; and yet it had to contain all of these diverse elements because it responded to numerous different social priorities. Meanwhile, on the pension front, such a compromise has been elusive so far, despite the institutional changes implemented during the 2000s, such as the multi-fund reform of 2002 and the introduction of the solidarity pillar in 2008. In this realm, stable compromises among coalitions that support opposing positions have been harder to obtain. Moreover, governance concerning this issue has not yet been consolidated, though it has inspired much political debate. Obviously, it does not help that the process of integration between capital markets and the pension system has plateaued.

The system causes unease partially because it reinforces inequalities, which raises questions about the effectiveness of the more consensual economic policy. Indeed, popular mobilizations in the late 2010s attest to this uneasiness (Araujo 2019; *Economist* 2016, 2019), showing that the population at large demands further changes to these arrangements.[69] Despite the consensus among the elites around the contours of economic governance, the same cannot be said about other sectors of society. Even if an authoritarian reversal is hard to imagine today, there are sectors of the population that consider problematic any significant departure from the status quo. Thus, I argue that in Chile economic governance is only partially consolidated despite the consensual strategy of creating growth while tackling inequality. The common interpretation that existed around economic policy did not extend to the pension system, and broader coalitions have been harder to assemble as a result. The institutional complementarity over which economic governance would stand, if it could, remains tentative and loosely built at best.

[69] As shown in footnote 34 above, people are finding ways of questioning the arrangements through both legal and political channels.

5.4 Conclusions

Whether the new pension system that replaced the old PAYG system was good for the country or not remains a contentious issue in Chilean politics. Answering this question is beyond the scope of this work. The matter at hand here is whether economic governance, broadly construed, is consolidated or not. The institutional reform of the new pension system and the debates that ensued indicate that it is only partially complementary to the financial system. And this incomplete institutional complementarity cannot truly buttress the new pattern of economic governance in Chile. As has been stressed several times above, it is a matter of open debate whether institutions that belong in the labor market are really used in complementary ways with other institutions from the financial market in order to create a virtuous circle of stability and growth. These debates around this issue show that there is as yet no consensus over the interpretation of institutional reforms: a fundamental component of the consolidation of economic governance.

Unequivocal evidence that the Chilean pension system fostered economic growth is scarce. Although there is some proof pointing in that direction, the limited number of pensions that the system actually pays should urge us to move carefully before drawing any conclusions. Had the system started to pay pensions in line with international standards, and had it helped the financial system to sustain some of its dynamism, an argument that it has contributed to fostering growth would be more convincing. But the system is perceived instead as reproducing the major inequalities in Chilean society; indeed, it prompted significant political mobilizations in 2019 (Andrade 2019). Regulation is seen as a way for the state to protect people from the uncertainties of the financial market, which exist due to its asymmetric information characteristics (Berstein and Chumacero 2003, 17–18), but it has failed to implement changes that would clearly improve the performance of such a market, such as more competition through a public AFP. Regulation does not fully address the system's inequality-reproducing biases.

Will these institutional reforms ever be able to buttress economic governance? The answer remains uncertain. If the response were affirmative, it would require that labor market savings (i.e., pensions) be part of a deep financial system of which enterprises can take advantage in order to finance their activities. This would have to be accomplished while paying the pensions—which is, after all, the main goal of the system.

This second condition does not yet exist, given that no pension depends entirely on the system. In 2020, at the time of writing, is not clear what the cash-flow profile of the system will be, since liabilities may still become as important as accumulated assets. Moreover, the pensions that the system currently pays still have as their main source the transitional transfers accrued when the old regime was closed to give way to the new one—Recognition Bonds—and thus new retirees are paid by the state. After forty years of existence, strangely, the pension system has not actually paid many pensions.[70] It is clear that these two systems have the potential to cohere as an example of institutional complementarity, but a double-decisive proof, in the sense of Collier (2011, 827–828), is not yet available.

Although many years have passed since the political and economic crises of the late twentieth century affected Chilean politico-economic stability, these events still play a role in everyday politics. Their influence has waned over the years, however, and is now much weaker than it was in the immediate aftermath of the transition to democracy, when an authoritarian reversal still seemed like a real possibility. The economic legacy of the authoritarian regime has been framed in a positive way, which in turn has empowered several associated interests, which has made the enactment of any significant changes to its landmark policies politically complicated. Nevertheless, many of these policies create uneasiness because they perpetuate a status quo that is perceived as unfair.[71] A broader consensus buttressing complementary institutions and a stable pattern of economic governance would be needed to address these concerns.

References

Andrade, Camila. 2019. "¿Cuánto más Soporta el Pilar Solidario? La Experiencia de la Vejez en el Chile Actual." In *Hilos Tensados. Para Leer el Octubre Chileno*, edited by Kathya Araujo, 217–242. Santiago: Colección IDEA/Editorial Usach.

[70] Gonzalo Cid. Interview with the author. Santiago. August 1, 2014.

[71] Mario Marcel, a prominent technocrat and current President of the Central Bank, said Chile "could become a country with a more solid and sustainable social contract that resolves the legacy issues [left by the Pinochet dictatorship]" (quoted in *Economist* 2020).

Araujo, Kathya, ed. 2019. *Hilos Tensados. Para Leer el Octubre Chileno*. Santiago: Colección IDEA/Editorial Usach.

Arellano, Jose Pablo. 1982. "Efectos Macroeconómicos de la Reforma Previsional Chilena." *Cuadernos de Economía* 19 (56): 111–122.

Arellano, Jose Pablo. 1985a. "De la Liberalización a la Intervención: El Mercado de Capitales en Chile 1974–1983." *El Trimestre Económico* 52 (207(3)): 721–772.

Arellano, Jose Pablo. 1985b. *Políticas Sociales y Desarrollo: Chile 1924–1984*. Santiago: CIEPLAN.

Arellano, Jose Pablo. 1988. "Una Mirada Crítica a la Reforma Previsional de 1981." In *Sistema Privado de Pensiones de Chile*, edited by Sergio Baeza and Rodrigo Manubens, 129–142. Santiago: Centro de Estudios Públicos.

Arellano, Jose Pablo. 2012. *Veinte Años de Políticas Sociales. Chile 1990–2009*. Santiago: CIEPLAN.

Arellano, Pablo. 2007. "Las AFP's No son un Producto de Exportación Verdaderamente Chileno." In *Working Paper*, edited by Associazione per gli Studi Internazionali e Comparati sul Diritto del lavoro e sulle Relazioni Industriali. Modena.

Arenas-de-Mesa, Alberto. 2000. "Cobertura Previsional en Chile: Lecciones y Desafíos del Sistema de Pensiones Administrado por el Sector Privado." In *Financiamiento del Desarrollo*. Santiago: CEPAL.

Arenas-de-Mesa, Alberto. 2010. *Historia de la Reforma Previsional Chilena. Una Experiencia Exitosa de Política Pública en Democracia*. Santiago: OIT.

Bacha, Edmar. 1994. "O Fisco e a Inflação: Uma Interpretação do Caso Brasileiro." *Revista de Economia Política* 14 (1(53)): 5–17.

Banco Central de Chile. 2020. "Tipo de Cambio Observado, Multilateral, Real e Índice de Precios Externos Relevantes" [Spreadsheet]. Banco Central de Chile, Last Modified February 29, 2020, accessed April 22, 2020. http://si3.bcentral.cl/estadisticas/Principal1/excel/EC/PARIDADES/xls/Tipo_cambio_Obs_Mult_Real_PrecExt.xls.

Barandiarán, Edgardo, and Leonardo Hernández. 1999. "Origins and Resolution of a Banking Crisis: Chile 1982–86." In *Documentos de Trabajo*, edited by Banco Central de Chile. Santiago.

Bennett, Herman, Klaus Schmidt-Hebbel, and Claudio Soto. 1999. "Series de Ahorro e Ingreso por Agente Económico en Chile 1960–1997." In *Documentos de Trabajo*, edited by Banco Central de Chile. Santiago.

Berstein, Solange. 2010. *El Sistema Chileno de Pensiones*. Edited by Superintendencia de Pensiones. Santiago.

Berstein, Solange, Pablo Castañeda, Eduardo Fajnzylber, and Gonzalo Reyes. 2009. *Chile 2008: Una Reforma Previsional de Segunda Generación*. Santiago: Superintendencia de Pensiones.

Berstein, Solange, and Rómulo Chumacero. 2003. "Quantifying the Costs of Investment Limits for Chilean Pension Funds." In *Documentos de Trabajo*, edited by Banco Central de Chile. Santiago.

Berstein, Solange, and Mario Marcel. 2019. "El Sistema Financiero en Chile: Lecciones de la Historia Reciente." In *Documentos de Política Económica*, edited by Banco Central de Chile. Santiago.

Berstein, Solange, and Alejandro Micco. 2002. "Turnover and Regulation: The Chilean Pension Fund Industry." In *Documentos de Trabajo*, edited by Banco Central de Chile. Santiago.

Biron, Miguel, Felipe Córdova, and Antonio Lemus. 2019. "Banks' Business Model and Credit Supply in Chile: The Role of a State-Owned Bank." In *Documento de Trabajo*. Santiago: Comisión para el Mercado Financiero.

Borzutzky, Silvia. 2019. "You Win Some, You Lose Some: Pension Reform in Bachelet's First and Second Administrations." *Journal of Politics in Latin America* 11 (2): 204–230. https://doi.org/10.1177/1866802x19861491.

Boylan, Delia M. 2001. *Defusing Democracy: Central Bank Autonomy and the Transition from Authoritarian Rule*. Ann Arbor: University of Michigan Press.

Braun, Matías, and Ignacio Briones. 2008. "Development of the Chilean Corporate Bond Market." In *Bond Markets in Latin America: On the Verge of a Big Bang?*, edited by Eduardo Borensztein, Kevin Cowan, Barry Eichengreen, and Ugo Panizza, 151–184. Cambridge, MA: MIT Press.

Bril-Mascarenhas, Tomás, and Antoine Maillet. 2019. "How to Build and Wield Business Power: The Political Economy of Pension Regulation in Chile, 1990–2018." *Latin American Politics and Society* 61 (1): 101–125. https://doi.org/10.1017/lap.2018.61.

Brunnermeier, Markus, Andrew Crocket, Charles Goodhart, Avinash D. Persaud, and Hyun Shin. 2009. *The Fundamental Principles of Financial Regulation*. Vol. 11, *Geneva Reports on the World Economy*. Geneva: International Center for Monetary and Banking Studies/Centre for Economic Policy Research.

Bustamante, Julio. 2006. "El Sistema de AFP: Su Aporte al Desarrollo Nacional." In *AFP: 25 Años. Un Modelo Exitoso*, edited by Mónica Titze, 63–80. Santiago: Fundación Libertad y Desarrollo.

Carrasco, Jorge. 2001. "Indicadores Económicos y Sociales de Chile 1960–2000." Banco Central de Chile, accessed July 16, 2020. https://www.bcentral.cl/documents/33528/133439/bcch_archivo_098139_es.pdf/9c630e90-825a-0e4a-1508-d215cd808413?t=1573279634953.

Cavallo, Ascanio. 1998. *Historia Oculta de la Transición*. Santiago: Editorial Grijalbo.

Chumacero, Rómulo, Rodrigo Fuentes, Rolf J. Lüders, and Joaquín Vial. 2007. "Understanding Chilean Reforms". In *Understanding Market Reforms in*

Latin America: Similar Reforms, Diverse Constituencies, Varied Results, edited by José María Fanelli, 94–134. Basingtoke: Palgrave Macmillan.

Cifuentes, Rodrigo, Jorge Desormeaux, and Claudio González. 2002. "Capital Markets in Chile: From Financial Repression to Financial Deepening." In *BIS papers*. Basel: BIS.

CNN-Chile. 2019. "TC acogió a trámite requerimiento por caso de profesora que quiere retirar ahorros de su AFP." Last Modified September 24, 2019, accessed September 15, 2020. https://www.cnnchile.com/pais/tc-acoge-tramite-requerimiento-profesora-ahorros-afp_20190924/.

Collier, David. 2011. "Understanding Process Tracing." *PS: Political Science & Politics* 44 (4): 823–830. https://doi.org/10.1017/s1049096511001429.

Corbo, Vittorio, and Klaus Schmidt-Hebbel. 2003. "Efectos Macroeconómicos de la Reforma de Pensiones en Chile." In *Resultados y Desafíos de las Reformas a las Pensiones*, 259–351. Santiago: Federación Internacional de Administradores de Fondos de Pensiones.

de-la-Cuadra, Sergio, and Salvador Valdés. 1992. "Myths and Facts About Financial Liberalization in Chile: 1974–1983." In *If Texas Were Chile: A Primer on Banking Reform*, edited by Philip L. Brock, 11–101. San Francisco: ICS Press.

Diaz-Alejandro, Carlos. 1985. "Good-bye Financial Repression, Hello Financial Crash." *Journal of Development Economics* 19 (1): 1–24. https://doi.org/10.1016/0304-3878(85)90036-7.

Economist. 2016. "The Perils of Not Saving." August 27.

Economist. 2019. "Piñera's Pickle." October 31.

Economist. 2020. "A Model Country in Need of Remodelling." March 12.

Edwards, Sebastian, and Alejandra Cox Edwards. 1987. *Monetarism and Liberalization: The Chilean Experiment*. Cambridge, MA: Ballinger Publishing Company.

Fajardo, Margarita. 2015. "The Latin American Experience with Development: Social Sciences, Economic Policies, and the Making of a Global Order, 1944–1971." PhD, Department of History, Princeton University.

Ffrench-Davis, Ricardo. 1973. *Políticas Económicas en Chile. 1952–1970*. Santiago: Centro de Estudios de Planificación Nacional/Ediciones Nueva Universidad-Universidad Católica de Chile.

Ffrench-Davis, Ricardo. 2014. *Chile entre el Neoliberalismo y el Crecimiento con Equidad. Cuarenta Años de Políticas Económicas y sus Lecciones para el Futuro*. 5th ed. Santiago: J.C. Sáez Editor. Original edition, 1999.

Fontaine, Juan Andrés. 1996. "La Construcción de un Mercado de Capital: El Caso de Chile." In *EDI Learning Resources Series*, edited by World-Bank. Washington.

Foxley, Alejandro. 1991. *Exposición sobre el Estado de la Hacienda Pública*. Edited by Ministerio de Hacienda. Santiago: Diprés.

Foxley, Alejandro. 1992. *Exposición sobre el Estado de la Hacienda Pública*. Edited by Ministerio de Hacienda. Santiago: Diprés.

Gárate, Manuel. 2012. *La Revolución Capitalista de Chile (1973–2003)*. Santiago: Ediciones Universidad Alberto Hurtado.

Garretón, Manuel Antonio. 1989. *La Posibilidad Democrática en Chile*. Santiago: FLACSO.

Harberger, Arnold C. 1985. "Observations on the Chilean Economy, 1973–1983." *Economic Development and Cultural Change* 33 (3): 451–462. https://doi.org/10.1086/451473.

Held, Günther. 1990. "Regulación y Supervisión de la Banca en la Experiencia de Liberalización Financiera en Chile (1974–1978)." In *Sistema Financiero y Asignación de Recursos. Experiencias Latinoamericanas y del Caribe. Colombia, Costa Rica, Chile, República Dominicana, Venezuela*, edited by Carlos Massad and Günther Held, 167–262. Buenos Aires: GEL.

Hepp, Margarita. 1980. *El Antiguo Sistema Previsional: Cómo era y a Dónde iba*. Edited by Ministerio de Hacienda. Santiago: Ministerio de Hacienda.

Iglesias-Palau, Augusto. 2009. "Pension Reform in Chile Revisited." In *OECD Social, Employment and Migration Working Papers*. Paris.

ILO-FACTS, The International Financial and Actuarial Service. 1998. *Internal Guidelines for the Actuarial Analysis of a National Social Security Pension Scheme*. Geneva: ILO.

Jud, Gustav Donald. 1978. *Inflation and the Use of Indexing in Developing Countries*. New York: Praeger.

Kaminsky, Graciela L., and Carmen M. Reinhart. 1999. "The Twin Crises: The Causes of Banking and Balance-of-Payments Problems." *American Economic Review* 89 (3): 473–500. https://doi.org/10.1257/aer.89.3.473.

Kinney, Jeanne. 1997. "Development and Democracy in Chile. Finance Minister Alejandro Foxley and the Concertación's Project for the 1990s." In *Technopols: Freeing Politics and Markets in Latin America in the 1990s*, edited by Jorge I. Domínguez, 229–275. University Park: Pennsylvania State University Press.

Krueger, Anne O. 1974. "The Political Economy of the Rent-Seeking Society." *American Economic Review* 64 (3): 291–303.

Larraín, Guillermo. 2006. "Compatibilizar Protección Social e Incentivos: Por una Reforma Previsional Integral." In *AFP: 25 Años. Un Modelo Exitoso*, edited by Mónica Titze, 93–113. Santiago: Libertad y Desarrollo.

Larraín, Mauricio. 1989. "How the 1981–83 Chilean Banking Crisis was Handled." In *Policy, Planning and Research Working Papers*, edited by World Bank. Washington.

Larrañaga, Osvaldo, Mariana Huepe, and María Eugenia Rodríguez. 2015. "Las Pensiones Solidarias: Análisis de una Reforma Exitosa." In *Las Nuevas*

Políticas de Protección Social en Chile, edited by Osvaldo Larrañaga and Dante Contreras, 159–188. Santiago: Uqbar Editores. Original edition, 2010.

Lüders, Rolf J. 1993. "El Estado Empresario en Chile. Las Bases de su Desarrollo hasta 1973, y la Privatización durante el Régimen Militar." In *El Modelo Económico Chileno*, edited by Daniel L Wisecarver, 131–169. Santiago: Centro Internacional para el Desarrollo Económico/Instituto de Economía Pontificia Universidad Católica de Chile. Original edition, 1992.

Marcel, Mario. 2012. "Participación Ciudadana en la Formulación de Reformas Estructurales: La Reforma Previsional de 2008 en Chile." In *Oportunidades y Desafíos de los Sistemas de Capitalización Individual en un Mundo Globalizado*, 153–202. Santiago: Federación Internacional de Administradores de Fondos de Pensiones.

Mas-Colell, Andreu, Michael D. Whinston, and Jerry R. Green. 1995. *Microeconomic Theory*. New York and Oxford: Oxford University Press.

Matte, Francisco. 2017. "Banking Regulation and Policy Recommendations for Chile." M.A. thesis, Public Policy Program, Stanford University.

McGillivray, Waren. 2006. "Structure and Performance of Defined Benefit Schemes." In *The Oxford Handbook of Pensions and Retirement Income*, edited by Gordon L. Clark, Alicia H. Munnell, and J. Michael Orszag, 223–240. Oxford: Oxford University Press.

Myers, Robert J. 1988. "Privatización en Chile del Sistema de Seguridad Social." In *Sistema Privado de Pensiones en Chile*, edited by Sergio Baeza and Rodrigo Manubens, 17–38. Santiago: Centro de Estudios Públicos.

Olson, Mancur. 1965. *The Logic of Collective Action: Public Goods and the Theory of Groups*. Cambridge, MA: Harvard University Press.

Ominami, Carlos. 2013. "El Desarrollo Esquivo." In *Radiografía Crítica al "Modelo Chileno"*, edited by Gonzalo D. Martner and Eugenio Rivera, 109–128. Santiago: LOM Ediciones/USACH.

Ostrom, Elinor. 1990. *Governing the Commons: The Evolution of Institutions for Collective Action*. Cambridge: Cambridge University Press.

Pérez, Francisco. 1988. "Fondos de Pensiones y Mercado de Capitales." In *Sistema Privado de Pensiones en Chile*, edited by Sergio Baeza and Rodrigo Manubens, 205–250. Santiago: Centro de Estudios Públicos.

Piñera, José. 1988a. "Discurso del Ministro del Trabajo y Previsión Social, con Motivo de la Aprobación de la Reforma Previsional." In *Sistema Privado de Pensiones en Chile*, edited by Sergio Baeza and Rodrigo Manubens, 305–318. Santiago: Centro de Estudios Públicos.

Piñera, José. 1988b. "Fundamentos de la Reforma Previsional." In *Sistema Privado de Pensiones en Chile*, edited by Sergio Baeza and Rodrigo Manubens, 319–337. Santiago: Centro de Estudios Públicos.

Plamondon, Pierre, Anne Drouin, Gylles Binet, Michael Cichon, Waren McGillivray, Michel Bédard, and Hernando Perez-Montas. 2002. *Actuarial Practice in Social Security*. Geneva: ILO/International Social Security Association.

Prat, Jorge. 1964. *Informe Sobre la Reforma de la Seguridad Social Chilena*. Edited by Comisión de Estudios de la Seguridad Social. Santiago: Editorial Jurídica de Chile.

Puryear, Jeffrey. 1994. *Thinking Politics: Intellectuals and Democracy in Chile, 1973–1988*. Baltimore: Johns Hopkins University Press.

Ramírez, Guillermo, and Francisco Rosende. 1992. "Responding to Collapse: Chilean Banking Legislation After 1983." In *If Texas Were Chile. A Primer on Banking Reform*, edited by Philip L. Brock, 193–216. San Francisco: ICS Press.

República de Chile. 1980. *Fundamentos Económicos, Sociales y Políticos del Anteproyecto de Reforma Previsional*. Edited by Ministerio del Trabajo y Previsión Social. Santiago.

Ruíz-Tagle, Jaime. 2001. *Reformas al Nuevo Sistema de Pensiones en Chile. Análisis de las Propuestas*. Santiago: Ministerio de Planificación y Cooperación.

Ruíz-Tagle, Jaime. 2013. "La Reforma Previsional de 2008: Antecedentes, Logros y Problemas Pendientes." In *Radiografía Crítica al "Modelo Chileno"*, edited by Gonzalo D. Martner and Eugenio Rivera, 497–509. Santiago: LOM Ediciones/USACH.

Schamis, Héctor E. 1992. "Política Económica Conservadora en América Latina y Europa Occidental: Las Fuentes Políticas de la Privatización." *Estudios Internacionales* 25 (99): 341–364. https://doi.org/10.5354/0719-3769.1992.15443.

Schmidt-Hebbel, Klaus. 1997. "Pension Reform, Informal Markets, and Long-term Income and Welfare." In *Documentos de Trabajo*, edited by Banco Central de Chile. Santiago.

Schmidt-Hebbel, Klaus. 1998. "Does Pension Reform Really Spur Productivity, Saving, and Growth?" In *Documentos de Trabajo*, edited by Banco Central de Chile. Santiago.

Schurman, Rachel A. 1996. "Chile's New Entrepreneurs and the 'Economic Miracle': The Invisible Hand or a Hand From the State?" *Studies in Comparative International Development* 31 (2): 83–109. https://doi.org/10.1007/bf02719329.

Silva, Eduardo. 1996. "From Dictatorship to Democracy: The Business-State Nexus in Chile's Economic Transformation, 1975–1994." *Comparative Politics* 28 (3): 299–320. https://doi.org/10.2307/422209.

Silva, Patricio. 2009. *In the Name of Reason: Technocrats and Politics in Chile*. University Park: Pennsylvania State University Press.

Sojo, Ana. 2014. "El Sistema Contributivo de Pensiones como Locus de Rivalidad y de un Nuevo Pacto Social en Chile." In *Serie Políticas Sociales*. Santiago: CEPAL.

Stallings, Barbara. 2006. *Finance for Development: Latin America in Comparative Perspective*. Washington: Brookings Institution Press/ECLAC.

Superintendencia de Pensiones - República de Chile. 2016. "Ficha Estadística Previsional N° 49." Superintendencia de Pensiones - República de Chile, Last Modified November 30, 2016, accessed April 28, 2020. http://www.spensiones.cl/portal/informes/581/w3-article-11138.html.

Superintendencia de Pensiones - República de Chile. 2020. "Superintendencia de Pensiones instruye a las AFP procedimiento para entregar fondos a los afiliados que soliciten retirar el 10%" [Press release]. Superintendencia de Pensiones, Last Modified July 23, 2020, accessed September 15, 2020. https://www.spensiones.cl/portal/institucional/594/w3-article-14027.html.

Uthoff, Andras. 2001. "La Reforma del Sistema de Pensiones y su Impacto en el Mercado de Capitales." In *Reformas, Crecimiento y Políticas Sociales en Chile desde 1973*, edited by Ricardo Ffrench-Davis and Barbara Stallings, 231–261. Santiago: LOM Ediciones.

Valdés, Juan Gabriel. 1995. *Pinochet's Economists: The Chicago School in Chile*. Cambridge: Cambridge University Press.

Valdés, Salvador. 1993. "Ajuste Estructural en el Mercado de Capitales: La Evidencia Chilena." In *El Modelo Económico Chileno*, edited by Daniel L Wisecarver, 401–444. Santiago: Centro Internacional para el Desarrollo Económico-Instituto de Economía de la Pontificia Universidad Católica de Chile. Original edition, 1992.

Valenzuela, J. Samuel. 1997. "La Constitución de 1980 y el Inicio de la Redemocratización en Chile." In *Working Papers*, edited by Kellogg Institute—The Helen Kellogg Institute for International Studies. Notre Dame.

Weyland, Kurt. 2006. *Bounded Rationality and Policy Diffusion: Social Sector Reform in Latin America*. Princeton: Princeton University Press.

CHAPTER 6

Institutionalizing Mexican Economic Policies: Limiting Presidential Discretion

This chapter is concerned with institutional reforms that underpin economic governance by limiting the possibilities for discretionary action of Mexican presidents. Some presidents have used the formal and informal powers of their office to implement economic policies that adhered to their political priorities instead of measures that were more prudent, even at a time when the Mexican economy was suffering its worst crisis in decades. Thus, in the Mexican context, presidential power over economic policy became associated with economic instability. The consolidation of economic governance, therefore, entailed limiting presidential discretion over the main instruments of economic policy. Even though, evidently, not all presidents act alike, institutional reforms seeking to curb their power were introduced—partly to quash the threat, in the early 2000s, of a serious new contender for the presidency, whose policies were expected to cause yet more instability. The candidate was defeated, but the reforms remained in place: Mexican presidents still maintain discretion over economic policies. An institutional complementarity never fully formed, however, and thus economic governance was not consolidated either.

There are two parts to the story of economic governance in Mexico in the late twentieth and early twenty-first centuries: the independence of the central bank in the early 1990s, and the budgetary reform that took

A. Angel, *Consolidating Economic Governance in Latin America*, Governance, Development, and Social Inclusion in Latin America, https://doi.org/10.1007/978-3-030-64522-9_6

place between 2003 and 2006. The former spanned a decade (1982–1993) during which bureaucrats sought to confirm their authority over monetary policy using a combination of ideological and material resources of both domestic and international origins. The latter occurred during the presidency of Vicente Fox (2000–2006), in response to the increasing popularity of left-wing politician Andrés Manuel López Obrador, whose opponents sought to restrict his possibilities both electorally and in terms of policy space. López Obrador lost the presidential election in 2006, and with this loss, the perceived threat of political instability disappeared (or was at least deferred).

This chapter explores how two institutions, the central bank and the budget, traditionally considered central to modern statecraft, were reformed, altering the way in which monetary and fiscal policies were implemented. These reforms occurred in different contexts, and they were shepherded by different political processes. First, I consider the autonomy of the *Banco de México,* Banxico (Mexican Central Bank).[1] Next, I consider the creation of a new budgetary act (the Budget and Fiscal Responsibility Act), in which fiscal responsibility is one of the central principles. Taken together, these two reforms show that political actors see new crises as reminiscent of previous ones, prompting them to coalesce and compromise over complementary reforms that might prevent the crisis from recurring, even while reducing, to some extent, their discretion over economic policies.

The first reform is important both because it changed how monetary policy was conducted and because it did not follow traditional models of central bank independence. The second institutional transformation is important because it imposed limits on debt accumulation, thereby changing economic authorities' use of debt as a policy instrument. Complementarity between the two institutions—the Bank and the budgetary act—would place a tight restriction on the president's discretion over economic policy. Actors in the Mexican political economy coalesced, compromised, and created such reforms in response to the legacy of the crisis in the early 1980s. However, once one institution—the Budgetary and Fiscal Responsibility Act—was in place, the threat of

[1] In this work, I use the acronym Banxico to refer the *Banco de México* because this is the way in which the institution is widely known in Mexico and abroad.

instability disappeared. In turn, complementarity between those institutions seeking to limit the Mexican president's discretion over economic policy also disappeared.

Historically, presidents in Mexico did not exercise significant authority over economic policy; rather, it was in the hands of the *Secretaría de Hacienda y Crédito Público* (Ministry of Finance).[2] And for many years, the country's economic model was generally agreed upon. Although there was some debate about how to implement this model, the authority of the Ministry was never fundamentally questioned until 1970. When President Luis Echeverría (1970–1976) took office, however, the violent events in Tlatelolco had instigated a crisis of legitimacy for the regime of the *Partido Revolucionario Institucional*—PRI (Institutional Revolutionary Party).[3] For Echeverría, the solution was to increase government spending; but the Ministry did not agree. In the middle of his term, around 1973, the President declared, "Economic policy is made at *Los Pinos*" (the presidential mansion). The phrase was intended to signal Echeverría's upper hand over the financial bureaucracy (Centeno 1994, 82–83).

The presidential influence over economic policy increased following Echeverría's claim. His successor, José López Portillo (1976–1982), reproduced the same pattern when he, too, began to conduct economic policy against the advice of his bureaucrats (Centeno 1994, 159–160). This occurred in the context of a broader conflict over the management of exchange policy (Maxfield 1997, 102). While 1982 can be considered a turning point in the broad reform agenda of the country, presidential influence over economic policy nonetheless continued to increase. The subsequent rise to power of Miguel de la Madrid (1982–1988) in the midst of a major crisis legitimized a new elite claiming their economic competence. It also catalyzed reforms that would change the

[2] For a long-term perspective on Mexican economic policy, see Maxfield (1990).

[3] Tlatelolco is a neighborhood in Mexico City in which the historic "Three Cultures Square" is a landmark where, on October 2, 1968, policemen and students clashed violently, leaving many students dead. The President was Gustavo Díaz Ordaz (1964–1970), and the *Secretario de Gobernación* (Minister of the Interior) was Luis Echeverría. Echeverría responded to a criminal process in the 2000s, for which he was acquitted in March 2009, for his responsibility in the violence against students (Avilés 2009). For details, see Zermeño (1981).

role of the Mexican state in the economy.[4] Indeed, presidential power over economic policy increased steadily under de la Madrid. He brought to the government a new bureaucratic style in which competence in economics was essential for promotion, and conflict ceased, in part for this very reason. However, his new vision was more a response to President Echeverría's and President López Portillo's "populist" deviations from orthodox economic policies than it was a triumph of sounder economic or bureaucratic doctrine.[5] It was also during these administrations that the new bureaucracy increased its power within the Mexican state (Centeno 1994).

The crisis occurred after Mexico had been "managing abundance," as López Portillo's government described it, for some years. This abundance was a consequence of the oil rents that started to flow into Mexico after big discoveries in the mid-1970s. With the hike in oil prices, the flow of foreign revenue increased substantially. These new resources piled up alongside some newly acquired debt (Moreno-Brid and Ros 2010, 350–351), increasing the permanent expenses and creating an unstable situation. Soon, the foundations of this strategy revealed their weaknesses. When oil prices fell in 1981, the market conditions for refinancing the running debt deteriorated. The following year was particularly unsettled. Mexico defaulted on its debt and nationalized its banks. The monopoly

[4] These reforms were incremental, however. At the end of his period, López Portillo nationalized the banking sector, enshrining this change in the constitution. De la Madrid sold the brokerage houses belonging to banks, as well as the maximum equity allowed to retain control of the banks (Mancera 2010, 360). With this approach, the government complied with the constitution by retaining ownership and control of the banks, while also changing the role of the state in the economy.

[5] Populism is defined as "a political strategy through which a personalistic leader seeks or exercises government power based on direct, unmediated, uninstitutionalized support from large numbers of mostly unorganized followers" (Weyland 2001, 14). In turn, Roberts (2007, 5) asserts that populism refers to "the top-down political mobilization of mass constituencies by personalistic leaders who challenge elite groups on behalf of an ill-defined *pueblo,* or 'the people'" (emphasis in the original). Among the many definitions discussed by Weyland, there is another one referred as the populist policy cycle that is "characterized by overly expansionary macroeconomic policies which lead to high inflation and severe balance of payments crises." "Economic populism," he continues, "has been adopted by governments representing a wide range of the political spectrum, and has not been the exclusive province of the left or right" (Sachs 1990, 139). High-end Mexican bureaucrats probably shared the latter definition.

of the PRI over the Mexican political system guaranteed that such bold measures would not be challenged.[6]

Lustig (2002, 48–52) asserts that while Mexican authorities were responsible for not taking the proper measures to address the situation, they were also victims of circumstance, as they were not the only group to misread the signals. On the domestic front, the mismanagement of the newly acquired resources derived from oil discoveries was the main issue. On the international front, the combination of a fall in oil prices with a significant hike in interest rates made debt service very difficult, because oil was the main source of foreign revenue (Everhart 2001). The response to these circumstances involved attempts by López Portillo to micromanage the exchange rate, which created conflicts with his bureaucrats, and the triggering of bank nationalization. The latter can be understood as an effort on the part of the Mexican government to secure at least some measure of financing when other sources were no longer available.

The bank nationalization had a lasting impact on Banxico's position within the financial structure of the Mexican state. Because the government was unable to divest itself from banking assets, the president charged Banxico with administering the nationalized banks. In the long run, this discretional action justified the views of those in favor of autonomy for the central bank.[7] The whole episode became a key symbol

[6]The PRI established a corporatist regime in 1929 after the Mexican Revolution, in which the bureaucracy always held the upper hand while the other members of the "Revolutionary Family"—workers, through its control of the *Confederación de Trabajadores Mexicanos,* CTM (Mexican Workers Confederation), and peasants, through the *Confederación Nacional Campesina,* CNC (National Peasant Confederation)—acquiesced, while providing a veil of democratic legitimacy. The president, in turn, as the head of state, had a say over the career path of the members of the bureaucracy who sought to advance through its ranks. Because the president controlled the bureaucracy, which in turn controlled both workers and peasants, no significant opposition could arise. Collier and Collier (1991) discuss how the PRI incorporated labor; Hamilton (1982) studies how the state became autonomous from peasants, labor, and capital in the aftermath of the Revolution; Centeno (1994) discusses the relationship between the bureaucracy and the broader Mexican political system, especially in Chapters 3 and 4, which include an extensive discussion and bibliography.

[7]While the *Banco de México* was created as an autonomous institution in 1925, its statutes changed to suit the new economic conditions after the Depression and the resolution of the Mexican Revolution during the government of Lázaro Cárdenas (1934–1940). Banxico did not therefore have autonomy during the five subsequent decades of its existence; rather, it served as the financial agent for the state. There were five reforms to the statute governing Banxico throughout the twentieth century (1934, 1954, 1972, 1983,

of political-economic instability, because it was based on the absolute power of the president over economic policy. This situation caused instability because no credible institutional checks and balances could have prevented it; thus, institutions were reformed to prevent future presidents from dictating economic policy at their discretion.

This was a critical moment in Mexican history because of both its political and its economic implications. Although the political consequences of the crisis did not lead to a regime change, political actors in Mexico did not want the event to repeat itself. Because the crisis was serious, a series of reforms, such as privatization and trade liberalization, started to gain traction. The events of 1982—including a decrease in exports due to the fall in oil prices, the debt moratorium, and the bank nationalization—were all manifestations of a deep economic crisis, indicating that the accumulation model was no longer viable (Pastor and Wise 2003, 180). Even if political decisions had only caused some of those traumas, decision-makers were closely associated with all of them. This created an enduring legacy, and it became important from a political standpoint not to allow any of the political and economic events of that time to reoccur.

The second reform studied here arose as a result of a confrontation between the two poles of the Mexican political system: President Vicente Fox (2000–2006) and the mayor of Mexico City, Andrés Manuel López Obrador (2000–2005), whose political allegiances fell to the right and left, respectively. The popularity of the latter throughout his tenure as mayor provoked his potential contenders, and two seemingly disconnected developments took place. First, López Obrador's mandate was challenged through judicial procedures in order to prevent his possible candidacy in the 2006 presidential elections. At the same time, in Congress, a bill reforming the budget and curbing the state's ability to run deficits was presented. The common motivation behind these two actions was the fact that the candidate was considered a menace to Mexican economic institutions, and authorities felt the need to prevent possible deficits. The implicit message was that a López Obrador government would reinstate Echeverría and López Portillo's policies, which would inevitably lead to a repeat of the 1982 crisis. Therefore, López Obrador's possible candidacy was interpreted as a crisis, prompting

and 1993) in which the autonomy of the bank was modified (Maxfield 1997, 91ff). For an institutional history of Banxico until the 1950s, see Turrent (2015).

political actors to coalesce and compromise, creating an institutional complementarity.

This chapter is divided into five sections including this introduction. The second and third sections analyze the political and economic processes behind the transformation of Banxico's status in relation to the federal government, as well as the budgetary rules surrounding the debt and its administration, respectively. The fourth analyzes the difficulty of controlling discretion. Finally, in the fifth section, I will draw some preliminary conclusions about the institutionalization of Mexican economic policy.

6.1 Banco de México

Conventional wisdom asserts that an independent central bank is essential to controlling inflation.[8] This perspective is the product of an intellectual trend that began in the 1970s and would consolidate in the 1990s. In 1993, *The Economist* declared, "The intellectual case for central bank independence is more or less won." However, when the Mexican experience is closely analyzed, the relationship between the control of high inflation and the independence of the central bank is less clear. Inflation in Mexico began to increase significantly in the second half of 1970s. It reached its peak in 1987, but was quickly controlled, with a reduction of 87% respective to its highest value within a two-year window (Fig. 6.1). The reform that granted independence to Banxico was enacted in 1993, after an easy journey through the National Congress. If the institutional reform that would theoretically bring inflation down was passed after the de-escalation had effectively already been achieved, then what truly motivated the reform?

The following section will analyze the reasons for this seemingly belated reform by looking at several key aspects of central bank independence. Notably, as will be explained further below, the Mexican

[8] A central bank is considered independent when its decisions do not depend politically on any other actor within the political economy. This independence normally implies that political authorities cannot change central bank governors, cannot change budgetary provisions for the bank, and in many occasions, do not participate in its decisions (Bade and Parkin 1988; Masciandaro and Tabellini 1988). The European Central Bank, modelled on the Bundesbank, is the main example of an independent central bank.

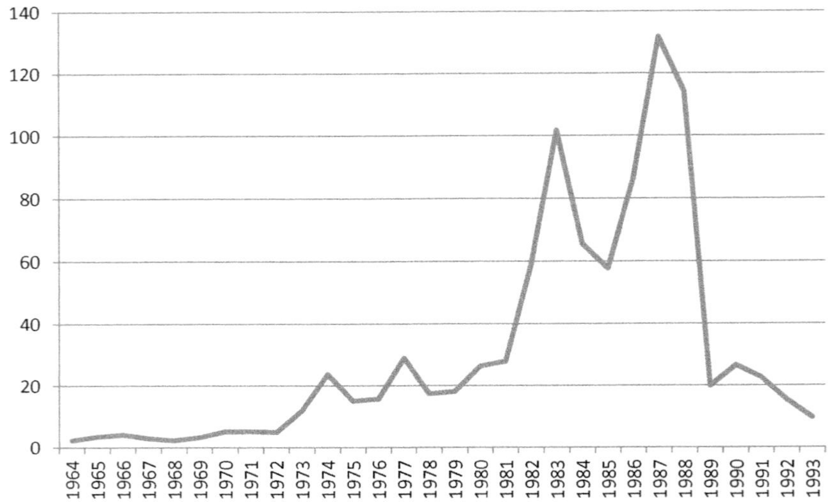

Fig. 6.1 Inflation, consumer prices. 1964–1993. Percentage (*Source* Own elaboration with data from IBRD [2016])

experience does not conform to traditional economic or political science models explaining central bank independence.

6.1.1 *Central Banks: Theory and Practice*

Coping with inflation became an intellectual as well as a policy challenge. Policymakers debated both rational expectations and inflation's implications for monetary policy (Lucas 1972). The argument was that the fully rational policymaker can change his policy path as the economy changes, which would result in suboptimal economic performance. Therefore, the best solution was to implement rules about how economic policy was to be conducted (Kydland and Prescott 1977). The literature argues that a sitting government would manipulate macroeconomic instruments to stimulate growth as a means of staying in office, which in turn disrupts both business and political cycles. When this is not possible, politicians instead tend to implement macroeconomic policies that make it more difficult for their successors to carry out their promises (MacRae 1977; Nordhaus 1975). Essentially, politicians will try to manipulate economic policy, disturbing key economic variables, and ultimately laying the blame for such disturbances on the shoulders of the incoming administration. These cycles would promote inefficiency and instability in the economy. Such volatility could be steadied by taking macroeconomic policy out of the hands of short-sighted politicians, and giving it over instead to a third party, preferably one with a more long-term vision. This would bring stability to macroeconomic policy (Alesina 1988, 39–40).

As Boylan (2001a, 30–35) argues, it is not clear why politicians value stability above everything else. Indeed, although right-leaning politicians might value stability and expenditure restraint, left-leaning politicians should value redistribution or state intervention in the economy. This argument raises an important point about the different preferences, both economic and political, of various agents. Because the models discussed above take a representative politician—without considering their position in the political spectrum—as the relevant agent,[9] they cannot take into account the crucial differences existing in the political arena. In this literature, the evidence—that is, stylized facts—suggests that countries with independent central banks had both lower inflation and a lower government expenditure/gross national product (GNP) ratio (Alesina 1988). Rogoff (1985, 1187) explains that this is "why many countries set up an independent central bank and choose their governors from conservative elements of the financial community."[10]

Even as further inquiries were carried out through the late 1980s and early 1990s, clear conclusions concerning the extent to which a causal relationship existed between central bank independence and low inflation remained elusive. According to Cukierman, Webb, and Neyapti (1992, 283), causality operates in two directions: When inflation is high, the turnover of central bank governors is high, which in turn causes higher inflation. Some new evidence, though less rigorous, put forward by Alesina and Summers (1993, 159) suggests that monetary discipline, when paired with central bank independence, reduces inflation levels. After offering some caveats about this relationship, these authors acknowledge, "Our results here do, however, create some presumption that the

[9] In microeconomics, normally the agent is the median consumer or the firm. This is a consequence of the condition for a competitive market demanding that all actors are alike.

[10] Adolph (2013) argues that socialization and the career paths of central bankers explain why at that moment in time such a trend was in place.

inflation benefits of central bank independence are likely to outweigh any output costs" (1993, 159). Again, theoretical models appear to confirm and validate conventional wisdom: An independent central bank reduces inflation.

Central bank independence has also been studied by scholars interested in the delegation of responsibilities to an independent government agency that exists within the realm of public administration. The main issue is how an agent—an independent bureaucracy—responds to its principal: Congress or the president, or both. Discretion would exist if the bureaucracy pursued a policy that the principal had not anticipated when it was appointed (Calvert, McCubbins, and Weingast 1989, 605). In such a setting, the independence of central banks would represent an attempt to delegate monetary policy to an outsider. In these terms, independent central banks do not exercise discretion insofar as they pursue the goal that politicians wanted them to pursue at the moment of delegation.[11]

Although these theoretical arguments were derived from the experience of both industrial and non-industrial economies (Cukierman, Webb, and Neyapti 1992, 355), there is a different explanation for central bank independence in developing economies. Maxfield argues that developing countries grant autonomy to their central banks for external reasons, and indeed, many transitional economies did so in the 1990s (Maxfield 1997, 51). Global finance became increasingly important during this period, and foreign investors began to have a stake in economic policymaking. Therefore, politicians would try to signal their country's creditworthiness to foreign investors by granting independence to their central banks (Maxfield 1997, 4). This decision depended on a number of factors, including balance of payments, politicians' tenure, expectations about the effectiveness of such a change, and the restrictions on financial transactions.

Boylan (2001a) argues that transitional politics also explain central bank independence. The cases in her study are Chile and Mexico. According to Boylan, reforms to institute central bank independence occur only when authoritarian elites expect to lose power. When the transition begins, they have a strong incentive to protect what they consider to be an important policy. If central banks control significant instruments

[11] New Public Management provides some explanation of the way in which public responsibilities are delegated to independent bodies (Thatcher and Sweet 2002) such as central banks (McNamara 2002).

of economic policy, then they are crucial for the continuation or rupture sought by authoritarian incumbents or democratic reformers, respectively. Relatedly, bureaucratic politics can also explain the move toward central bank independence, as incumbent bureaucrats push for reform in order to secure their own autonomy *vis-à-vis* politicians (Ballinas-Valdés 2011, 111).

Thus, theoretical arguments look to many arenas to explain central bank independence, from macroeconomic policymaking to transitional and bureaucratic politics. However, none of these arguments fully describes the Mexican experience. For example, a central assumption in the literature, that central bank independence *causes* low inflation, does not apply to the situation in Mexico at all. Likewise, managerial and bureaucratic isolation does not fully account for the Mexican case either, as will be shown below. The creditworthiness hypothesis founders when one considers that there was neither a crisis on the horizon nor even foreseeable financial constraints when the Mexican reform was enacted. And while the idea of policy isolation in transitional times does explain some aspects of the reform, the transition had not actually begun at the moment of legal change.

6.1.2 *Brewing a Reform*

In this section, I will discuss the hypotheses that explain the reasons for granting independence to a central bank, specifically with regard to the case of Mexico. The first hypothesis is that such reform seeks to control inflation—in other words, that having an independent central bank allows countries to control inflation. The second hypothesis is that politicians delegate highly technical policies, such as monetary policy, to an independent body such as a central bank. The third hypothesis is that some countries grant independence to their central banks to demonstrate their country's creditworthiness to foreign investors. Finally, the fourth hypothesis concerns transitional politics and proposes that authoritarian elites facing an imminent transition seek to protect monetary stability by granting independence to their central bank. Let us begin by considering the first hypothesis.

For many years, Banxico was just an organization within the federal government. During the period of "Stabilizing Development," when the Minister of Finance was Antonio Ortiz Mena (1958–1970), Banxico enjoyed moments of stability in its roles and functions.[12] This encouraged a relationship of mutual respect between the Ministry and the Bank in which the former did not push for policy measures not supported by the latter. During the second half of López Portillo's government, however, on several occasions, the President managed exchange policy himself, ignoring the advice of his own counselors and also overriding Banxico's directors.[13] Admittedly, these two situations represent extreme cases of Banxico's position within the structure of Mexican economic policymaking; in a broader sense, it was really just another organization, among many, at the disposal of those who exercised power.

Banxico's bureaucrats recognized this secondary status. There was, however, some ambiguity in the relationship between Banxico and other economic authorities. Because Banxico held a certain prestige among economists and the financial community in general, not following its advice had symbolic consequences. This was especially the case when bank officials were called to deal with the consequences of politicians' actions on behalf of the Mexican state. Notably, such situations tended to arise during financial crises, which inevitably affected the Bank's reputation. In the short term, the roles of the two parties—the federal government and Banxico—would not change and therefore neither would not have any reputational costs to bear, but in the long term, the Bank held the upper hand.

In 1982, because the international reserves were a central part of the debt crisis, the exchange policy was paramount to crisis management. When the President decided to impose exchange controls, Miguel Mancera, Director General of Banxico, expressed his disapproval of the policy in a rather abstract way that nonetheless left little doubt about his

[12] "Stabilizing Development" is how economists and historians refer to the period between 1956 and 1970 when economic growth was combined with low inflation. Lustig (2002, 41–46), Moreno-Brid and Ros (2010, 149–169), and Ortiz (1970) himself provide details about this period.

[13] In the final days of his presidency, López Portillo met with his then-Minister of Finance David Ibarra and Banxico Director General, Gustavo Romero Kolbeck. They argued that the peso should be devaluated and deficits could not be perpetual, but the President simply told them "not to worry" and eventually dismissed them (Centeno 1994, 159–160). Maxfield (1997, 102) says that after Romero had argued several times for the devaluation, the President responded by refusing to meet with him again because López Portillo was not going to leave a "depreciated" president. These events say a great deal about the hubris of López Portillo concerning Mexico's oil exportation and about his command of the country at the time.

position (Mancera 1982).[14] This opposition between the President and the bureaucrats at Banxico then eased somewhat following the change of government in December of that year. In fact, Maxfield (1997, 103) argues that Miguel de la Madrid's government (1982–1988) actually began increasing the bank's autonomy. This, however, requires some qualification, since the improved relationship between the President and Banxico's bureaucrats did not translate directly into greater autonomy for the bank.

Miguel de la Madrid and his government were sensitive to the cost of nationalization to Banxico, which López Portillo had carried out just before leaving his post. A move toward even more autonomy for the Bank, however, could have been counterproductive, since it might have signaled that the government was taking a hands-off approach to a serious problem. Furthermore, de la Madrid was not ready to relinquish the tools and privileges of controlling monetary policy—and thus also controlling Banxico. Although his government did eventually enact a reform of the Bank's statutes in 1985, this reform did not contain any provision indicating increased autonomy. It merely sought to reinstate the kind of relationship between the Presidency and the Bank that had prevailed before the governments of Luis Echeverría and José López Portillo.

The political legacies of these administrations persisted. The power struggles between the presidents and the economic bureaucracy were closely tied to the economic conditions in Mexico. In 1973, President Echeverría reaffirmed his authority over economic policy in hopes of legitimizing his regime. And the way in which López Portillo managed the oil discoveries of the late 1970s created economic disequilibria that proved crucial when the conditions of the international economy changed. Indeed, Echeverría's populism and López Portillo's hubris would continue to shape Mexican economic governance for many years after they had left office.

As far as de la Madrid was concerned, meanwhile, Banxico's autonomy was not a priority; he believed the president should control

[14]When the banks were nationalized, Mancera quit Banxico and the President nominated a counselor in his place who was behind the nationalization. This change was short-lived however, because a new president had already been elected, and when he took office, he re-nominated Mancera (Maxfield 1997, 102).

economic policy.[15] Therefore, under his government, Banxico remained an economic agent of the federal government. Indeed, one of the measures taken by the federal government following the debt crisis in 1982 was the reinstatement of the former Director General of Banxico, in an effort to regain the confidence of creditors. Two additional elements influenced the relationship between the federal government and Banxico during de la Madrid's government. First, there was a need for stability. Inflation was soaring and relations with the private sector had deteriorated following the nationalization of the banking sector.[16] Therefore, avoiding any disagreement concerning Banxico was key to recovering the trust of the private sector. Second, the critical situation seemed to require the centralized command of every available instrument, which meant that the circumstances were not optimal for granting independence to Banxico. Furthermore, at the time, there was little evidence about the convenience of independent central banks—hardly enough to guide policymakers.

Conditions did improve under the government of Carlos Salinas de Gortari (1988–1994), but no significant change took place at first. Although some literature (discussed above) suggests a correlation between central bank independence and low inflation, in fact, a non-autonomous central bank controlled Mexican inflation. A pact involving various actors was crafted to control prices in as many sectors as

[15] Miguel Mancera. Interview with the author. Mexico City. March 25, 2015. Mancera was Banxico's longest serving Director General. He oversaw the transition from a completely dependent institution toward a formally independent one. He entered the bank in 1958 and climbed its ranks until his appointment as Director General in 1982. He retired in 1998 as Governor.

On the control that the president should have over economic policy, Romero (2010, 188) signals that de la Madrid sought to increase monetary authority and sovereignty to avoid further cyclical crises, while Sales (2010, 446–448) briefly describes the role of Banxico in the transformation of the Mexican financial system post-nationalization, indicating that control over Banxico was key to achieving the desired goals.

[16] Espinosa and Cárdenas (2010) provide an interesting compilation of testimonies of the people involved in the nationalization, including former presidents, whereas Espinosa and Cárdenas (2011) delve into the consequences of the nationalization, re-privatization, and rescue of the banking sector.

possible.[17] Because inflation decreased in the first year of Salinas's term,[18] it was a *fait accompli* well before any serious discussion about central bank independence was on the horizon. Even if the highest economic authorities, the President, Carlos Salinas, and the Minister of Finance, Pedro Aspe, were supportive of a stable market-oriented economy, such an idea seemed unrealistic at first. Banxico's Director General received a renewed mandate, a rare measure given the bureaucratic changes that normally take place with each new government. Banxico's bureaucrats sought to learn from relevant experiences abroad and the Minister of Finance kept a balanced budget showing that financing for government activities did not depend solely on primary emission.[19] And if primary emission was unnecessary in the eyes of these officials, then subsequent Mexican governments could also relinquish it.

Thus, the first hypothesis proposing that the shift toward an independent central bank was intended to control inflation does not adequately explain the course of events in Mexico. For one thing, inflation was controlled by a dependent central bank in the 1980s. For another, inflation was not an issue during the 1960s, when the bank was fully subordinate to the Ministry's authority. Instead, the PRI, under the leadership of the President, forced the acquiescence of the most affected actors. This was not advanced economic theory in practice, but traditional carrot-and-stick politics. At the beginning of Salinas's government, the priorities in economic policy were elsewhere. Foreign debt was still a concern, even if the preceding government had made significant efforts to improve the situation on that front.[20] Although the advantages of

[17] The *Pacto de Solidaridad Económica* (Economic Solidarity Pact), regularly known as *Pacto* or Pact, was a corporatist arrangement to conduct macroeconomic policy. It was signed by the federal government, workers, agrarian producers, and organized businesses. Its main components were fiscal deficit reduction, tighter monetary policy, commercial liberalization, and an income policy covering the whole range of prices and wages (Lustig 1991).

[18] Mexican presidential terms begin on December 1 of the inauguration year. Therefore, 1989, when inflation was around 20%, was the first year of Salinas's term.

[19] Jorge Chávez Presa. Interview with the author. Mexico City. March 9, 2015. During the 1990s, Chávez Presa was a mid- to high-level bureaucrat at the Ministry of Finance. In the period 2000–2003, he was elected to the Chamber of Deputies, representing the PRI. He currently runs a consulting firm in Mexico City. He suggested that high-end officials pressed both formally and informally for expenditure restraint.

[20] Debt negotiations were difficult within and outside Mexico. De la Madrid's government implemented orthodox measures to repay the debt and gain the confidence of

Salinas's solutions are debatable,[21] he used them to achieve a political victory, presenting himself as a competent defender of Mexican interests.[22] Furthermore, Salinas signaled his intention to seek a free trade agreement with the United States,[23] which was a clear departure from traditional Mexican policy (Serra 2010).

Central bank independence was not a priority at this point, but it began to gain momentum as one of a series of other liberalizing reforms.[24] It was not itself considered urgent because inflation was already under control in the first two years of the Salinas government (ca. 1990). The motivation for granting autonomy to Banxico might have had more to do with the insulation of monetary policy from elected officials, as was also the case elsewhere (Roberts 2010). Indeed, politicians and bureaucrats alike wanted to avoid a repeat of López Portillo's presidency, and granting formal independence to the Bank was a feasible solution. Whatever the reason, there has been considerable debate surrounding the reasons for and timing of the Salinas government's reform granting autonomy to the central bank (Ballinas-Valdés 2011; Boylan 2001b; Maxfield 1997),

external creditors. However, as oil prices fell in 1986, making it harder to maintain the payment schedule, negotiations became acrimonious. This gave traction to domestic advocates for radical measures. Finally, an agreement was brokered with relatively soft conditions for Mexico (Kaufman 1988, 89–90).

[21] As debt continued to be a problem, Salinas's administration sought a new deal to accelerate the recovery that the debt was supposedly preventing. Mexico was among the first to adhere to the Brady Plan of debt relief brokered by the US Treasury Secretary (after whom the plan was named); however, savings in terms of cash-flow were less than expected, amounting to only 9–10% of yearly interest payments for five years, or a billion dollars in the same time span. In 1992, with the decrease in interest rates, savings were even lower. Therefore, the new conditions were not a great relief to the Mexican economy (Lustig 2002, 90–91).

[22] This was possible because Salinas had a reputation for being a strong and "serious" leader (*un hombre serio*); therefore, his strategy could only be good for Mexico (Centeno 1994, 236–237).

[23] Salinas and George H. W. Bush signaled their intention to establish a free trade agreement between Mexico and the US in June 1990. In August, Salinas asked Bush for the formal opening of negotiations (Lustig 2002, 23 fn. 1). Mexico's entry into the General Agreement on Trade and Tariffs, GATT, after 1985 was a precedent (Olea Sisniega 1990).

[24] Other changes were the end of agrarian reform (Appendini 2010), privatization (MacLeod 2004), and the North American Free Trade Agreement, NAFTA (Morales 1999).

as it is hard to assess the relative weight of the different factors. Moreover, the government did not make their decision public right away, which only heightened the confusion—even though the first draft of the independence statute had existed since the early 1990s.[25]

Banxico's Director General sought to learn from the situation in Chile. In 1989, Chile granted operational, legal, and political independence to its central bank.[26] Other countries soon followed suit (Maxfield 1997, 51), but the Chilean influence was fundamental for Mexico. This was the case not only because Chile had been the first country in the region to experiment with such policies, but also because the two heads of the Chilean and Mexican central banks, Andrés Bianchi and Miguel Mancera respectively, were friends and communicated with each other in several fora about their experiences.[27] After the decision to grant autonomy to Banxico was made, the Chilean example became even more useful. In essence, it provided practical lessons on central bank independence of which the future statute could take advantage. A political argument justifying the decision was no longer necessary by this point, since the reform was already underway. Bianchi became a kind of role model for Mancera, and the latter was able to learn a lot. At first, their exchange was sporadic, since both officials were tied up with numerous responsibilities in their respective institutions. However, when Bianchi's appointment

[25] Roberto del Cueto. Interview with the author. Mexico City. March 24, 2015. Member of the Board of Governors of Banxico (2007–2018). Del Cueto entered the Bank in 1973 and had ascended to Deputy Director by 1994 when he resigned. He worked in the financial sector as CEO of *Banco Nacional de México,* Banamex (National Bank of Mexico), and held other posts in the Mexican financial sector. He also held academic positions in the Law School of the *Instituto Tecnológico Autónomo de México,* ITAM (Autonomous Technological Institute of Mexico), a private university, and was re-nominated as a member of the Board of Governors of Banxico in 2007.

[26] The constitution established by the authoritarian government in 1980 contemplated an autonomous central bank. However, it was not until 1989, just after Pinochet had lost the plebiscite in 1988, that a detailed legislation was enacted. As Boylan (2001a, 75ff) discusses at length, what mattered most in that reform was the threat of a new democratically elected government. The importance of Boylan's argument is that it questions the extent to which such reforms were enacted in the quest for economic credibility vis-à-vis markets, but for political reasons involving mainly domestic considerations. Bianchi (2009) offers a broader historical account of this policy change from an insider's perspective.

[27] Miguel Mancera. Interview with the author. Mexico City. March 25, 2015. Ariel Buira. Interview with the author. Mexico City. March 6, 2015. Buira served as a member of the Board of Governors of Banxico from 1994 to 1996 and previously was Director for International Organizations and Agreements within the Bank (1985–1993).

period (1989–1991) ended, he was able to assist his Mexican counterpart in a more sustained and intimate way to shape a statute granting independence to Banxico.[28]

The statute was enacted in December 1993, after a six-month legislative process. At the same time, other reforms were either being implemented (e.g., privatization and agrarian reform) or realized (e.g., NAFTA). The Bank's new statute was certainly a triumph for Banxico's bureaucrats, who had seen how presidential authority often trumped their priorities. The perception of political interference as a threat was critical to advancing the reform, even though President Salinas and Secretary Aspe were not interested in intervening as their predecessors had. This is significant because other reforms to economic governance were also enacted in order to prevent the possible interference of political authorities.

While it was clear that primary emission must remain out of the reach of politicians, exchange policy affected more than just monetary variables and, consequently, the federal government maintained control over it. To achieve these conditions—to surrender a source of monetary emission while still continuing to control it—an Exchange Commission was created. The Commission was composed of three members of Banxico's Board and three members of the Ministry of Finance—the Minister and two of his deputies. Every decision had to receive at least one vote of support from the Ministry, who were deterred from making arbitrary decisions because the proceedings of the Commission were public. Interested parties could observe the respective positions and could make the federal government bear the cost in other markets, such as bonds.

The second hypothesis about the reasons for central bank independence in Mexico, which concerns the delegation of macroeconomic policy to an autonomous agency, is worth some consideration. While the delegation of monetary policy to an autonomous body means isolating it from everyday political debates, Mexico does not conform to the archetypal example. For one thing, although Banxico had a reputation for being a highly technical agency, both the President and the Minister of Finance at the time were professional economists. Delegation was therefore not simply a matter of handing responsibilities over to a more qualified technical agency. Even if some international experiences seem to suggest that savvy bankers saved the world from inflation (Roberts 2010), Mexican

[28] Miguel Mancera. Interview with the author. Mexico City. March 25, 2015.

inflation was not controlled by savvy bureaucrats but, as explained above, through corporatist politics.

As McNamara (2002, 51) suggests, some see delegation as a solution to electoral and partisan politics, whereby left-leaning parties try to stimulate the economy in order to get elected, but this does not fit the Mexican experience either. First, authorities were not keen to stimulate the economy because they thought the role of the state in the economy should be reduced, not expanded.[29] Second, the PRI was hegemonic in Mexican politics. It did not face any serious threat from the left that would force it to stimulate the economy—not even from the left-leaning faction of the party that had long been isolated. And third, when the reform was enacted, there was no credible menace to the PRI's hegemony at the federal level that might force the government into fiscal profligacy.

The third hypothesis, developed by Maxfield (1997, 4), argues that a country's desire for its creditworthiness to be recognized will lead to a change in the status of its central bank. This factor was especially salient as reforms took place around the world, partially because the liberalization of capital accounts allowed international actors—both international organizations and individual investors—to play significant roles in the definition of economic policies.[30] The weakness of Maxfield (1997)'s argument concerning the relevance of international creditworthiness when applied to Mexico is that the financial crisis that might, under other circumstances, have prompted the move toward Banxico's independence, happened after the reform had already been enacted. Not only that, but because the crisis occurred after independence the reform was actually severely questioned. In 1994, political turmoil would have serious economic consequences as capital flight followed several major events. On January 1, a guerrilla uprising, the Zapatista movement, started in the southern state of Chiapas, reminding the world that there were serious challenges to the government's claims that Mexico had entered a new stage of modernity and stability.

[29] Salinas's cabinets were composed mainly of economists, which represented a departure from traditional Mexican cabinet politics (Centeno 1994). In fact, this trend had begun at least as early as de la Madrid's cabinet, which was the first cabinet composed for the most part by professional economists, giving it a high degree of homogeneity (Hernández 1987).

[30] In reality, the main international factor leading to central bank independence in Mexico, discussed above, was the cooperation established between the heads of Banxico and the Central Bank of Chile, who had been friends since their time in graduate school.

Some months later, the political assassinations of the PRI presidential candidate, Luis Donaldo Colosio, in April, and of the party's Secretary General, José Francisco Ruíz Massieu, in September, showed foreign investors that political stability was not assured in Mexico. Again, there were significant capital flights (Banxico 1995, 48, 2015): manifestations of instability and vulnerability. Perhaps because the political threats demanded the government's attention, the economic cabinet did not meet as frequently as it had before,[31] which led to a lack of coordination among authorities and increased the country's economic vulnerability. When the new government took office in December 1994, exchange rate policy once again became a salient issue. The depreciation of the peso at this time was so extreme that foreign reserves were almost depleted in an effort to contain devaluation, creating a situation that became known as the peso crisis.[32] Although this was mainly under the purview of the federal government, Banxico bore the brunt of the reputational costs of the crisis. There were no formal challenges to Banxico's autonomy, but market actors began to doubt the extent to which it was truly independent.

In turn, Banxico officials argued that political factors were responsible for the capital flights and subsequent crisis (Gil-Díaz and Carstens 1996). This situation was nevertheless a blow to an institution that had made significant efforts to build a political consensus around its independence, relying, to a certain degree, on its reputation—which now seemed to be tainted. Responding to the crisis required a political and financial effort from Guillermo Ortiz, President Ernesto Zedillo's (1994–2000) Minister of Finance, who brokered a solution to the financial mayhem after the

[31] Jorge Chávez Presa. Interview with the author. Mexico City. March 9, 2015.

[32] The literature about the peso crisis is abundant and its review is beyond the scope of the present work. International reserves declined substantially in 1994 because of the political events of that year. The need for a depreciation increased with the lost reserves; however, the outgoing Salinas administration delayed decisions on that issue. The later *Error de Diciembre* (December Mistake) refers to a comment by the new Minister of Finance, Jaime Serra Puche, concerning the necessity of changing the exchange regime. This led investors to speed up the accumulation of foreign exchange. Serra was dismissed from his post as Minister of Finance shortly after taking office. Whitehead and Kravis (1996) provide a detailed account of the events surrounding the peso crisis and its resolution, while GAO (1996) is an official report to the US Congress. Serra (2011, 194–195) insists such versions are inaccurate.

crisis bottomed out.[33] His career at Banxico and his tenure as Deputy Minister of Finance during Salinas's government were essential to gathering the support, both political and financial, to solve the crisis. The resolution of the crisis gave Ortiz a powerful position within the cabinet. He now had substantial political influence, which outweighed questions about his previous responsibilities as President of the Banking Privatization Committee. In 1998, Ortiz was appointed Governor of Banxico. The significance of this appointment cannot be underestimated, as his predecessor had served for sixteen years, through the administrations of four different presidents.

The fourth hypothesis about central bank independence in Mexico concerns the impact of transitional politics. Boylan (2001a) proposes a model in which the degree of autonomy ceded to the central bank depends on the electoral threat faced by authoritarian elites. If authoritarian elites fear that they will soon be ousted, they would try to insulate monetary policy. This was the case in Chile, when insulation happened between the referendum of October 1988 and the arrival of the *Concertación* to power in March 1990. Meanwhile, it follows that if the electoral threat was only partial, then the insulation would also be partial. This was the case in Mexico, where the electoral threat faced by the PRI was weak, and thus so was the insulation.

Officials generally consider the 1993 reform to be the instrument through which Banxico acquired its autonomy. The regulation of internal credit supply and the interest rate remained Banxico's prerogatives. Exchange policy, as per the rules of the Exchange Commission, remained under the federal government's control, in spite of its importance to monetary policy. As Boylan (2001b)'s work implies, the weak electoral threat faced by the PRI would explain this partial insulation. However, despite exchange policy arrangements, the insulation of monetary policy following the 1993 reform was complete[34]; the argument thus loses

[33] The solution consisted mainly of a credit from the US Treasury, the IMF, and other lenders of the Paris Club amounting to USD 53 billion. In late January 1994, there was already some clarity about the contours of the credit; it was signed in mid-February and implemented in March, when the decline of the peso was finally under control (Pastor 1998, 141).

[34] Miguel Mancera, Director General of Banxico from 1982 to 1998, Roberto del Cueto, member of the Board of Governors (2007–2018) and former Deputy Director General of Banxico in 1993, and Ariel Buira, member of the Board of Directors in 1990s, confirmed this condition in the interviews conducted by the author. Ballinas-Valdés (2011,

some traction, since the transition to democracy only took place in 2000. Nevertheless, when the transition did take place, the practical autonomy of the Bank was tested, suggesting that insulation, as well as electoral and political threats, is relevant to understanding central bank autonomy.

In 1998, before the beginning of the formal transition and after the PRI's lackluster electoral results in 1997 (Rubio 1998, 33–35), President Zedillo nominated Guillermo Ortiz, the Minister of Finance behind the resolution of the peso crisis, as Governor of Banxico. Electoral threats were no longer simply an idea but a reality with which the Zedillo government had to cope. Zedillo had refused to use the nomination powers of his office for either presidential or gubernatorial candidates,[35] which allowed for significant electoral change. His nomination of Ortiz, however, implied that a powerful Minister of Finance could become a powerful central banker. This would become even more important when in 2000 President Vicente Fox (2000–2006), of the *Partido Acción Nacional*, PAN (National Action Party), was elected.

The insulation of monetary policy in the face of electoral threats seems relevant to the question of central bank autonomy, but perhaps not as one might expect. That is, insulation is both a matter of institutional design and a consequence of the political power projected by the bureaucratic leader at the head of an organization such as Banxico. Insulation, then, depends critically on how political actors perceive the organization, and is not only a matter of formal powers granted through institutional reforms. In this case, these formal powers existed, but it was chiefly Ortiz's stature that led President Fox to nominate him once again in 2003 as Governor of Banxico. The Minister of Finance, Francisco Gil-Díaz, was instrumental to that nomination, as he emphasized Ortiz's good performance thus far in his post, not to mention his long-standing reputation in the financial community.[36] The need for continuity after the transition supported Banxico's ongoing independence throughout the PAN governments.

As demonstrated above, none of the four hypotheses presented can fully explain central bank independence in Mexico. Nevertheless, some of them do offer valuable insights. The perceived need to keep monetary

129–132) suggests that a 1997 reform to the *Banco de México*'s Act completed the process of granting autonomy to Banxico. Nevertheless, Banxico's website does not mention such a reform (México 1993).

[35] The metaconstitutional powers doctrine will be further discussed below.

[36] Roberto del Cueto. Interview by the author. Mexico City. March 24, 2015.

policy out of the presidential reach was central to all actors involved—both to bureaucrats who acquiesced to presidential authority and to new incumbents who thought past policies were not economically wise. Because the President had to relinquish his authority over monetary policy, the question was simply when to do so. Bureaucrats, eager to be autonomous, tried to learn from the experiences of other countries so that they could offer a model that would fulfill presidential expectations on the matter without seeming to override presidential authority. International financial markets were increasingly important in the consolidation of the reform. And finally the respect enjoyed by a Director General in both financial and political circles meant continuity in the post even after a transition to democracy.

Evidently, then, the autonomy of the central bank was not brought about by one single event. Rather, an accumulation of undesirable situations convinced officials of its desirability. In the middle of the reform process, adjustments were made to accommodate issues affecting other areas of economic policy. The institutionalization of monetary policy was a gradual process in which the margin for discretionary action was severely reduced, allowing other actors to play a more significant role. Therefore, it is best to have a long-term view of the process. This kind of broad perspective points to the enduring legacy of the conflict-ridden relations between President López Portillo and Banxico's upper-level bureaucrats during the 1982 crisis. Even two decades after these events, the president under whom the PRI's dominance foundered still hesitated to re-nominate the first governor appointed after institutional reform. Indeed, presidential power over monetary policy, through the appointment of a sympathetic Governor, was still a temptation, even if such power was contained within a frame of formal independence. Despite the various steps taken to achieve the reform, the president maintained substantial sway over monetary policy throughout the process of institutional change.

The next section presents another instance where the legacy of a president willing to risk economic stability as a political strategy appeared in the political arena, once again fostering new institutional reforms.

6.2 Budget and Fiscal Responsibility Act

Balanced budgets were not a priority of Mexican authorities—or at least, economic conditions generally have not allowed for balanced budgets. However, presidential priorities have prevailed in questions of economic governance. Under the right circumstances, there were no restrictions on the president's discretion over economic policy, other than what domestic and international conditions allowed. Therefore, it is important to study why and how the Budget and Fiscal Responsibility Act, a piece of legislation that pretended to restrain the president's authority to run deficits, was enacted. It was, in broad strokes, another attempt to reduce the president's authority to make economic policy decisions at his sole discretion. Like the reform concerning the status of Banxico, the Act sought, among other things, to establish rules for the federal government's implementation of economic policies. These two forms of restriction—on monetary and fiscal affairs—had the potential to become complementary.

Transitional politics are contentious because there is much at stake for governments and the population alike. New incumbents embody hopes for change, and people are led to believe that democracy will deliver all that they desire. While some policies can fulfill these expectations, the effects of economic policy are beyond a government's control. This engenders political debate, attracts criticism, and may even result in the fall of elected governments.[37] Mexican politics followed this pattern after the transition to democracy in 2000[38]—but with one key unique feature. Those in charge of economic policy stayed in power (Hernández 2011, 89–93). President Fox's inability to reach consensus with other actors only increased the conflict in an already contentious transition. Moreover, his appeal to public opinion through electronic and mass media only complicated things further. Instead of privileging fluid communication with legislators, the presidential communication strategy created uneasiness among elected representatives and an even more tense political environment (Hernández 2005, 208). This strategy affected not only the relationship between the two branches of power, but also other political opponents. The main opponent was Andrés Manuel López Obrador, who as mayor of Mexico City (2000–2005) was caught up in several scandals during which the President did not remain neutral.

[37] The Alfonsín government (1983–1989) in Argentina is a case in point.

[38] The transition to democracy in Mexico is commonly considered to be when the government of Vicente Fox, of the PAN, took office, ending seventy years of PRI dominance. However, the seeds of this shift were sown at least as far back as the election of Carlos Salinas in 1988, when doubts about the electoral results were aired, eroding the veil of legitimacy on which the PRI had relied for decades. Domínguez and Lawson (2004) analyze the transition in depth.

While these confrontations dominated the political environment, the first draft of a new budgetary regulation called *Ley Federal de Presupuesto Público* (Public Budget Federal Act) was presented in the Chamber of Deputies. The congressmen who authored this initiative stated that one of their motivations was to adapt the budgetary rules issued in 1976 to the new transitional environment (Chávez 2003, 37). Also proposed was the reorganization of public finance, by establishing a clear framework for expenses and revenues, and of the budgetary process, by prohibiting last-minute adjustments intended to avoid proper scrutiny on the part of congressmen. The point was to strengthen the planning process within the Executive Branch (Chávez 2003, 38). The second explicit goal of the future Act was "To assure fiscal discipline" (Chávez 2003, 39). Those presenting this initiative wanted a thorough reorganization of the budgetary process, including a comprehensive examination of public finances including debt, expenses, revenues, and assets, among other issues.[39] Around the same time, the *Partido del Trabajo* (Labor Party) submitted another text to the Chamber, in this case with the aim of limiting budgetary imbalances. These limits would depend on the preservation of macroeconomic stability as well as on access to the international credit of private agents (Regis 2003, 176). Clearly, fiscal discipline remained paramount within broad parliamentary debates.

Most likely, these projects represented a way to oppose the government; in other words, they were intended to hold the government accountable and restrain its margin for action, during a political campaign in which small parties had much at stake.[40] In the mid-term elections of

[39] Jorge Chávez. Interview with the author. Mexico City. March 9, 2015.

[40] Those outside the mainstream Mexican political establishment comprising PRI, PAN, and *Partido de la Revolución Democrática,* PRD. These parties are *Partido Verde* (Green Party), *Partido del Trabajo* (Labor Party), *Movimiento Ciudadano* (Citizen's Movement), *Nueva Alianza* (New Alliance), *Movimiento de Regeneración Nacional*—Morena (National Regeneration Movement), and *Encuentro Social* (Social Gathering). Electoral legislation favored the creation of political parties at the time, explaining their proliferation (Flores Andrade 2006), which, in consequence, led to the fragmentation of the party system (Sonnleitner 2017). In turn, the electoral process of 2006 had a considerable impact in the Mexican party system since many parties appeared after such process, some as political associations, such as Morena—strongly linked to the figure of López Obrador (Bolívar Meza 2014), Encuentro Social—with a strong evangelical base and program (de la Torre Castellanos 2020, 16–17), and some others directly as political parties, such as Nueva Alianza, a transformation of the *Sindicato Nacional de Trabajadores de la Educación,* SNTE (National Union of Education Workers), in a political party (Leyva 2007).

June 2003, the first since the transition, a portion of the lower Chamber was in contest. The PAN had much to lose, because it had not realized the promises made during its ascension to power in 2000. This opened the door for smaller parties, who had the opportunity to consolidate themselves as political alternatives—a goal they actually achieved during this election (Concha 2004, 11). In addition, the PRI kept most of its core voters and representation (Camacho 2004).

In the second half of Fox's government, between 2003 and 2006, the increasing importance of the future PRD candidate, López Obrador, dominated Mexican politics. While López Obrador was mayor of Mexico City (2000–2005), he used a clever communication strategy to become the most visible politician in the country, aside from the president (Espino-Sánchez 2007, 294). This position, however, made him the target of several legal controversies involving either his own actions as an elected official or those of his cabinet. The most significant of these sought to remove his legal immunity in 2004–2005 so that he would be unable to participate in the presidential contest of 2006 (Espino-Sánchez 2007, 299).[41] But his opponents' strategy backfired. After the legal procedure was over, López Obrador's popularity increased to historic heights (Espino-Sánchez 2007, 302).

As tensions between the federal government and the mayor escalated, public finance remained a way to oppose the government. The Chamber presented two different proposals about budgetary procedures. The PRI parliamentary group presented the first text, following the general guidelines established during the preceding legislative period. This proposal included provisions to organize the budgetary process, changing the balance between the Executive and the Legislative Branches in favor of the latter. It also contained as a major theme fiscal responsibility principles

[41] López Obrador was accused of contempt of court because the Government of Mexico City unduly expropriated land to build an entrance to a hospital back in 2001. The judge ordered a restitution, which was not carried out until after the allotted time. Because the head of the city's government was accountable for this, the Attorney General started a prosecution process. In accordance with an outdated legislation, all those subject to a legal process would not have the right to participate in any election. This was important for all potential contenders, given López Obrador's popularity and his intention to participate in the presidential elections of 2006. Given his post as elected official, his legal immunity could only be taken away by the Chamber of Deputies, which is indeed what happened. After this stage of the process was completed, the judge decided that the case was inconsistent and the charges were withdrawn (Espino-Sánchez 2007, 298–304).

that would allow for the maintenance of macroeconomic stability through sound public finances (Rojas 2004, 58–61). The *Diario de los Debates* (Journal of Debates) of the Chamber of Deputies published this project on April 15, 2004, which was about one month before the Attorney General announced, on May 17, the beginning of the case that would remove López Obrador's immunity (*Latinnews-Daily* 2004).

The Labor Party presented the second proposal, which was consistent with its position during the preceding legislative period. Although it contained some key differences from the PRI's project, its core proposition was also budgetary balance with fiscal responsibility. Congress would authorize a deficit if its objective was to promote national economic and social development (Padilla 2004, 23). Two characteristics of this plan should be noted. First, the details surrounding the proposed authorization to carry deficits were actually quite vague, and second, the project was presented on May 26, 2004, roughly one week after the process against López Obrador began. While the subject was not new either to the parliamentary debate or to the Labor Party's initiatives, the timing of the proposal would later make it an important factor in a broader debate regarding the left and López Obrador.

At the same time as these proposals were being formulated, opposition to the most visible, and viable, candidate from the left was rising. The process against López Obrador was supported by the view, as expressed by one former Foreign Minister, that he must be stopped at any cost (*Reforma* 2004, 6). This perspective was taken up again two years later during the presidential campaign in which López Obrador competed against Felipe Calderón, the PAN candidate, and Roberto Madrazo, the PRI candidate. Hostilities against López Obrador continued, eventually fueling a negative campaign against his presidential intentions. This campaign tried to suggest a number of connections between López Obrador's political style and that of Hugo Chávez, the populist Venezuelan president (Treviño 2009, 640–641)—an association that had only begun to circulate when López Obrador first became a viable presidential candidate. During his time as mayor, however, López Obrador had never shown any signs of fiscal profligacy, as a comparison with the Venezuelan president might imply.[42] If he had done, such criticisms

[42] Anonymous. Political Operative. Interview with the author. Mexico City. 2015. Paradoxically, the response of López Obrador's government to the global pandemic in 2020 was considered excessively austere (*Economist* 2020c).

would have emerged earlier. Instead, they only surfaced when the presidential contest was actually on the horizon. The characterization of the candidate as a danger to fiscal and macroeconomic stability was thus a political strategy rather than a true warning based on past behavior. Nevertheless, the theme of fiscal responsibility was prominent in political debates, even if the consequences for López Obrador remained mild,[43] since his record as mayor was enough to deter the accusations.[44]

The year 2005 was pivotal in discussions surrounding the legal process against López Obrador and the release of the definitive text of the Budget and Fiscal Responsibility Act. In the first part of the year, Congress discussed the case of López Obrador's legal immunity, which was finally removed on April 7 (*Latin American Regional Report. Mexico & NAFTA* 2005a). During the President's Annual Report to Congress in September, some concerns had arisen about his neutrality. His government's actions related to López Obrador, as well as sudden changes made to certain policies that presumably favored the PAN candidate, had prompted these concerns (*Latin American Regional Report. Mexico & NAFTA* 2005b). Later, the federal government presented the text of the Budget and Fiscal Responsibility Act, with some modifications, to Congress, so that the normal legislative process could proceed.[45]

In December 2005, when the final procedures for the approval of the new Act were taking place, it became clear that the Executive Branch had played an active role in the elaboration of the new text. An opposing member of Congress signaled that many of the amendments presented by the federal government had been approved by the Chamber as part of the final text of the Act (México 2005, 351). This powerful and long-standing influence of the Mexican federal government over the legislative process

[43] It is hard to assess how much the candidate was affected by the claims about his fiscal profligacy. In November 2003, it was clear that Mexico City's debt was rising, but so were its revenues—with the consequence of keeping the debt under control (*Economist* 2003). Nevertheless, in May 2005, only eighteen months later, López Obrador was compelled to clarify that if he became President he would respect macroeconomic stability, potentially indicating that there were doubts about his record as Mayor (*Economist* 2005). In any case, it was the framing that mattered more rather than his actual behavior.

[44] Anonymous. Political Operative. Interview with the author. Mexico City. 2015.

[45] Part of the normal legislative procedure. In Mexican legal jargon, this document is called *Controversias*, which refers to disagreements or amendments that the federal government introduces to the legal text initially proposed in Congress, including to their own respective positions on these issues.

was summarized in the metaconstitutional powers doctrine (Carpizo 2002).[46] Nevertheless, after the transition, the President lost a substantial amount of his influence, because elections now determined politicians' careers. Thus, during the first PAN government, the relationship between the Executive and the Legislative branches was not as rigidly defined as it had been during the PRI regime (Hernández 2005).[47] Both López Obrador's immunity and the new Act, as well as the actors involved, are important for the present discussion. It is quite remarkable that the 59th Congress (2003–2006) decided not only to remove the legal immunity of an elected official, the opposition leader, but also to accept, with almost no modifications, a bill written by the Executive Branch at a time when interactions between the two branches were less than fluid. The majority parties who had voted to strip López Obrador of his legal immunity and for a bill restricting the formal feasibility of running deficits probably considered both moves to be strategic, although each would carry a different weight.

The electoral campaign in 2006 merely extended the tensions that already existed between the post-transitional poles of the Mexican political system: the President and his party, the PAN, on the right; and López Obrador and his coalition[48] on the left. While the President stressed the importance of keeping the macroeconomic model in place, López Obrador emphasized the role that the state should play in the war against social inequality (Escamilla 2007, 258). The government's concerns about maintaining economic policy had actually preceded the campaign; more precisely, they had arisen in the second half of 2005, in the amendments to the Budget and Fiscal Responsibility Act. But the technicalities of fiscal responsibility were not nearly as important to the campaign as the ways in which both the President and López Obrador

[46] The metaconstitutional powers of the Mexican president refer to the overwhelming powers he held during the PRI dominance. They included the president's power to nominate and remove governors, and to nominate his own successor. As far as Congress was concerned, what mattered most was that the president controlled the career path of congressmen, possibly by making appointments out of the federal bureaucracy or a governorship.

[47] For a discussion of post-transition Executive and Legislative branches' relations, see Nacif (2010).

[48] The official name of the coalition was *Coalición por el bien de todos* (Coalition for the Good of All) representing the PRD, of which López Obrador was officially a member, *Convergencia Democrática* (Democratic Convergence), and the Labor Party.

attacked one another, each claiming that the other was irresponsible or unqualified for the job.[49] In other words, while economic policy might have hovered in the background throughout the political campaign, what mattered most was López Obrador's presumed irresponsibility concerning those very issues, which—as the government threatened—could affect Mexicans just as they had been affected by previous economic crises.

Those who opposed López Obrador argued that his becoming president would represent a return to the early 1980s, when President López Portillo (no relation) had declared the debt moratorium and nationalized the banks. That such an argument could be mobilized during a presidential campaign a quarter of a century later speaks to the wounds that this crisis caused. In Congress, the same argument arose when an unlikely coalition formed between the PRI and the PAN to pass the new Budget and Fiscal Responsibility Act. These steps completed the consolidation of economic governance in Mexico: a crisis reminiscent of past struggles, a consensus over the causes of the new threat, and a broad coalition willing to prevent its re-edition—all taking place alongside incremental institutional reforms that sought to address the crisis that had toppled the previous development model.

Once the campaign was over and Felipe Calderón (2006–2012), the PAN candidate, had been elected President, all questions about López Obrador's potential and supposed mismanagements vanished. However, the legacy of these debates endured. The Budget and Fiscal Responsibility Act reduced the federal government's ability to autonomously run deficits. And yet, while one would expect deficits to become a rarity in the aftermath of this institutional change, what happened was quite the opposite (Fig. 6.2). The global financial crisis, starting in 2007–2008, led many governments around the world to run deficits, both because of countercyclical policies and because their finances had been crushed by the decrease in revenues. Therefore, even with legislation demanding a balanced budget, sometimes it still makes sense to run a deficit, if circumstances require. The consensus in Mexico was that the federal government

[49] An indication of such disqualifications is provided by two instances: first, the way in which López Obrador referred to the President by using the Mexican popular bestiary and second, the construction of the former as a "danger" to the Mexican society because of his lack of interest in maintaining macroeconomic stability, among other values cherished by Mexican society (Bruhn 2009; Hiller 2011; Treviño 2009).

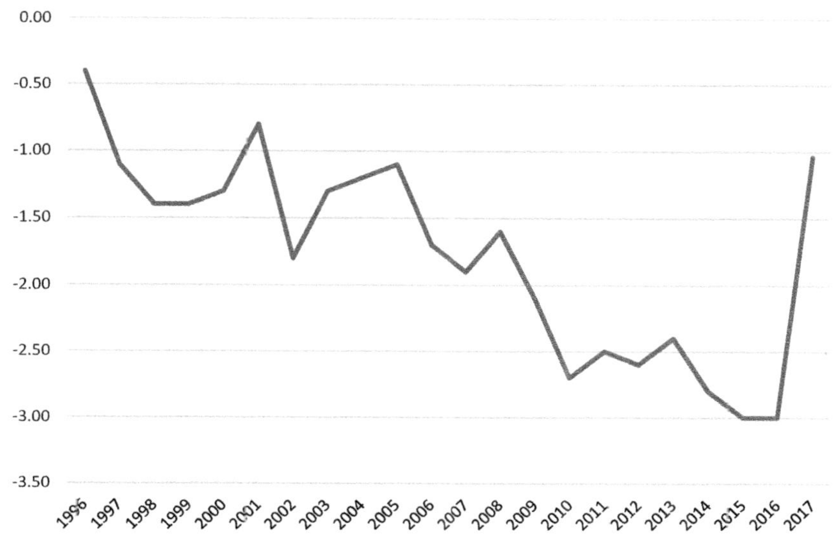

Fig. 6.2 Overall fiscal balance. GDP percentage. 1996–2017 (*Source* Own elaboration with data from ECLAC [2019])

would be able to obtain authorization from Congress without significant difficulty.[50] In other words, from a political point of view, the possibility of running deficits was not severely constrained, and from the economic point of view, conditions were favorable to that course of action. However, the new fiscal rule reinforced the pro-cyclical character of Mexican policy and has not prevented deficits in the long run (Esquivel 2010, 54; IMF 2010, 21–22).

6.3 Difficulties in Controlling Discretion

The discretionary power of Mexican presidents over economic policy has caused conflicts both within and beyond the state. Economic governance is about limiting the discretion of actors who are able to shift the costs of their actions to others. Even if the discretionary actions of an elected

[50] Anonymous. Political Operative. Interview with the author. Mexico City. March 2015.

representative are legitimate, they do not happen in a void, and they have consequences. However, complementary restrictions on presidential powers over economic policy can consolidate economic governance. In the case of Mexico, first, an independent central bank prevented possible episodes of expansionary monetary policy, and second, a fiscal rule was introduced that lowered the possibility of running deficits and promised to prevent further attempts to expand governmental expenses unnecessarily. If we consider that both reforms aimed, in their own ways, to restrain presidential discretion over some instruments of economic policy, then it is clear that they are complementary—at least when both sets of restrictions operate effectively.

Each reform pursued other goals, too, of course; the central bank reform sought to keep inflation low, for instance, whereas the Budget and Fiscal Responsibility Act sought also to reorganize outdated budgetary procedures. Other liberalizing reforms such as trade liberalization, first with Mexico's entry into the GATT in 1985, and later consolidated with the signature of NAFTA, as well as the transformation of the role of the state in the economy, also restricted the discretion of Mexican authorities over economic policy.[51] It is clear, then, that several different reforms have worked together to restrict, at least to some extent, the discretion of the Mexican presidency over the management of economic policy. However, some reforms have been more successful than others in achieving that goal.

The Mexican case lays bare the different parts of the mechanism that leads to the consolidation of economic governance. In general, consolidation occurs when several actors interpret a new critical situation in a similar fashion and create a broad coalition to enact reforms that will prevent the repetition of past crises. And, indeed, in Mexico, the possibility of López Obrador becoming president in 2006 led some political actors to believe that a new crisis was in the making. They responded by forming a broad coalition to create a fiscal rule that would force the federal government to negotiate with Congress before making decisions on fiscal and budgetary issues, thereby reducing the possible discretionary actions of the president. In theory, the elements for the consolidation of economic governance were present, and so we should see the president's

[51] Although it is beyond the scope of the present work to discuss these reforms, they might have played an important role in the success of the Economic Solidarity Pact through which Mexican inflation was controlled.

discretion over fiscal policy significantly reduced. Yet, as discussed above, this was not the case.

The Mexican case illustrates the importance, in the consolidation of economic governance, of the way in which a given critical situation is interpreted. The fact that the risk apparently posed by López Obrador in 2006 completely disappeared when the other candidate won the election highlights two significant points. First, if the interpretation of a possible crisis changes, then the coalition for reform may disband, which means that institutional complementarities and economic governance will disappear in turn. Second, when no complementarity exists and economic governance is consequently not consolidated, political actors are able to maintain a degree of discretion over economic policy. The situation in Mexico also underlines the role of perception in understanding institutions and their role in the political economy (Widmaier, Blyth, and Seabrooke 2007). When interpretations change, we should expect their effects to change as a result. In the case of the present study, the interpretation of a new critical situation is not merely a step, but a constitutive part of a mechanism, without which the latter is no longer effective.

As the example of the central bank independence in Mexico makes clear, perceptions around the role of institutions are at least as important as any formal regulations outlining the roles themselves. Neither independence nor complete subordination alone reduced inflation in Mexico. It was the way in which certain institutions were perceived that made them effective. Moreover, actors have to behave as expected in order for an institution to carry out its own intended role. So far, central bank independence in Mexico has encouraged actors to reinforce the policy path that was established along with it. Their positive feedback, however, arose more in response to the possible costs associated with breaking this policy path than because they believed it was truly the best course of action. This was certainly the case when Guillermo Ortiz was nominated as Governor of Banxico for a second time, even though the president's political associates would have preferred another person (Luhnow 2003).

While central bank independence has been successful in structuring Mexican political economy, the opposite can be said about the fiscal rule. The fiscal rule has had some effects, as the pro-cyclicality of expenses has increased and the federal government still has significant latitude in running deficits. But two factors have limited its impact. First, because López Obrador did not win the presidency in 2006, the threat built around him was voided. Second, many governments around the world—including Mexico's—responded to the global financial crisis by expanding deficits and debt. The Mexican economy was deeply integrated with the American market, which was the center of the 2008–2009 crisis, affecting it particularly hard. However, even so, deficits continued to exist even after the most intense phase of the crisis abated. Had the deficits been only a consequence of the worst moments of the crisis, the federal government would have had trouble obtaining authorization to continue running them.[52] But this was not the case during the government of President Enrique Peña Nieto (2012–2018), and deficits thus remained prevalent in the Mexican political economy, despite the fiscal rule (Revilla 2019).

As President, López Obrador (2018–2024) has enjoyed support in Congress thanks to the dominance of his party, Morena, in the Chamber of Deputies, which has meant few constraints on deficits. The continuation of this situation will depend on the results of the 2021 elections and the extent to which expansionary policies are needed to respond to the 2020 coronavirus pandemic. In broad terms, then, the example of the Mexican fiscal rule shows just how much the effects of a given institution depend on the way in which actors use it. Institutions, it must be remembered, are resources (Hall and Thelen 2009). Once the critical situation to which the institution initially responded has been resolved, the institution is no longer useful—or at least no longer as urgently needed. This suggests that sometimes economic governance is difficult to consolidate even when its institutional components exist.

In Mexico, attempts to restrict political authorities' discretionary powers were only partially successful. While the state conceded the role of resource allocator to the market through trade liberalization and privatization, it is unclear to what extent the government's hands are actually tied. It is true that monetary policy is no longer fully controlled by the government, as rates are fixed by the independent central bank taking into consideration market trends. But the government still commands significant resource allocation capabilities, and thus possesses a significant degree of control over the economy. Whether this capability will be used in the future is an open question. What should be clear is that it exists. The Mexican presidency still has considerable power, especially through

[52] Journalistic accounts indicate that deficits are contentious and their exact level is subject to intense political negotiations happening every year (*Aristegui-Noticias* 2012; Luna 2014; Mendoza 2013; Pazos 2016).

its control of strategic resources such as mining, and it continues to hold the authority to grant the use of many other resources, such as public infrastructure contracts.[53]

The institutionalization of Mexican economic policy still has the potential to consolidate economic governance through the effects created by an institutional complementarity. The consolidation of the structuring characteristics of its components has, after all, been partially successful. But while the independent central bank has succeeded in restricting presidential control over monetary policy, thus regulating agents' behavior, the fiscal rule and its limits on debt tell another story. It is possible that the different legal statuses of the two reforms (Banxico's independence is in the Constitution whereas the Budget and Fiscal Responsibility Act is not) can tell us something about their weight, but this line of reasoning could also prove misleading. The difference in the type of legal instruments required to enact reforms is not necessarily an indicator of their importance.[54]

In any case, the reforms have already taken place. The legal framework required to enforce tight limits on the discretionary power of the federal government, with the president at the top, exists for when actors deem its use necessary. However, while the legal reform was enacted during a presidential campaign when a threat was thought to be imminent, the full application of the law no longer demands complicated legal and political procedures to function. If a president is considered a threat to the political-economic stability of Mexico because of his or her supposed fiscal profligacy, Congress could simply enforce the Budget and Fiscal Responsibility Act. Naturally, such a scenario would require the opposition to control the Chamber of Deputies, and thus, there would be a window of opportunity of at least three years between legislative elections.[55]

[53] Even after the liberalization of the oil market in 2014, Pemex continues to be as strategic as ever (Tacuba and Chávez 2018), and there will not be any listing of the company's shares for the foreseeable future, mainly because it would imply a prohibitive political cost for a party to propose such a policy. On the other hand, the company itself is at the center of a big corruption scandal concerning contracts and previous joint-ventures (*Economist* 2020a, b), which further complicates any listing.

[54] A case in point is the bank nationalization López Portillo enshrined in the Constitution, reversed just a decade later.

[55] In the first half of López Obrador's presidency, there have been questions about the personalization of economic policy (*Economist* 2019a, b).

Beyond the legal character of each reform, what mattered most was the way in which economic agents used the institutions that resulted. Liberalization brought about significant changes in Mexican economic policymaking, while economic authorities kept significant allocation capabilities. Institutions have certainly been reformed to some extent, but less than is generally thought. The coalition supporting an independent central bank was stronger because there had been a recent breach of trust concerning the role of Banxico. The coalition behind the fiscal rule, on the other hand, was built in anticipation of a change that never happened: Felipe Calderón was elected President in 2006, not the left-leaning López Obrador, and the new rule's perceived pertinence diminished as a result.

6.4 Conclusions

This chapter has discussed two institutional transformations that were carried out by different actors within the Mexican political economy, in the context of different political struggles. First, the autonomy of the central bank was brokered by a coalition of bureaucrats and the incumbent government, influenced by a few factors from abroad. Second, the short-term fiscal rule was enacted at a time when a left-leaning candidate appeared as the most likely winner of a presidential contest. This threat helped to gather a coalition to create a formal restriction on the president's authority to run deficits. When the "populist" candidate did not win the election, the institutional complementarity that had arisen around the rule's creation became latent. Nevertheless, presidents now have to negotiate with other political actors in order to be allowed to run deficits. Thus, the basic institutional setting for the consolidation of economic governance in Mexico is in place.

These required negotiations with political actors indicate that the Budget and Fiscal Responsibility Law does constrain, at least to a degree, the federal government's ability to run deficits. This is, evidently, a restriction on presidential discretion. In other words, even if the president has continued to be able to run deficits, the fact that negotiations must take place at least suggests the potential for restriction that the fiscal rule carries. The forbearance of the fiscal rule observed during the 2010s could certainly become a stricter enforcement if political conditions change, and particularly if the government is divided. Even with the formal institution in place, it has been used only at the margins and with significant political negotiations.

A rigid budget with little margin for debt in conjunction with an independent and restrictive monetary policy can set the stage for another reform that would restrict even further the economic authority of the federal government. That said, although such a development could diminish the discretion of the president in the management of economic policy, it would hardly imply consolidated economic governance. Such restrictive situations, apparently consensual, tend to elicit struggles further down the road. Negotiations among political actors allow for the consolidation of economic governance because a broad range of actors participate in the definition of economic policy. Thus, the way in which actors use institutions is more important than reforms themselves.

At the present moment, monetary and fiscal policies will not be restrictive because of the necessity of responding to the coronavirus pandemic. It is possible, however, that both institutions will continue to coexist without any further consequences either for the institutional development of the Mexican political economy, or for the economic performance of the country as a whole. In fact, it seems that some political actors are using the restrictions on debt as a way of promoting debate around the federal government's actions. The fiscal rule has been applied inconsistently because of the economic situation but also because there has been a coalition supporting the turn of economic policy in that direction. Presidential discretion continues to loom large over Mexican economic governance.

References

Adolph, Christopher. 2013. *Bankers, Bureaucrats, and Central Bank Politics. The Myth of Neutrality*. New York: Cambridge University Press.

Alesina, Alberto. 1988. "Macroeconomics and Politics." In *NBER Macroeconomics Annual 1988*, edited by Stanley Fischer, 13–62. Cambridge, MA: MIT Press.

Alesina, Alberto, and Lawrence H. Summers. 1993. "Central Bank Independence and Macroeconomic Performance: Some Comparative Evidence." *Journal of Money, Credit and Banking* 25 (2): 151–162. https://doi.org/10.2307/2077833.

Appendini, Kirsten. 2010. "La Regularización de la Tierra después de 1992: La 'Apropiación' Campesina de PROCEDE." In *Los Grandes Problemas de México. Tomo XI. Economía Rural*, edited by Manuel Ordorica, Jean-François Prud'homme, and Antonio Yúnez, 63–94. México: El Colegio de México.

Aristegui-Noticias. 2012. "Paquete Económico de EPN, Cero Déficit Presupuestal." Last Modified December 7, 2012, accessed April 28, 2020. http://aristeguinoticias.com/0712/mexico/paquete-economico-2013-de-epn-cero-deficit-presupuestal/.

Avilés, Carlos. 2009. "Tribunal exonera a Echeverría de Matanza del 68." *El Universal*, March 26. http://archivo.eluniversal.com.mx/notas/586879.html.

Bade, Robin, and Michael Parkin. 1988. "Central Bank Laws and Monetary Policy." University of Western Ontario, accessed June 26, 2020. http://economics.uwo.ca/people/parkin_docs/CentralBankLaws.pdf.

Ballinas-Valdés, Cristopher. 2011. *Political Struggles and the Forging of Autonomous Government Agencies*. Basingstoke: Palgrave Macmillan.

Banxico. 1995. Informe Anual. 1994. México: Banco de México.

Banxico. 2015. "Reserva Internacional." Banco de México, accessed May 20, 2015. http://www.banxico.org.mx/graph/test/?s=SF7,CF1,41&period=Men&l=es.

Bianchi, Andrés. 2009. "La Autonomía del Banco Central de Chile: Origen y Legitimación." *Economía Chilena* 12 (3): 11–23.

Bolívar Meza, Rosendo. 2014. "Morena: el partido del lopezobradorismo." *Polis* 10 (2): 71–103.

Boylan, Delia M. 2001a. *Defusing Democracy: Central Bank Autonomy and the Transition from Authoritarian Rule*. Ann Arbor: University of Michigan Press.

Boylan, Delia M. 2001b. "Democratization and Institutional Change in Mexico: The Logic of Partial Insulation." *Comparative Political Studies* 34 (1): 3–29. https://doi.org/10.1177/0010414001034001001.

Bruhn, Kathleen. 2009. "López Obrador, Calderón, and the 2006 Presidential Campaign." In *Consolidating Mexico's Democracy: The 2006 Presidential Campaign in Comparative Perspective*, edited by Jorge I. Domínguez, Chappell Lawson, and Alejandro Moreno, 169–188. Baltimore: Johns Hopkins University Press.

Calvert, Randall L., Mathew D. McCubbins, and Barry R. Weingast. 1989. "A Theory of Political Control and Agency Discretion." *American Journal of Political Science* 33 (3): 588–611. https://doi.org/10.2307/2111064.

Camacho, Manuel. 2004. "México 2003: Evaluación Preliminar y Previsiones Electorales." In *México 2003: Elecciones Intermedias, Resultados y Perspectivas*, edited by Hugo A. Concha and Mario Melgar, 1–5. México: UNAM/Tribunal Electoral del Poder Judicial de la Federación.

Carpizo, Jorge. 2002. *El Presidencialismo Mexicano*. 18 ed. México: Siglo Veintiuno Editores. Original edition, 1978.

Centeno, Miguel Angel. 1994. *Democracy Within Reason: Technocratic Revolution in Mexico*. University Park: Pennsylvania State University Press.

Chávez, Jorge Alejandro. 2003. "Ley Federal de Presupuesto Público." *Diario de los Debates. Órgano Oficial de la Cámara de Diputados del Congreso de los Estados Unidos Mexicanos*, April 10, 39–98.

Collier, Ruth Berins, and David Collier. 1991. *Shaping the Political Arena: Critical Junctures, the Labor Movement, and Regime Dynamics in Latin America*. Princeton: Princeton University Press.

Concha, Hugo A. 2004. "Significados Políticos de las Elecciones Intermedias de México en 2003." In *México 2003: Elecciones Intermedias, Resultados y Perspectivas*, edited by Hugo A. Concha and Mario Melgar, 7–25. México: UNAM/Tribunal Electoral del Poder Judicial de la Federación.

Cukierman, Alex, Steven B. Webb, and Bilin Neyapti. 1992. "Measuring the Independence of Central Banks and Its Effect on Policy Outcomes." *The World Bank Economic Review* 6 (3): 353–398. https://doi.org/10.1093/wber/6.3.353.

de la Torre Castellanos, Renée. 2020. "Genealogía de los movimientos religiosos conservadores y la política en México." *Ciencias Sociales y Religión* 22: e020014.

Domínguez, Jorge I., and Chappell H. Lawson, eds. 2004. *Mexico's Pivotal Democratic Election: Candidates, Voters, and the Presidential Campaign of 2000*. Stanford and La Jolla: Stanford University Press/Center for US-Mexican Studies-UCSD.

ECLAC, Economic Commission for Latin America and the Caribbean. 2019. "Overall Fiscal Balance" [Online Database]. ECLAC, Last Modified September 28, 2018. https://cepalstat-prod.cepal.org/cepalstat/tabulador/ConsultaIntegrada.asp?idIndicador=1246&idioma=i.

Economist. 1993. "Narrow Money." August 28.

Economist. 2003. "The Man Who Would Be President." November 13.

Economist. 2005. "Will the Real Andrés Manuel López Obrador Please Stand Up?" May 28.

Economist. 2019a. "It's All About Him." November 29.

Economist. 2019b. "Life After Neoliberalism." November 7.

Economist. 2020a. "Bombshells on Board." September 4.

Economist. 2020b. "How Not to Handle a Scandal." September 4.

Economist. 2020c. "Shoestring King." April 16.

Escamilla, Alberto. 2007. "La Actuación del Poder Ejecutivo en la Elección Presidencial de 2006." In *México 2006: Implicaciones y Efectos de la Disputa por el Poder Político*, edited by Roberto Gutiérrez, Alberto Escamilla, and Luis Reyes, 245–268. México: UAM-Azcapotzalco.

Espino-Sánchez, Germán. 2007. "El Nuevo Escenario de la Comunicación Política en las Campañas Presidenciales de México." PhD, Departamento de Ciencia Política y Derecho Público, Universidad Autónoma de Barcelona.

Espinosa, Amparo, and Enrique Cárdenas, eds. 2010. *La Nacionalización Bancaria, 25 Años Después la Historia Contada por sus Protagonistas*. 2nd ed. 3 vols. México: Centro de Estudios Espinosa Yglesias. Original edition, 2008.

Espinosa, Amparo, and Enrique Cárdenas, eds. 2011. *Privatización Bancaria, Crisis y Rescate del Sistema Financiero. La Historia Contada por sus Protagonistas*. 5 vols. México: Centro de Estudios Espinosa Yglesias.

Esquivel, Gerardo. 2010. "De la Inestabilidad Macroeconómica al Estancamiento Estabilizador: El Papel del Diseño y la Conducción de la Política Económica." In *Los Grandes Problemas de México. Tomo IX. Crecimiento Económico y Equidad*, edited by Manuel Ordorica, Jean-François Prud'homme, and Nora Lustig, 35–77. México: El Colegio de México.

Everhart, Stephen Duval-Hernandez Robert. 2001. Management of Oil Windfalls in Mexico: Historical Experience and Policy Options for the Future. In *Policy Research Working Papers*, edited by World-Bank.

Flores Andrade, Anselmo. 2006. "Pluralismo y democracia. Partidos nuevos y agrupaciones políticas en México (1977–2003)." *Revista Venezolana de Economía y Ciencias Sociales* 12 (2): 65–93.

GAO, U.S. Government Accounting Office. 1996. *Mexico's Financial Crisis: Origins, Awareness, Assistance, and Initial Efforts to Recover*. Washington: US Government Accounting Office.

Gil-Díaz, Francisco, and Agustín Carstens. 1996. "One Year of Solitude: Some Pilgrim Tales About Mexico's 1994–1995 Crisis." *American Economic Review* 86 (2): 164–169.

Hall, Peter A., and Kathleen Thelen. 2009. "Institutional Change in Varieties of Capitalism." *Socio-Economic Review* 7 (1): 7–34. https://doi.org/10.1093/ser/mwn020.

Hamilton, Nora. 1982. *The Limits of State Autonomy: Post-Revolutionary Mexico*. Princeton: Princeton University Press.

Hernández, Rogelio. 1987. "Los Hombres del Presidente De la Madrid." *Foro Internacional* 28 (2): 5–38.

Hernández, Rogelio. 2005. "Conflicto y Colaboración entre Poderes. La Experiencia Reciente de los Gobiernos Divididos en México." *Mexican Studies/Estudios Mexicanos* 21 (1): 183–211. https://doi.org/10.1525/msem.2005.21.1.183.

Hernández, Rogelio. 2011. "¿Aprende a Gobernar la Oposición?: Los Gabinetes Presidenciales del PAN, 2000–2010." *Foro Internacional* 51 (1): 68–103.

Hiller, Fernando Rudy. 2011. "En Busca del Voto del Miedo: La Construcción Mediática de López Obrador como un Peligro para México Durante la Campaña Presidencial de 2006." *Foro Internacional* 51 (4): 715–748.

IBRD, The World Bank. 2016. "Inflation, Consumer Prices (Annual %)" [Spreadsheet]. World-Bank, accessed December 12, 2016. http://data.wor

ldbank.org/indicator/FP.CPI.TOTL.ZG?end=1993&locations=MX&start=1964.

IMF, International Monetary Fund. 2010. *Mexico: 2010 Article IV Consultation—Staff Report and Public Information Notice on the Executive Board Discussion*. Washington: IMF.

Kaufman, Robert R. 1988. *The Politics of Debt in Argentina, Brazil, and Mexico. Economic Stabilization in the 1980s, Research Series*. Berkeley: Institute of International Studies. University of California.

Kydland, Finn E., and Edward C. Prescott. 1977. "Rules Rather Than Discretion: The Inconsistency of Optimal Plans." *Journal of Political Economy* 85 (3): 473–492. https://doi.org/10.1086/260580.

Latin-American-Regional-Report-Mexico-&-NAFTA. 2005a. "The Lopez Obrador Saga. Swings and Roundabouts." April.

Latin-American-Regional-Report-Mexico-&-NAFTA. 2005b. "The President. Concerns About Impartiality." September.

Latinnews-Daily. 2004. "MEXICO: Government Goes After Lopez Obrador Again." May 18, Mexico & NAFTA. https://www.latinnews.com/component/k2/item/26341.html?full=true&period=May%202004&archive=3&cat_id=3744:mexico:-government-goes-after-lopez-obrador-again.

Leyva, Marco Antonio. 2007. "Partido Nueva Alianza: La Metamorfosis del SNTE en Partido." *El Cotidiano* 21 (141): 54–64.

Lucas, Robert E. 1972. "Expectations and the Neutrality of Money." *Journal of Economic Theory* 4 (2): 103–124. https://doi.org/10.1016/0022-0531(72)90142-1.

Luhnow, David. 2003. "Mexico's Central Bank Head Is Likely to Be Renominated." *The Wall Street Journal*, December 4, accessed April 28, 2020. https://www.wsj.com/articles/SB107049787734092300.

Luna, Carmen. 2014. "El Gobierno Busca Mayores Déficit y Deuda en 2015." *Expansión*, Last Modified September 9, accessed December 16, 2016. http://expansion.mx/economia/2014/09/08/gobierno-echa-mano-de-un-deficit-presupuestario-creciente.

Lustig, Nora. 1991. "El 'Pacto de Solidaridad Económica': Heterodoxia Puesta en Marcha en México." In *Elecciones y Política Económica en América Latina*, edited by Guillermo Rozenwurcel, 357–385. Buenos Aires: Editorial Tesis. Grupo Editorial Norma.

Lustig, Nora. 2002. *México. Hacia la Reconstrucción de una Economía*. Translated by Eduardo L. Suárez and Peter Lustig. 2nd ed. México: El Colegio de México/Fondo de Cultura Económica. Original edition, 1992.

MacLeod, Dag. 2004. *Downsizing the State: Privatization and the Limits of Neoliberal Reform in Mexico*. University Park: Pennsylvania State University Press.

MacRae, C. Duncan. 1977. "A Political Model of the Business Cycle." *Journal of Political Economy* 85 (2): 239–263. https://doi.org/10.1086/260561.
Mancera, Miguel. 1982. "Consideraciones sobre el Control de Cambios." *Comercio Exterior* 32 (6): 670–675.
Mancera, Miguel. 2010. "Recuerdos y Reflexiones acerca de la Nacionalización Bancaria." In *La Nacionalización Bancaria, 25 Años Después la Historia Contada por sus Protagonistas. Tomo I. Presidentes y Altos Funcionarios*, edited by Amparo Espinosa and Enrique Cárdenas, 347–367. México: Centro de Estudios Espinosa Yglesias. Original edition, 2008.
Masciandaro, Donato, and Guido Tabellini. 1988. "Monetary Regimes and Fiscal Deficits: A Comparative Analysis." In *Monetary Policy in Pacific Basin Countries*, edited by Hang-Sheng Cheng, 125–152. Norwell: Kluwer Academic Publishers.
Maxfield, Sylvia. 1990. *Governing Capital: International Finance and Mexican Politics*. Ithaca: Cornell University Press.
Maxfield, Sylvia. 1997. *Gatekeepers of Growth: The International Political Economy of Central Banking in Developing Countries*. Princeton: Princeton University Press.
McNamara, Kathleen. 2002. "Rational Fictions: Central Bank Independence and the Social Logic of Delegation." *West European Politics* 25 (1): 47–76. https://doi.org/10.1080/713601585.
Mendoza, Viridiana. 2013. "EPN Propone el Mayor Déficit desde 1989." *Forbes México*. Last Modified September 14, accessed December 16, 2016. http://www.forbes.com.mx/epn-propone-el-mayor-deficit-desde-1989/-gs.DBNEWnM.
México, Estados Unidos Mexicanos. 1993. *Ley del Banco de México*. December 15, Accessed July 7, 2020. http://www.banxico.org.mx/disposiciones/marco-juridico/ley-del-banco-de-mexico/%7B6A70B07F-127A-0079-220C-83843B089097%7D.pdf.
México, Estados Unidos Mexicanos. 2005. "Ley Federal de Presupuesto y Responsabilidad Hacendaria." *Diario de los Debates. Órgano Oficial de la Cámara de Diputados del Congreso de los Estados Unidos Mexicanos*, December 13, 289–375.
Morales, Isidro. 1999. "NAFTA: The Governance of Economic Openness." *The Annals of the American Academy of Political and Social Science* 565: 35–65. https://doi.org/10.1177/000271629956500103.
Moreno-Brid, Juan Carlos, and Jaime Ros. 2010. *Desarrollo y Crecimiento en la Economía Mexicana*. México: Fondo de Cultura Económica. Original edition, 2009. Reprint, 2014.
Nacif, Benito. 2010. "El Fin de la Presidencia Dominante: La Confección de las Leyes en un Gobierno Dividido." In *Los Grandes Problemas de México.*

Tomo XIII. Políticas Públicas, edited by Manuel Ordorica, Jean-François Prud'homme, and José Luis Méndez, 45–83. México: El Colegio de México.

Nordhaus, William D. 1975. "The Political Business Cycle." *The Review of Economic Studies* 42 (2): 169–190. https://doi.org/10.2307/2296528.

Olea Sisniega, Miguel Angel. 1990. "Las Negociaciones de Adhesión de México al GATT." *Foro Internacional* 30 (3 (119)): 497–535.

Ortiz, Antonio. 1970. "Desarrollo Estabilizador: Una Década de Estrategia Económica en México." *El Trimestre Económico* 37 (146(2)): 417–449. https://doi.org/10.2307/20856136.

Padilla, Joel. 2004. "Con Proyecto de Decreto, que crea la Ley de Presupuesto de Egresos de la Federación, presentada por el Diputado Joel Padilla Peña, del grupo parlamentario del PT, en la sesión de la Comisión Permanente del miércoles 26 de mayo de 2004." *Gaceta Parlamentaria. Cámara de Diputados del Congreso de los Estados Unidos Mexicanos*, May 28, 17–26.

Pastor, Manuel. 1998. "Pesos, Policies, and Predictions: Why the Crisis, Why the Surprise, and Why the Recovery?" In *The Post-NAFTA Political Economy: Mexico and the Western Hemisphere*, edited by Carol Wise, 119–147. University Park: Pennsylvania State University Press.

Pastor, Manuel, and Carol Wise. 2003. "A Long View of Mexico's Political Economy: What's Changed? What Are the Challenges?" In *Mexico's Politics and Society in Transition*, edited by Joseph S. Tulchin and Andrew D. Selee, 179–213. Boulder: Lynne Rienner Publishers.

Pazos, Luis. 2016. "Tres Años de Finanzas Erróneas de EPN." *El Financiero*. Last Modified May 4, accessed June 30, 2020. http://www.elfinanciero.com.mx/opinion/tres-anos-de-finanzas-erroneas-de-epn.html.

Reforma. 2004. "Pugna ex Canciller por Derrota de AMLO." May 19.

Regis, Juan Carlos. 2003. "Ley de Presupuesto, Contabilidad y Gasto Público Federal." *Diario de los Debates. Órgano Oficial de la Cámara de Diputados del Congreso de los Estados Unidos Mexicanos*, April 29, 174–177.

Revilla, Ernesto. 2019. "La Regla Fiscal en México." In *Reglas Fiscales Resilientes en América Latina*, edited by Alberto Barreix and Luis F. Corrales, 101–118. Washington: BID.

Roberts, Alasdair. 2010. *The Logic of Discipline: Global Capitalism and the Architecture of Government*. Oxford: Oxford University Press.

Roberts, Kenneth M. 2007. "Latin America's Populist Revival." *SAIS Review of International Affairs* 27 (1): 3–15. https://doi.org/10.1353/sais.2007.0018.

Rogoff, Kenneth. 1985. "The Optimal Degree of Commitment to an Intermediate Monetary Target." *The Quarterly Journal of Economics* 100 (4): 1169–1189. https://doi.org/10.2307/1885679.

Rojas, Francisco José. 2004. 'Ley Federal de Presupuesto." *Diario de los Debates. Órgano Oficial de la Cámara de Diputados del Congreso de los Estados Unidos Mexicanos*, April 15, 50–97.

Romero, Gustavo. 2010. "Testimonio sobre las Condiciones que Prevalecían en México y que Llevaron a la Nacionalización de la Banca." In *La Nacionalización Bancaria, 25 Años Después la Historia Contada por sus Protagonistas. Tomo I. Presidentes y Altos Funcionarios*, edited by Amparo Espinosa and Enrique Cárdenas, 169–189. México: Centro de Estudios Espinosa Yglesias. Original edition, 2008.

Rubio, Luis. 1998. "Coping with Political Change." In *Mexico Under Zedillo*, edited by Susan Kaufman Purcell and Luis Rubio, 5–36. Boulder: Lynne Rienner Publishers.

Sachs, Jeffrey D. 1990. "Social Conflict and Populist Policies in Latin America." In *Labour Relations and Economic Performance*, edited by Renato Brunetta and Carlo Dell'Aringa, 137–169. Houndmills and Basingstoke: Macmillan Press.

Sales, Carlos. 2010. "La Banca Nacionalizada y la Regulación Hacendaria." In *La Nacionalización Bancaria, 25 Años Después la Historia Contada por sus Protagonistas. Tomo I. Presidentes y Altos Funcionarios*, edited by Amparo Espinosa and Enrique Cárdenas, 419–450. México: Centro de Estudios Espinosa Yglesias. Original edition, 2008.

Serra, Jaime. 2010. "La Apertura Comercial." In *Los Grandes Problemas de México. Tomo X. Microeconomía*, edited by Manuel Ordorica, Jean-François Prud'homme, and Alejandro Castañeda, 175–212. México: El Colegio de México.

Serra, Jaime. 2011. "Reflexiones sobre la Crisis de 1994." In *Privatización Bancaria, Crisis y Rescate del Sistema Financiero. La Historia Contada por sus Protagonistas. Tomo I. Funcionarios*, edited by Amparo Espinosa and Enrique Cárdenas, 177–201. México: Centro de Estudios Espinosa Yglesias.

Sonnleitner, Willibald. 2017. "Rastreando las dinámicas territoriales de la fragmentación partidista en México (1991–2015)." *América Latina Hoy* (75): 23–54. https://doi.org/10.14201/alh2017752354.

Tacuba, Angélica, and Luis Augusto Chávez. 2018. "Gestión de Pemex como Empresa Productiva del Estado." *Problemas del Desarrollo* 49 (193): 119–144. https://doi.org/10.22201/iiec.20078951e.2018.193.60235.

Thatcher, Mark, and Alec Stone Sweet. 2002. "Theory and Practice of Delegation to Non-Majoritarian Institutions." *West European Politics* 25 (1): 1–22. https://doi.org/10.1080/713601583.

Treviño, Javier. 2009. "Pánico Moral en las Campañas Electorales de 2006: la Elaboración del 'peligro para México'." *Foro Internacional* 49 (3): 638–689.

Turrent, Eduardo. 2015. *Historia del Banco de México.* 6 vols. México: Banco de México.

Weyland, Kurt. 2001. "Clarifying a Contested Concept: Populism in the Study of Latin American Politics." *Comparative Politics* 34 (1): 1–22. https://doi.org/10.2307/422412.

Whitehead, John C., and Marie-Josée Kravis. 1996. *Lessons of the Mexican Peso Crisis. Report of an Independent Task Force*. New York: Council on Foreign Relations.

Widmaier, Wesley W., Mark Blyth, and Leonard Seabrooke. 2007. "Exogenous Shocks or Endogenous Constructions? The Meanings of Wars and Crises." *International Studies Quarterly* 51 (4): 747–759. https://doi.org/10.1111/j.1468-2478.2007.00474.x.

Zermeño, Sergio. 1981. *México: Una Democracia Utópica: El Movimiento Estudiantil del 68*. 2nd ed. México: Siglo Veintiuno Editores. Original edition, 1978.

CHAPTER 7

Conclusions: Limiting Discretion—The Problem of Economic Governance

The association between economic governance and economic performance elicited significant interest from political economists during the 1990s (Kaufmann, Kraay, and Zoido-Lobatón 1999; Knack and Keefer 1995). They sought to explain variations in economic performance, which seemed tied to differences in institutions. Some argued that particular institutions were effective across the board and would inevitably lead to better performance. Conversely, others argued that each economy should adopt its own set of institutions, adapted to their specific priorities and experiences. The literature of comparative capitalisms has tended to embrace the latter standpoint. The hypothesis of institutional complementarity, which emerged from this body of work, explains why there was similar economic performance across advanced economies in the wake of liberalization, despite their institutional differences. The idea that order, stable rules, and economic performance were linked was implicit throughout this literature.

In the context of scholarly discussions that focus broadly on the link between economic performance and institutional complementarities, the literature on comparative capitalisms also considers the complementarities that exist in non-advanced economies. However, non-advanced economies exhibit differences in performance even when they are

A. Angel, *Consolidating Economic Governance in Latin America*, Governance, Development, and Social Inclusion in Latin America, https://doi.org/10.1007/978-3-030-64522-9_7

supported by institutional complementarities, which weakens the hypothetical link between complementarity and performance. Instead, complementarity explains how capitalism is organized differently across the globe, an argument that strengthens the association, previously neglected, between complementarity and economic order. Scholars of Latin American economics have identified the institutions that underlie capitalism in the region, and analyzed the variability in its organization. This is a complex task, however, because despite some continuities, the reform processes that have been launched as each successive development model ends have represented significant changes in the structure of Latin American economies.

Thus, instead of describing the particular complementarities that are prevalent in Latin America, or assessing how specific institutions have affected economic performance, this study analyzes a link between institutional complementarities and economic governance. An institutional complementarity is a situation in which the functioning of one institution depends on the functioning of another institution, and vice versa (Höpner 2005, 383), and thus it implies stability—at least insofar as institutions represent credible limits to actors' behavior. Economic governance, meanwhile, refers to the effective enforcement of rules that constrain different actors' discretionary power. The present work has emphasized the relationship between the two concepts, arguing that the prevalence of institutional complementarities led to the consolidation of economic governance in Latin America. If institutions depend on the presence of other institutions to be effective, this means that actors cannot avoid compliance with one institution without also ignoring other institutions, and this could represent significant losses.

Latin America has long struggled to establish stable economic governance. Its consolidation has been an ongoing process of institutional change that has, in some cases, limited the discretion of powerful economic actors. This occurs when institutional complementarities ensure that institutions are functioning properly, thus constraining the behavior of certain economic and political actors. The cyclicality of economic crises means that there have been repeated opportunities to gather coalitions that support institutional reforms, and that are able to ease the uncertainty surrounding the cost of reducing actors' discretion. Broad coalitions provide stability in the long run, since they quiet opposition to the reforms that mitigate the short-term effects of economic crises. However, if the threat to stability that led actors to coalesce in the first place disappears, then the reform implemented as a result of that coalition will no longer be effective. In other words, coalitions must be sufficiently broad and the threats around which they form must remain credible in order for institutions to remain complementary and economic governance to remain consolidated.

7.1 Complementarity and Economic Governance

Economic governance can be understood as an outcome of political processes rather than as the presence of certain features, whether these processes are substantive (e.g., best practices) or procedural (e.g., conditions to create rules). This perspective helps to explain the notion of predictability in the political economy. When governance is consolidated, political and economic actors are willing to earmark their resources to that order, because they expect such commitments to hold in the long run. Since institutions represent regularities that structure actors' behaviors, and complementarity represents an instance in which the performance of one institution depends on the presence of another institution and vice versa, this study has argued that institutional complementarity buttresses economic governance. In essence, complementarity implies that institutions function effectively, meaning that actors obey the rules that they instate. In this way, the autonomy of economic agents is reduced.

Economic governance is consolidated when complementary institutions successfully reduce the discretion economic agents enjoy. The path to consolidating institutional complementarities and economic governance involves three key steps: first, an economic crisis that seems poised to recreate the effects of previous crises; second, the emergence of broad coalitions created in response to actors' perception that the new crisis will once again represent substantial costs; and third, the enactment by the coalition of a broad institutional reform that will prevent the worst effects of the crisis from taking place. Actors agree to such a compromise because they recognize that the consequences of the crisis could cost them dearly. This consolidation considerably reduces the discretion of powerful political or market actors over economic outcomes—since in the past, they might have been able to pass on the costs of their actions to the rest of the society.

The many debates around institutional complementarity reflect the diverse ways in which the concept can be understood (Crouch et al.

2005). Scholars of political economy all agree, however, that institutional complementarity explains the resilience that capitalist economies display faced with the challenge of liberalization. The existence of complementary institutions prevented the convergence of liberal institutional arrangements like those that prevail in the most important economy in the world, the US economy. Instead, economies with different arrangements, whether in labor or financial markets, exhibited remarkable resilience both in terms of the stability and the performance of their institutions in an increasingly liberalized world. Even if there was consensus around the consequences of complementary institutions in the political economy, the processes that produced these effects were less clear. This was in part because there are different ways of understanding complementarity. The most accepted version involves increasing returns: that is, institutional complementarity exists when the presence of one institution increases the efficiency of another institution.

This was the view of both Varieties of Capitalism (Hall and Soskice 2001) and the Regulation Theory (Boyer 2002–2003, 2004). Another view that has held wide appeal was the notion of complementarity as compensation: one institution compensates for the deficiencies of the other (Crouch 2005). In this case, the concept of two complementary goods, drawn from microeconomics, was applied to institutional analysis. The empirical examples used to illustrate complementarity made reference primarily to the Japanese economy, where the main bank system was complementary with controls of team-oriented output (Aoki 1994). Debates arose about whether that particular arrangement of the Japanese economy was complementary because it created increasing returns, as argued by Aoki (1994, 675), or because one of its institutions compensated for the shortcomings of the other, as argued by Crouch (2010, 124).

The evidence has not been conclusive. In some instances, it seems that performance depends on the institutions being motivated by similar incentives (Hall and Gingerich 2009); in others, it seems that performance depends on the compensation that each institution provides for the shortcomings of others (Campbell and Pedersen 2007). Later, some studies proposed that institutional complementarities could actually lead to poor economic performance (Campbell 2011): an observation that has made it difficult to pin down the scope and the utility of institutional complementarities.

In the study of Latin American economies, the concept of institutional complementarities has supported the idea that the region has its own distinct type of capitalism. The link between complementarities and economic performance has been less clear, because the latter has exhibited significant instability in recent decades. Moreover, given the ways in which these economies have transformed throughout this period, it is hard to assess whether institutional complementarities in Latin American capitalism are stable or in flux. The present work reprises the concept of institutional complementarity to explain the consolidation of economic governance in contexts of institutional change that take place as a response to frequent economic crises. In effect, this standpoint emphasizes how institutional complementarities explain capitalist organization and stability, rather than simply performance. In the present study, the focus is on how economic governance has evolved, a perspective that avoids the debate about economic performance as well as the persistence or not of certain institutional complementarities in the different Latin American economies. It is argued that to consolidate economic governance, the discretion of political and economic actors must be limited.

7.2 The Legacies of Crises and Economic Policymaking

Latin America is a region with a long history of institutional disruptions. Time and again, there are events that seem to put economies off course. Their causes are less relevant to this analysis than the consequences. Institutional disruptions led to a profound resetting of the prevailing arrangement within the cases analyzed in this study. These changes in economic policy implied for the most part a change in the model of the economy around which the different interventions of public authorities were organized. The institutional crises that took place as a result of changes in the world economy forced Latin American governments to break with their past policies, whether these were more or less interventionist. As the ISI model faltered, some governments continued with their previous policies until the consequences were impossible to ignore. However, this was not simply a matter of good policy vs. bad policy or ISI model vs. neoliberalism.

With the crises of the early 1980s, big Latin American economies had no choice but to reform the arrangements governing their economic policies. Institutional disruptions created turmoil within the patterns of economic governance that had long guided policymakers. These disruptions had long-term consequences, too, and for years they represented the kind of situation policymakers sought to avoid. Against the backdrop of a looming crisis that can potentially produce dire outcomes, despite the different circumstances and the numerous reforms, powerful political and economic actors have agreed to reduce their discretion to ensure long-term stability. When they could not agree on whether a crisis constituted a threat, however, or when their expectations were not realized, these actors retained significant discretion, because they no longer had reason to relinquish it. Therefore, the way in which policymakers evaluate a crisis is what leads them to push for institutional changes that will reduce their possibilities for action in exchange for a more predictable political economy—in other words, the consolidation of economic governance.

In Brazil, the disruption that marked the need to change the pattern of economic governance was hyperinflation. Although inflation was simply considered a fact of life in Brazil, it attained previously unseen levels during the 1980s. Hyperinflation resulted from the political and economic strategies of many actors who were all attempting to externalize their costs. At a moment when the state could no longer arbitrate these conflicts because its own resources—both political and economic—were exhausted, the externalization of costs had systemic consequences. Many attempts to solve hyperinflation were implemented, but none of them represented the silver bullet that some had hoped they would be. After institutional reforms finally succeeded in preventing the externalization of costs, inflation was under control, at least in the short to medium term. Despite these accomplishments, however, the threat of inflation continued to loom over Brazilian policymakers well into the 1990s.

The possibility that an inflationary crisis would reoccur in Brazil was deemed too real to ignore. Brazilian policymakers feared that the return of inflation could derail the government they worked for. They also considered it to be the same kind of disruption to economic governance that inflation had represented in the past. In the face of this threat, they implemented reforms that allowed two different institutions to function thanks to the presence of the other, thus creating an institutional complementarity. It is important to underscore the fact that they did not seek this outcome from the beginning of the process of institutional reform. The institutional complementarity that arose was more a solution to a pressing problem than the result of a preconceived notion of how the political economy should be organized.

The theory proposed in the present study can be helpful in analyzing the political-economic crises that Brazil experienced throughout the 2010s. In the late 2000s, new reforms rolled back earlier efforts to reduce the role of the Brazilian state in the economy. While there were some technical *faux pas* (*Latin-American-Weekly-Report* 2014; Mendes 2016), the main objective was to reintroduce interventionism in the midst of an international financial crisis (Singer 2015, 47–49)—which in some cases created new opportunities for certain actors to act discretionally (Cagnin et al. 2013, 184). However, the main consequence of these changes was an incremental erosion of the consensus around the best way to achieve economic stability (Franco 2018, 709ff). Today, even if costs are no longer externalized to the same extent, the polarized viewpoints on economic governance make it difficult to compromise around competing goals. For instance, in 2020, some want to prioritize the stable organization of public finances, while others push for state intervention to counteract the economic shock of the coronavirus pandemic. The main lesson that emerges from the story of Brazil's economy over the last half-century is that the consolidation of economic governance can always unravel in response to changing conditions.

In Mexico, the disruption that launched the process of reform was caused by the choice of two successive presidents to break the tacit agreement that, as far as economic policy is concerned, the president is a mere referee between two bureaucracies. Presidents Echeverría and López Portillo intervened in part in an attempt to restore the lost legitimacy of the regime, and amid the poor administration of a windfall of oil resources respectively. The most direct consequence of these presidential actions was the nationalization of the banking sector, but the more lasting outcome was a realization that the power of Mexican presidents over economic policy should be checked. A long process of institutional reform was launched in which the Mexican Central Bank was granted operational and political autonomy.

Nevertheless, a return to an unstable situation in which the president could carry out a more interventionist approach, mainly through unchecked policymaking, loomed on the horizon in the early 2000s with the presidential candidacy of López Obrador. For the Mexican government as well as a large majority of legislators at the time, this new threat to the Mexican economy had to be stopped. A fiscal responsibility law was enacted to prevent any possible mismanagement by a president who, in their view, would not prioritize macroeconomic equilibrium. More precisely, Mexican policymakers and legislators interpreted the increasing appeal of a left-leaning politician over the electorate as a menace to their cherished macroeconomic stability, as represented by a balanced budget. Institutional reforms were enacted to further tie the hands of the President, in order to quash the risk of fiscal profligacy.

Once all these reforms were in place, however, their *raison d'être* disappeared. López Obrador lost the election in 2006 by a narrow margin, and the perception of a credible threat to macroeconomic stability vanished thereafter. In the wake of the 2007–2008 global financial crisis, many governments, including Mexico's, ran deficits to counter the downturn in economic activity caused by the unstable conditions in the United States. However, more than a decade after the financial crisis, the Mexican federal government was still running deficits, which suggests that the fear of a fiscally profligate president's discretional power was indeed the real motive behind the reform.

When the threat of a left-leaning president's potential intervention in the economy had apparently vanished, so too did the political will to strictly enforce the fiscal rule, which would have further restrained the latitude of the Executive in terms of their control over the economy. The independence of the Central Bank prevents the use of monetary policy to finance government initiatives, and the fiscal rule prevents the government from running deficits unless a plan to pay this deficit down is explicitly articulated. It is important to note that if either one of these two institutions is not strictly enforced, the federal government possesses significant leeway in terms of economic policy, which is what has, in fact, occurred. Even after further modifications to the fiscal rule enacted in 2014, it still allows for significant discretion (Revilla 2019, 113). Had the constraints been strictly applied to the Executive, the fiscal rule would have complemented the independent Central Bank. Both institutions may still become complementary, if agents' perceptions change and the fiscal rule is implemented as strictly as possible.

This is the kind of transformation that might take place in the context of a divided government, where opposition parties control the Chamber of Deputies. So far, the presidency of López Obrador (2018–2024) has not brought about the economic chaos foreseen in the early 2000s, and the control of his party, Morena, over the Chamber has meant that there has been minimal oversight of the President in the first half of his term.

Moreover, some tension around presidential discretion surfaced during López Obrador's first year in office with the acrimonious resignation of his Minister of Finance (*Economist* 2019). The Mexican experience thus offers several important warnings to reformers. While institutional reforms are crucial to effecting substantial changes within the political economy, a mere technocratic solution is not enough. Even after a new reform sought to fine-tune the fiscal rule, without a foreseeable threat, reformers left ample space for the President to exercise discretion. Whether that discretion manifests the will of Mexico's authoritarian past, or whether, in the context of the current democratic polity, it is more salutary, is an open empirical question.

In the case of Chile, the threat to politico-economic stability was acknowledged on both the right and the left, but for different reasons. For the left, the arrangements left in place by the authoritarian government had many problems, but often had to be upheld in order to stave off an authoritarian regression. For the right, every change in the institutional architecture left by the military represented a step toward a socialist government. The left possessed political legitimacy, but, following the socialist government of the 1970s, economic actors were not confident in its ability to rule the economy. The right was in exactly the opposite situation. It lacked significant political legitimacy, having lost the plebiscite for a renewed mandate, but it could claim positive results in the economic arena. Such was the complex backdrop of institutional reforms that were first enacted during authoritarian rule but were then incrementally changed by successive democratic governments.

In the political arena, a democratic reversal seemed unlikely by the mid-1990s, and the governing coalition was loath to repeat the mistakes made in the 1970s in terms of economic policy. Moreover, by this point there was no clear threat to stability, insofar as there was no credible factor that might lead to a complete demise of Chile's post-transition arrangements. The privately administered pension system, created during authoritarian rule, helped to strengthen capital markets because its resources had to be channeled through them. However, because of its regulatory architecture as well as the size restrictions of domestic capital markets, the pension system eventually started to reveal its limitations. It went through different phases of reform, but aside from the reform of 2008, none represented a significant overhaul of the system or a definite change that would consolidate Chilean capital markets.

The reforms sought to deepen capital markets while opening new investment opportunities for pension funds on the one side, and diversifying risk profiles and regulating administrative fees on the other. Until the mid-2010s, every Chilean government on the left enacted a reform to the pension system, and some also implemented changes in the financial system.[1] The financial heft of the accumulated savings was not enough, however, to transform Chilean financial system from a bank-based structure to one rooted in capital markets. Even if some companies can fund themselves with bonds floated in the domestic market, banks remain the core of the Chilean financial system. That said, change might be on the horizon once again: after a series of massive protests in October 2019, Chileans began a major national conversation about the kind of state, society, and state-society relationships they should have (Pizarro-Hofer 2020).

This is a testament to the increasing malaise that has been accumulating in the three decades since Chile's transition from military rule. The left has tried to improve the social situation inherited from the military government within the margins of the market-oriented "Chilean model," while the right regards any changes with disdain. A consensus around economic policy, involving hard compromises, was not enough for the majority of Chileans. This is in large part because even after successive attempts to reform the pension system, the results that ordinary Chileans expected have not materialized, and powerful economic and political actors retain significant discretion. In this context, the consolidation of economic governance can only take place when a satisfactory social pact is crafted, one that provides a more level playing field. This would open a clear path forward for the reforms that would lead to the consolidation of economic governance in Chile. The socio-political processes triggered by the protests in October 2019 might well lead the way to such reforms (Escudero and Gajardo 2020; Faure and Maillet 2020).

In all three cases—Chile, Mexico, Brazil—previous crises represented situations that policymakers sought to avoid. Reforms were conducted in response to those crises, and in order to reduce the ability of powerful actors to act discretionally or to externalize the costs of their actions. Critical events affected economic policymaking insofar as they remained in the background as a reminder of the conditions that should be avoided.

[1] During the second government of Michelle Bachelet (2014–2018), there was an unsuccessful reform to the pension system (Borzutzky 2019).

However, various interests continued to mobilize in an effort to retain some of the privileges that previous development models had allowed, even if these were not feasible anymore. Indeed, previous models left both economic and political legacies that policymakers had to deal with. Political compromises were the answer to both types of legacy, because they allowed institutional reforms to advance, while preventing the alienation of potential coalition partners that top-down path-breaking reforms can cause. Even when these reforms were implemented with relative success, however, they were often contested later on. After four decades, old problems still lurk, emphasizing the fact that economic governance is dynamic and must constantly adapt to new political challenges.

7.3 The Continuous Struggle for Economic Governance

At its core, economic governance attempts to ensure the existence of a predictable environment in the political economy, in which no actor can discretionally flout the rules that shape economic life. But these rules might not serve all interests equally and are thus subject to contestation and change, making predictability hard to achieve. Thus, creating and maintaining stable and uncontested routines require much in the way of political mobilization. Developing and implementing new rules that effectively structure actors' behavior within a stable setting involves long processes of institutional change in a variety of arenas. These institutional changes tend to be incremental, since actors have neither the intellectual capacity to devise complex reforms in different arenas of the economy nor the political resources to implement them all at once. The political compromises required to enact the desired reforms are also easier to agree upon when the proposed changes are incremental.

Nevertheless, economic governance is frequently imagined as a technocratic endeavor. The key supposition supporting this perspective is that once the best possible rule is implemented, stable governance is assured. In other words, the struggle for economic governance in this scenario is simply a matter of devising the best possible rule that the political arena allows. But this theory of governance does not always play out in reality. What the cases analyzed in this study tell us is that technical expertise does not suffice if it does not come with political support, whether to implement the necessary measures, to prevent their erosion in the mid- to long term, or to shield them from opposing political attacks. In all the countries analyzed, there was no shortage of experts who could identify the most economically sound institutions, and yet in all cases economic governance has proven contentious. In Brazil, the consensus around how best to lower inflation waned; in Chile, technocratic solutions did not take into account the needs of the majority of Chileans, who are now asking for constitutional change; and finally in Mexico, the political reality of the president's discretionary power continues to overshadow technocratic considerations.

The struggles that took place in all three cases revealed that political and economic actors, both old and new, were able to act discretionally, and that a level playing field could therefore not be maintained. Institutional complementarities, by contrast, provide a wide space within a political economy where actors must abide by the rules, and risk substantial losses or hefty penalties if they fail to do so. Exceptions can be important in certain cases and should be considered if need be, but within a sound institutional complementarity they cannot become the rule, as they did in the case of Brazilian trade before the 1980s, or of Chilean corporatist retirement schemes. Regulations must be put in place to prevent vested interests from bending institutions to their own advantage, and at their own discretion—which we know for a fact that they will try to do. The struggle for economic governance involves the strengthening of rules that will be able not only to adapt to the changing economic environment but also to account for shifting political realities.

A long-term perspective on economic governance also underscores the danger of grandiose schemes in economic policymaking. Such initiatives tend to create resistance from the interests that they challenge, which will contest them sooner or later. While institutional complementarities refer to the correct functioning of one institution alongside another institution and vice versa, they also, as the literature on comparative capitalisms has documented extensively, explain the institutional stability within political economies. This study has shown that these arrangements consolidate after compromises and bargains are agreed upon. Stability and predictability are the product of ongoing political processes rather than of measures that have been imposed, no matter how technically sound or well-intentioned these measures might be.

Although some vested interests are able to veto certain policy initiatives and thus fit the definition of veto players, whose agreement is required to change the status quo (Tsebelis 2000, 442), their actions can be potentially damaging to stable economic governance. More specifically, their actions cause deviations and policy changes that have the potential to impose additional costs on other actors. To consolidate economic governance, the discretional powers of these dominant actors should be constrained through the creation of institutions that will limit them with costs, both political and economic. While institutions provide predictability and stability, however, they are also subject to changes that can open new possibilities for discretionary actions. Thus, even if policymakers rely on their bounded rationality, they must watch carefully for any indication that new possibilities for discretionary actions might be appearing on the horizon.

Institutional complementarities and the processes leading to their constitution result from the political struggles at the core of economic governance. The fact that they underpin political-economic stability shows that successful economic governance must take into account both political and economic considerations. In other words, is not enough simply to establish the right institutions and then expect them to have the desired effect; instead, it is necessary that they be accepted by the interested parties if they are going to play any significant role. The stability created by the consolidation of institutional complementarities is nothing more than the acquiescence of actors to a given order, which is a key feature of economic governance. But such stability cannot be taken for granted indefinitely. Indeed, as the present study has argued, economic governance involves actors' behaviors and preferences as well as the institutions that structure them. Frequently, only the latter is taken into account.

In addition to the technocratic debates around economic governance that obscure its political realities, there are also scholarly debates that tend to play a similar role. The state-market continuum has had a considerable impact on political discussions about economic governance, particularly in Latin America, where successive governments on both the right and the left have emphasized one or the other as the main pillar of economic governance. These positions are echoed in some of the scholarly literature on economic governance, particularly works on modes of governance (e.g., Levi-Faur 2012, 339ff). Both points of view—the one that privileges technocratic solutions and the one that focuses on modes of governance—tend to see economic governance as the result of a one-time solution that responds effectively to the problem at hand. While these existing discussions are certainly important in understanding economic governance, they do not sufficiently consider the dynamism that this study has emphasized.

This study concludes that the consolidation of economic governance in Latin America was an incremental process buttressed by complementarity among institutional reforms. Moreover, since governance is achieved through gradual and ongoing change, it is never completely settled. Even if some countries have, in the past, succeeded in consolidating new patterns of economic governance that effectively limit the discretion of a wide variety of agents, nothing prevents those arrangements from becoming ineffective through further actions. Moreover, in order to understand how economic governance is consolidated it is essential also to understand the role that political consensus plays in determining both the causes and possible solutions to economic crises. For instance, the European Union's difficulty in handling their debt crises was due to the absence of consensus about their origins and potential resolutions. In addition, the difficult moments that some Latin American countries have faced in recent years underscore that economic governance is not a static feature of political economies; instead, it is a dynamic and continuous struggle. Indeed, the complexity of this process will only intensify in the wake of the global pandemic of 2020, which precipitated sweeping changes to economies around the world. The ways in which states respond to the crisis, once again, redefining their role in the economy, will continue to shape economic governance for years to come.

References

Aoki, Masahiko. 1994. "The Contingent Governance of Teams: Analysis of Institutional Complementarity." *International Economic Review* 35 (3): 657–676. https://doi.org/10.2307/2527079.

Borzutzky, Silvia. 2019. "You Win Some, You Lose Some: Pension Reform in Bachelet's First and Second Administrations." *Journal of Politics in Latin America* 11 (2): 204–230. https://doi.org/10.1177/1866802x19861491.

Boyer, Robert. 2002–2003. "Variété du Capitalisme et Théorie de la Régulation." *L'Année de la Régulation* 6 (Économie, Institutions, Pouvoirs): 125–194.

Boyer, Robert. 2004. *Une Théorie du Capitalisme Est-elle Possible?* Paris: Odile Jacob.

Cagnin, Rafael Fagundes, Daniela Magalhães Prates, Maria Cristina P. de Freitas, and Luís Fernando Novais. 2013. "A Gestão Macroeconômica do Governo

Dilma (2011 e 2012).” *Novos estudos CEBRAP* (97): 169–185. https://doi.org/10.1590/s0101-33002013000300011.

Campbell, John L. 2011. “The US Financial Crisis: Lessons for Theories of Institutional Complementarity.” *Socio-Economic Review* 9 (2): 211–234. https://doi.org/10.1093/ser/mwq034.

Campbell, John L., and Ove K. Pedersen. 2007. “The Varieties of Capitalism and Hybrid Success: Denmark in the Global Economy.” *Comparative Political Studies* 40 (3): 307–332. https://doi.org/10.1177/0010414006286542.

Crouch, Colin. 2005. *Capitalist Diversity and Change*. New York: Oxford University Press.

Crouch, Colin. 2010. “Complementarity.” In *The Oxford Handbook of Comparative Institutional Analysis*, edited by Glenn Morgan, John L. Campbell, Colin Crouch, Ove K. Pedersen, and Richard Whitley. Oxford: Oxford University Press.

Crouch, Colin, Wolfgang Streeck, Robert Boyer, Bruno Amable, Peter A. Hall, and Gregory Jackson. 2005. “Dialogue on ‘Institutional Complementarity and Political Economy’.” *Socio-Economic Review* 3 (2): 359–382. https://doi.org/10.1093/ser/mwi015.

Economist. 2019. “Resigning with Rancour.” July 11.

Escudero, María Cristina, and Jaime Gajardo. 2020. “Nueva Constitución y Proceso Constituyente.” *IdeAs* 15. https://doi.org/10.4000/ideas.8417.

Faure, Antoine, and Antoine Maillet. 2020. “*Chile despertó*. Mobilisations sociales et politisation au Chili.” *IdeAs* 15. https://doi.org/10.4000/ideas.8364.

Franco, Gustavo H. B. 2018. *A Moeda e a Lei. Uma História Monetária Brasileira. 1933–2013*. 2nd ed. Rio de Janeiro: Zahar. Original edition, 2017.

Hall, Peter A., and Daniel W. Gingerich. 2009. “Varieties of Capitalism and Institutional Complementarities in the Political Economy: An Empirical Analysis.” *British Journal of Political Science* 39 (3): 449–482. https://doi.org/10.1017/s0007123409000672.

Hall, Peter A., and David Soskice, eds. 2001. *Varieties of Capitalism: The Institutional Foundations of Comparative Advantage*. Oxford: Oxford University Press.

Höpner, Martin. 2005. “Epilogue to ‘Explaining Institutional Complementarity’.” *Socio-Economic Review* 3 (2): 383–387. https://doi.org/10.1093/ser/mwi016.

Kaufmann, Daniel, Aart Kraay, and Pablo Zoido-Lobatón. 1999. *Aggregating Governance Indicators*. Washington: World Bank.

Knack, Stephen, and Philip Keefer. 1995. “Institutions and Economic Performance: Cross-Country Tests Using Alternative Institutional Measures.” *Economics & Politics* 7 (3): 207–227. https://doi.org/10.1111/j.1468-0343.1995.tb00111.x.

Latin-American-Weekly-Report. 2014. “Breaking the Rules.” November 13.

Levi-Faur, David, ed. 2012. *The Oxford Handbook of Governance*. New York: Oxford University Press.

Mendes, Marcos. 2016. "A Lei 11803/2008 e a Relação Financeira entre Tesouro Nacional e Banco Central." In *A Crise Fiscal e Monetária Brasileira*, edited by Edmar Bacha, 205–239. Rio de Janeiro: Civilização Brasileira.

Pizarro-Hofer, Roberto. 2020. "Chile: Rebelión contra el Estado Subsidiario." *El Trimestre Económico* 87 (2(346)): 333–365. https://doi.org/10.20430/ete.v87i346.1055.

Revilla, Ernesto. 2019. "La Regla Fiscal en México." In *Reglas Fiscales Resilientes en América Latina*, edited by Alberto Barreix and Luis F. Corrales, 101–118. Washington: BID.

Singer, André. 2015. "Cutucando Onças com Varas Curtas – O Ensaio Desenvolvimentista no Primeiro Mandato de Dilma Rousseff (2011–2014)." *Novos Estudos CEBRAP* 34 (2(102)): 43–71. https://doi.org/10.25091/s0101-3300201500020004.

Tsebelis, George. 2000. "Veto Players and Institutional Analysis." *Governance* 13 (4): 441–474. https://doi.org/10.1111/0952-1895.00141.

List of Interviews

The semi-directed interviews were conducted between February 2014 and March 2015. Each interview lasted between thirty minutes and two hours and was held in Portuguese or Spanish. These authors accepted the use of their names in the text.

José Pablo Arellano was Head (1990–1996) of the *Dirección Nacional de Presupuesto*—Diprés (National Budget Directorate) and Minister of Education (1996–2000). He was a prominent member of the *Corporación de Investigaciones Económicas para América Latina*—CIEPLAN (Corporation of Economic Research for Latin America) from its foundation in 1976 and has served as Senior Researcher, Member of the Board of Directors and Executive Director of it.

Edmar Bacha is a founding partner and Head of the Instituto de Estudos em Política Econômica/Casa das Garças. He was President of the *Instiuto Brasileiro de Geografia e Estatística*—IBGE (Brazilian Institute of Geography and Statistics) during the Cruzado Plan in 1986. Later he was nominated as President of different institutions during the Real Plan and was a member of the team behind it.

Luiz Carlos Bresser-Pereira is Emeritus Professor of Getúlio Vargas Foundation in São Paulo. He was Finance Minister from April 29 to December 18, 1987 and Minister of Federal Administration (1995–1998).

A. Angel, *Consolidating Economic Governance in Latin America*, Governance, Development, and Social Inclusion in Latin America,
https://doi.org/10.1007/978-3-030-64522-9

Ariel Buira served as a member of the Board of Governors of Banxico from 1994–1996 and previously was Director for International Organizations and Agreements within the Bank (1985–1993).

Gonzalo Cid was Head of the Pension Studies Directorate within the Chilean Ministry of Labor (2014–2018). Before that he was the Head of the Pension Unit of *Centro de Estudios Nacionales de Desarrollo Alternativo—CENDA* (Center for National Studies on Alternative Development), a Chilean think-tank at the left of the political spectrum.

Roberto del Cueto was Member of the Board of Governors of Banxico (2007–2018). Del Cueto entered the Bank in 1973 and had ascended to Deputy Director by 1994 when he resigned. He worked in the financial sector as CEO of *Banco Nacional de México*—Banamex (National Bank of Mexico), and held other posts in the Mexican financial sector. He also held academic positions in the Law School of the *Instituto Tecnológico Autónomo de México*—ITAM (Autonomous Technological Institute of Mexico), a private university, and was re-nominated as a member of the Board of Governors of Banxico in 2007.

Jorge Chávez Presa. During the 1990s, Chávez Presa was a mid- to high-level bureaucrat at the Ministry of Finance. In the period 2000–2003, he was elected to the Chamber of Deputies, representing the PRI. He currently runs a consulting firm in Mexico City.

Gustavo H.B. Franco was President of the Brazilian Central Bank, head of the International Directorate of the same institution and Deputy Secretary of Economic Policy of the Brazilian Ministry of Finance. He is now Chief Strategy Officer of Rio Bravo Investimentos.

Miguel Mancera was Banxico's longest serving Director General. He oversaw the transition from a completely dependent institution towards a formally independent one. He entered the bank in 1958 and climbed its ranks until his appointment as Director General in 1982. He retired in 1998 as Governor.

Carlos Ominami was Minister of the Economy (1990–1992) during the government of Patricio Aylwin, and was elected Senator in 1993 and reelected until 2009. He participated in the transition team from the military government to the democratically elected government.

Andre Lara Resende is an Adjunct Senior Research Scholar at the School of International and Public Affairs, Columbia University. He is a founding partner of the *Instituto de Estudos em Política Econômica da Casa das Garças*. He thought economics at PUC-Rio de Janeiro, was a member of the board of directors of the Central Bank of Brazil and President of BNDES. He was part of the team behind the Cruzado and Real Plans.

Jaime Ruíz-Tagle is a sociologist; he was Director of the Labor Economics Program, Head of the Office of Forecasting Studies at the Ministry of Planning, and has been involved in social security issues since the 1980s.

Alfonso Serrano Spoerer was the Under-Secretary of Social Protection from 1976 to 1985, making him an important member of the team in charge of shepherding the pension reform from conception to completion. He was later nominated (in 1985) as Vice-President of the Central Bank and, after the reform granting independence to the institution, in 1989, he was chosen to be a Member of the Board of Directors.

Licínio Velasco Jr was the Chief of the Department of Privatization Services of the BNDES in 1999. He entered the bank through one of its subsidiaries in the 1970s and made his career in the BNDES bureaucracy; he completed a Master's and a Ph.D. in Political Science at the *Instituto Universitário de Pesquisas do Rio de Janeiro*—IUPERJ (Institute for Advanced Research of Rio de Janeiro) in the 1990s and the early 2000s.

Joaquín Vial is Deputy Governor of the Chilean Central Bank. He was the Chief Economist of the Global Trends Unit of the Economic Research Department at BBVA (a bank), and was Chief Macroeconomic Adviser to the Minister of Finance (1992–1994) and Head (1997–2000) of the *Dirección Nacional de Presupuesto*—Diprés (National Budget Directorate).

Index

A. Angel, *Consolidating Economic Governance in Latin America*, Governance, Development, and Social Inclusion in Latin America, https://doi.org/10.1007/978-3-030-64522-9

Printed by Printforce, the Netherlands